How Historians Work

How Historians Work

RETELLING THE PAST —
FROM THE CIVIL WAR TO THE WIDER WORLD

Judith Lee Hallock

John C. Waugh

Drake Bush

StateHouse
Press

Buffalo Gap, Texas

Library of Congress Cataloging-in-Publication Data

How historians work : retelling the past, from the Civil War to the wider world / edited by Judith Lee Hallock ; interviewed by John C. Waugh, interviewed by Drake Bush.

    p. cm.

    Includes index.

    ISBN-13: 978-1-933337-43-2 (pbk. : alk. paper)

    ISBN-10: 1-933337-43-5 (pbk. : alk. paper)

    1. Historians–United States--Interviews. 2. Historiography. 3. History–Research. 4. History–Methodology. 5. History–Study and teaching. I. Hallock, Judith Lee, 1940- II. Waugh, John C. III. Bush, Drake, 1937

E175.45.H69 2010

973'.007'202–dc22

2010040012

State House Press
P. O. Box 818, Buffalo Gap, TX 79508
325.572.3974 • 325.572.3991 (fax)
www.mcwhiney.org/press

Printed in the United States of America

Distributed by Texas A&M University Press Consortium
800.826.8911
www.tamu.edu/press

ISBN 13: 978-1-933337-43-2
ISBN 10: 1-933337-43-5
10 9 8 7 6 5 4 3 2 1

Cover design by Hist & Fritz Creative Media, Inc.

Book design by Deborah M. Lindberg

Contents

In Appreciation

THREE OF US HAVE BEEN THE PRINCIPAL COLLABORATORS IN PUTTING this book together; but as with any project such as this, many more helpful hands have pitched in.

Above all, we would like to thank the twenty-four marvelous historians who endured with great patience and consideration first the interview process and then all the subsequent steps necessary to make this book what it is. They are at the heart of this work.

Others have played most helpful roles along the way in making it all come true. The historian team at the Grady McWhiney Research Foundation associated with McMurry University has been most considerate, patient, and supportive—Donald S. Frazier and Robert F. Pace from the beginning, and more recently, Stephen L. Hardin and Robert T. Maberry.

A trio at the Foundation's State House Press has played a critical role as well. Amy Smith, coordinating it all, has been a pleasure to work with throughout the process. Gina Lockley was equally helpful earlier in the project. We are particularly appreciative of Claudia Gravier Frigo, who edited the manuscript after we put it together. Her work has been highly professional and intelligent, enabling us to see it all to the end in the speediest manner.

In the long journey this project has required, we have occasion also to be grateful to Ernest Albee, who helped with the editing of the original interviews; to Carolyn Acciarito, who proofread them; to Ingeborg Kelly, who critiqued the essay on McWhiney; to Ellen Barcel, Dolores DiStefano, and Mary Ellen Fornsel for their special help; and to Mary Bush, the perfect hostess who endured with us throughout the process.

Of course, we must thank Grady McWhiney himself, who brought all of us together to participate in and finish this work.

Finally, the three of us who appear as authors of this book must thank one another. We have, from the start, worked together in the friendliest, most collegial, and cooperative manner, disagreeing where we needed to, but agreeing most of the time. It has been a delightful process.

Judith Lee Hallock
John C. Waugh
Drake Bush

August 2010

OBJECTIVE

IT IS OUR HOPE, AND WAS DOUBTLESS GRADY MCWHINEY'S TO WHOM THIS volume is dedicated, that this project—to quote one of our historian-interviewees, Perry Jamieson—"will have value for young historians starting out, and a larger value for the profession, and you would hope even for the general public. I think people are very ignorant of how historians work and think. People have a general idea of how lawyers work, or medical doctors, but most people either don't know how historians work, or, worse yet, they think they know what we do and they really don't."

The interviews conducted to produce these profiles were pegged to a particular time—the then and there. And times change. Some of the historians in this book have since moved on to other jobs or other institutions or new interests. Some have retired. Three have passed on. These sketches therefore present where they were, what they were thinking, and how they were working at the time they were interviewed.

The full text of the interviews will be posted on the Grady McWhiney Research Foundation website at www.mcwhiney.org.

DEDICATION

Grady

THE MAN

THIS BOOK WAS GRADY MCWHINEY's idea, another of his thoughtful contributions to history, which so much moved him and which he so much loved. Unfortunately, McWhiney passed on before this project could be finished.

Now, instead of a book edited by him, it has become a book dedicated to him and his enormous legacy. As we finish the work he started, we do it out of affection for him and what he meant to us and to so many others in his fruitful lifetime.

McWhiney was drawn irresistibly to the great drama that is the past. Many times he told us that like the protagonist in Somerset Maugham's *The Razor's Edge,* he made his life's quest the search for wisdom. But wisdom first requires knowledge, and McWhiney found both of them in the study of the past. He was celebrated by his students, his colleagues, and the history-reading public for both knowledge and wisdom in his teaching and his writing.

He researched exhaustively and wrote brilliantly, shedding a clear, incandescent light on the past, and in particular on the culture of the antebellum South. His books were often not comfortable for those who thought they had the past pegged. With *Cracker Culture* and *Attack and*

Die, he rattled the history establishment. He did this simply, he said, by "just trying to recount the history of the South as I have found it." And when he found it, he fearlessly told it.

The compass by which he navigated through history was the fixed idea that we owe it to ourselves to learn about the past and to pass it on to others. "What would you do," he asked, "if you didn't know where you came from, what your ancestors were like?" To him, not knowing was to be rudderless with no horizon toward which to sail and no stars by which to steer.

He was avid in his desire to pass that navigational skill on to others. One of his students, Robert Pace, says McWhiney taught him generosity. He was ever generous with his knowledge, his wisdom, and his time, not only with his students, but also with his colleagues and anyone else who came into his life.

His graduate students adored him for who he was, for the grace he brought into their lives, and for the helping hand he held out to them in their search for careers in history. A few affectionately called him "Doc," and they thought of themselves as his family. Many of them have gone on to become productive and influential historians. Several of them were interviewed for this book where their love and gratitude shines throughout.

McWhiney always looked first at prospective students to see if they had passion. He urged them to go home and think overnight of every possible career except history that they might go into. If after this soul-searching they decided that history was the *only* way for them—what they passionately desired—they were to come back to him. Many did, and when they did, he taught them with every ounce of his own passion.

Bob Maberry, another of his students, says McWhiney "made it possible for me to really become a historian.... [H]e gave me the best tools, more than any other person, and that's all you need. If you have Grady McWhiney, that's all you need."

Steve Hardin, another of McWhiney's students, says, "Whenever one of us publishes a new book, it is as much his as ours. Every time we draw strength and wisdom from his example, he remains as vital and prominent as ever he was. As long as his 'kids' continue to learn, teach, and write, Doc will impart his vigor to our lives and the lives of *our* students."

McWhiney was hooked on the great story of history. He indefatigably hammered that into the heads of his students: history is a great story; write it and teach it that way. "You can be a great historian," he told Maberry, "but if you don't tell a good story, no one's going to have the benefit of your expert research and all of your hard work."

Colleagues, too, recognized McWhiney's influence. One of those colleagues described the "deep respect and love that his students have for him." Attachments that deep, that colleague said, "do not happen willy-nilly; they happen only when a good soul spreads itself out and touches those nearby." Another called him an "academic pathfinder." Yet another said, he "is one of the outstanding Southern historians of our day. There are very few historians in any field today who have his combination of solid scholarship and creative insight, carried out at a high level and so prolifically." And McWhiney's own teacher and mentor, the great David Herbert Donald, said of him, he is "among a small handful of the ablest and the most respected historians practicing their craft in America."

His graduate students revered McWhiney for his great evening seminars, events always preceded by dinner together. His hope for this book, we believe, is that it will be another of his seminars in absentia, that it will bring many others together in the love of the past. We rather like to think this is McWhiney's last great seminar on Earth.

Farewell, good friend. We hope this book makes you proud.

JCW

The Biography

Henry Grady McWhiney (pronounced *whinny*) was born July 15, 1928, in Shreveport, Louisiana. After a brief stint in the marines at the end of World War II, he began his life of scholarship. He earned a bachelor of science degree from Centenary College of Louisiana in Shreveport in 1950. It was there, under the tutelage of W. Darrell Overdyke, that McWhiney first became interested in the history of the South.

From Centenary, he moved on to Overdyke's alma mater, Louisiana State University, where he studied under Francis Butler Simkins. McWhiney greatly admired Simkins, affectionately known as "Doc," and modeled his own professional demeanor on Simkins's. "A great teacher whose technique was simple," McWhiney wrote in an essay on his beloved mentor. "He made friends with his students and treated them as a patient father would treat his children." Years later, McWhiney clearly remembered a day when Doc helped him rewrite an article. "He explained why he thought certain words or phrases belonged or did not belong here or there.... It seems to me, looking back, that I learned a good bit about writing that day." Throughout his life, it delighted McWhiney to share stories of Doc and his many eccentricities; his devotion to and admiration for Simkins were always apparent.

To further his education, Simkins urged McWhiney to attend his (Simkins's) own alma mater, Columbia University, believing it important for McWhiney to study outside the South. So, after earning his master's degree in 1951, McWhiney went to New York, where he earned his doctorate in 1960 from Columbia University. There, he had the good fortune to study under David Herbert Donald, who further honed McWhiney's writing and teaching skills. Donald insisted on concise, precise language, and on telling a good story. He gave freely and generously of his time, carefully critiquing every paragraph and sentence that his graduate students wrote. His seminar students became family, socializing with Donald and his wife Aida in their home. He encouraged them to develop close ties with one another, connections that they have maintained and treasured throughout their lives.

McWhiney's teaching career began at Troy State University in Alabama in 1952. He subsequently taught at Millsaps College, the University of California, Northwestern University, the University of British Columbia, the University of Michigan, and Wayne State University. In 1975, after spending two decades in the North, McWhiney returned to his roots in the South, moving to the University of Alabama, Tuscaloosa, where he established and directed the Center for the Study of Southern History and Culture. His final move took him to Texas Christian University in Fort Worth, Texas, where he spent the final thirteen years of his career before retiring in 1996.

Over that long career Grady wrote, edited, or coauthored more than a dozen books and numerous articles for journals and magazines. In 1969, he published two books: *To Mexico with Taylor and Scott, 1845–1847*, coauthored with his wife, Sue Baca McWhiney; and *Braxton Bragg and Confederate Defeat, Vol. I.* Originally, he intended to write an entire biography, but when he completed half of it, his attention had been drawn in other directions. The Bragg biography remained incomplete until Judith Lee Hallock, a graduate student at the University at Stony Brook, New York, asked if McWhiney would approve of her completing it. McWhiney was delighted. He not only shared the research notes that he gathered, but he also became a mentor, reading and critiquing each chapter and serving as an outside reader on her dissertation defense. Twenty-one years after the publication of volume one, the second volume appeared, and Bragg was finally laid to rest.

In 1973, McWhiney published *Southerners and Other Americans*, a volume of essays he wrote beginning in 1954. Over the years, he had worked to prove that Southerners and Northerners shared most traits and that many historians had greatly exaggerated and distorted regional differences. Although he recognized that there were indeed some differences, he believed that, "Too often writers have lumped large numbers of people together into poorly defined groups and generalized about their attitudes and characteristics." Writers, he was convinced, "have tended to magnify the differences between Northerners and Southerners out of all proportion." In one of the essays he declared, "attacking myths…is one of a historian's most enjoyable activities."

Before long, however, the myth he attacked was the one he had promoted. The major emphasis of the last decades of McWhiney's work was what he referred to as his Celtic thesis: Southerners are different from

Northerners because they are primarily people from the Celtic areas of Europe, whereas Northerners were largely of English and Germanic descent.

The seed of this thesis appeared in a 1942 book by Wilbur J. Cash, *The Mind of the South.* Cash described a Southerner as "proud, brave, individualistic, courteous, honorable, generous, and loyal; but he was also swift to act, violent, intolerant, romantic, narrow in his concept of social responsibility, [and] sentimental." Several times throughout the book, Cash attributes these characteristics to the fact that Southerners were primarily Celtic peoples: "He had much in common with the half-wild Scotch and Irish clansmen of the seventeenth and eighteenth centuries whose blood he so often shared," Cash wrote. "The Gaelic...strain...dominated in so large a part of the original Southern stocks.... He was of the blood of the Scotch and Irish." Cash, however, did not present any proof of his contention that Southerners are primarily Celtic, nor did he include the words Scotch, Irish, or Gaelic in his index.

Writing an article on Cash for the *Encyclopedia of American Biography* piqued McWhiney's curiosity. Suspecting that Cash might be on to something, he decided to test Cash's claim in a coherent manner. He did this through name analysis techniques and by scouring contemporary accounts by travelers, primarily English and Northern, to both the American South and the Celtic areas of Great Britain—Scotland, Ireland, and Wales. Finding evidence that he believed proved Cash's assertions correct, McWhiney boldly stated his Celtic thesis in a series of articles on the continuity of Celtic culture in the American South. Many of these were coauthored with Forrest McDonald, who had noted the same cultural continuity and differences from a different path.

By 1980, after writing more than twenty articles on the Celtic roots of Southerners, Grady put his thoughts into a book, *Attack and Die: Civil War Military Tactics and the Southern Heritage.* The bulk of that study was written by Perry D. Jamieson, a graduate student of McWhiney's, who described Civil War tactics and weapons in the infantry, cavalry, and artillery. McWhiney added two chapters, the first and last, in which he argued that the tactics of the Confederate armies owed much to the Celtic background. Repeatedly assaulting strong Federal positions, the Confederacy virtually bled itself to death, McWhiney argued, and that way of fighting grew out of their cultural heritage. This was the first major publication of the Celtic thesis, and as one historian said, it created a "firestorm of controversy" within the historical community.

In his article on Cash, McWhiney discussed the debate among historians about Cash's conclusions. "This scholarly disagreement," McWhiney wrote, "which one contemporary reviewer predicted Cash's book would excite, seems likely to continue." And continue it did. In 1988, McWhiney published *Cracker Culture: Celtic Ways in the Old South.* Although criticized by historians, many Southerners took the book to heart, seeing themselves, at long last, honestly portrayed and explained. In his final publication on the Celtic thesis, *Confederate Crackers and Cavaliers,* McWhiney continued his explication of Southern Celtic cultural continuity.

McWhiney's espousal of the Celtic thesis led to unforeseen consequences. One of his graduate students founded the League of the South to celebrate and preserve what he believed to be the true essence of the region. At first McWhiney supported the movement, even serving as a director. In time, however, the movement became more radical and McWhiney felt obligated to distance himself from its activities.

Although he will best be remembered for his Celtic thesis work, McWhiney also wrote extensively on the Civil War and edited several collections of essays on Civil War-related subjects, among them *Battle in the Wilderness: Grant Meets Lee* (1995); *An American Civil War Primer* (1992); *Jefferson Davis—The Unforgiven* (1989); *Robert E. Lee's Dispatches to Jefferson Davis, 1862–1865,* ed., (1957); *Grant, Lee, Lincoln and the Radicals: Essays on Civil War Leadership,* ed., (1964); *Reconstruction and the Freedmen,* ed., (1963); and *Fear God and Walk Humbly: The Journal of James Mallory, 1843–1877,* (1995) co-edited with Warner O. Moore and Robert Pace.

At the same time that he researched, wrote, and published, McWhiney mentored nineteen graduate students in their doctoral pursuits, passing on the lessons he had learned from each of his mentors to his own students. In the interviews that follow, many of those students clearly remember and appreciate the lessons he taught. McWhiney emphasized that in their writing they needed to tell a good story, making the work accessible to everyone, not just to other academics. He spent time with them, both academically and socially, setting an example of how to be professional. McWhiney always made himself available to his graduate students; something, they discovered, from conversations with contemporaries trained elsewhere, was not the norm.

Although McWhiney retired from active teaching in 1996, his dedication to the profession continued. The pride he took in his graduate students kept him involved with their accomplishments, and he always extended a helping hand. He was a favorite speaker at Civil War Round Tables around the country and abroad, having an honorary membership in the Civil War Round Table in London, England.

After his retirement, both McWhiney and Sue began experiencing health problems. McWhiney suffered a series of strokes, and Sue was diagnosed with Parkinson's disease. Married in 1947, the McWhineys had no children. As their health deteriorated, McWhiney decided to put his estate to good use by establishing an organization to fund research and education in primarily Southern and Civil War history. This became the Grady McWhiney Research Foundation, which is associated with McMurry University in Abilene, Texas. The Foundation owns and operates the Buffalo Gap Historic Village, a collection of Texas frontier buildings and artifacts, located several miles south of Abilene. It also runs two presses, publishing books on the Civil War, on Texas, and on military history in general. McWhiney took great pride in the accomplishments of the Foundation.

In 2000, after more than fifty years of marriage, Sue passed away. About the same time, McWhiney began showing symptoms of Alzheimer's disease. As the illness progressed, he became unable to care for himself; so in 2004, Hallock, who had maintained a friendship with the McWhineys since working on Bragg, became his primary caregiver, which allowed McWhiney to remain in his home in Abilene. Even as his mental abilities declined and frustrations crept in, McWhiney continued to enjoy life by socializing with friends old and new, dining out, attending concerts and plays, listening to music—Irish, classic country, gospel, and bluegrass were special favorites—and spending time with his several cats.

McWhiney passed away on April 18, 2006, at his home.

JLH

· PART 1 ·

THE INTERVIEWER INTERVIEWED

THE FIRST, AND PERHAPS MOST IMPORTANT, DECISION TO BE MADE in creating this work was choosing someone to interview the participating historians. John C. Waugh came to mind immediately. A close friend of McWhiney's, and an integral part of the planning of the project, Waugh's many years of experience as a newspaper journalist made him the natural choice.

But Waugh's career path made him more than an interviewer; he is also a historian with several published works on the Civil War and on Abraham Lincoln. McWhiney insisted that Waugh be included among the historians presented, and so we begin with his story—to introduce him to the reader before moving on to those he interviewed.

For this interview, Waugh drew on the dispassionate services of another passionate lover of the past, Scott Martin of Austin, Texas.

John C. Waugh

HISTORICAL REPORTER

"You can set yourself down anywhere in the past, I don't care where it is or when it is, and something fascinating is going on."

"I live much of my life in the nineteenth century. That's where I go every day and I love it. My wife Kathleen is never sure whether I'll be home in time for dinner."

"Nothing is inconsequential. I think what makes good history is not just the big facts, but the little facts. A little thing that somebody said...can make a whole page shine."

"I see the Civil War as being fought twice. It was actually fought during that tremendous, bloody, nation-changing war, but ever since then it has been re-fought by great historians."

"I believe in many cases the writing is viewed by too many historians as a necessary evil, and it doesn't receive the same attention that is paid to research. That shouldn't be."

"DOING HISTORY IS AN ART, LIKE ANY OTHER KIND OF ART OR writing," says our interviewer-historian, John C. Waugh. He believes there are two kinds of history: studies and stories. "The kind of history that I do, called narrative history, has one aim, and that is to tell a story." Within the story, however, he believes the study part, the historical perspective, must be seamlessly woven. And the art is in pulling this off in an accurate, readable, compelling, engaging manner.

Although he always had an interest in history, Waugh became a full-time historian later in life. His interest in the past began long before in the public schools of Tucson, Arizona, and when he attended the University of Arizona he "almost" majored in history. His desire to be a writer, however, steered him to a major in journalism with a minor in history. He admits, though, that through a long career as a newspaper journalist and other career paths, "I've been a closet historian."

It was his years of interviewing and writing about people as a journalist that made him Grady McWhiney's choice to interview the historians whose stories appear in this book. "I've interviewed hundreds of people and written millions of words," Waugh said. "By the time I got to this, I was doing what comes naturally."

"Grady wanted to do another book," he explains, "one that reflected the artistic process of putting history together, and we talked about it a lot." Waugh remembered interviews with writers that appeared in the *Paris Review* years ago that had been edited by George Plimpton into a series of books. He and McWhiney discussed the possibility of doing a similar project with historians, describing "how they work and how they engineer the creative process." McWhiney liked the sound of that and asked Waugh to do the interviewing. It soon became a team effort: "Judith Lee Hallock, a fine historian and a long-time associate of Grady's, has transcribed the interviews and is writing these companion features on each historian. Drake Bush, a retired editor for Harcourt and a close friend of Grady's, is also on board to edit and organize the text."

The Grady McWhiney Research Foundation's mission, Waugh explains, is to encourage "doing history right." McWhiney wanted the book "to reflect the kind of history that was really important to him. He wanted a book that would be a guidepost for doing history right, i.e., telling a great story, and he selected historians to be interviewed who he believed do that."

Before beginning his career as a journalist, Waugh served for five years in the U.S. Navy. He then spent seventeen years with *The Christian Science Monitor,* starting as the secretary to the bureau chief in Los Angeles and doing writing assignments on the side before becoming a staff correspondent. A nonspecialist, his beat was eclectic. Waugh reported the Watts Riots, wrote a Hollywood column, covered sports, politics, and science—"just about everything," he recalls. He spent two years in the home office in Boston before returning to the West Coast eventually as the bureau chief. By the time his years with the *Monitor* wound down, he had done special series on such subjects as U.S. prisons, American Indians, and the American family. During political campaigns, he was one of the "boys on the bus," traveling with presidential candidates—Adlai Stevenson, Richard Nixon, and Ronald Reagan.

After leaving the *Monitor* in 1973, Waugh moved into the political arena. He first joined the senior staff of New York Governor-Vice President Nelson Rockefeller as a media specialist. When Jeff Bingaman, a friend from New Mexico, won election to the U.S. Senate in 1982, Waugh became the new senator's first press secretary. After Bingaman won reelection for a second term, Waugh left his staff to devote himself to writing history—his first love—full-time.

He is passionate about the past. "I've always loved history," he says. "You can set yourself down anywhere in the past, I don't care where it is or when it is, and something fascinating is going on. Someone is doing something fascinating, and probably doing it to somebody else, so you always have a continuing great story."

That passion, beginning early, became focused primarily on the era of the American Civil War. Part of that strong interest was rooted in Waugh's "great admiration for Lincoln, who I always thought was an absolutely unique figure in the American past." So when Waugh made his move from politics to book writing, out of all the subjects in the world of history, he focused on the Civil War. Since 1989, he has written nearly a dozen books on and around the subject.

In 1994, his first book, *The Class of 1846: From West Point to Appomattox: Stonewall Jackson, George McClellan and Their Brothers* appeared. In it, Waugh followed the careers of several Civil War generals, North and South, from their days at West Point to the surrender at Appomattox. All those he wrote about were members of the Academy's class of 1846. Some became major figures of the war; others played more minor roles—but all were distinctive in some way.

Although he has written of widely differing events, they are all related to the era of the Civil War. *Surviving the Confederacy: Rebellion, Ruin, and Recovery—Roger and Sara Pryor During the Civil War* tells the story of one Confederate couple's trials, joys, and agonies from 1861 to 1865, and their subsequent postwar success in New York City. In *On the Brink of War: The Compromise of 1850 and How It Changed the Course of American History,* Waugh reached back to study the early issues and forces that would eventually tear the country apart. He has even written *20 Good Reasons to Study the Civil War,* in which he shares his enthusiasm for this dramatic passage in our nation's history.

Lincoln, the dominating figure of the Civil War era, is always on Waugh's mind. His great admiration for the war president comes through in three of his books: *Reelecting Lincoln: The Battle for the 1864 Presidency; One Man Great Enough: Abraham Lincoln's Road to Civil War;* and *Lincoln and McClellan: The Troubled Partnership between a President and His General.*

In all of his books, Waugh taps extensive primary resources—letters, diaries, memoirs, newspapers, and periodicals—that allow Lincoln and his contemporaries to carry the story forward in their own words, with the author playing the role of interpreter and guide for the reader.

Part of Waugh's veneration for Lincoln comes from his great admiration of the president's literary ability. He quotes Shelby Foote, who talked about Lincoln's speeches and writing as "Lincoln music"—writing that sings. "Lincoln was not only one of the greatest politicians in American history," Waugh believes, "but also one of the greatest writers, a giant of American literature. He was a pioneer in the kind of brief, cohesive, coherent, punchy writing that we have today. Most politicians in his day were very verbose, very wordy. Lincoln got to the point with sublime eloquence."

"I live much of my life in the nineteenth century. That's where I go every day and I love it. My wife Kathleen is never sure whether I'll be home in time for dinner. It's a great trip back, and I'm together with people that I love and that I've always admired for one reason or another. All those characters back there are fascinating to me. They're my people. I love it there." As with most historians, the people he spends his days with become real. "When I'm writing about them, if something sad is going on, I cry; if something is humorous, I laugh. You really get involved in their lives, and you either love them or hate them, as you would anybody." But at the end of each day, he eventually returns to the twenty-first century: "I come back here to play tennis."

The secret to writing readable and enjoyable history is passion, something Waugh believes writers must have if readers are going to feel what they feel. "You're trying to let readers share the great drama and the passion you have for these people in the past. You're trying to bring them back to life. You want the reader to see how these people lived and died. They're not that different from who we are; they have the same passions, the same love, the same envy, the same foibles as we do today. Their experiences and feelings are no different from ours, only the setting is different, the times are different."

"The passions, the living, the loves and hates, are all the same; they are lived over and over and over again," Waugh believes. "There are lessons in history that will help guide what we do today and how we think." Harry Truman, Waugh recalls, studied *Plutarch's Lives,* short biographies of famous Greeks and Romans, and discovered from it that people were basically the same in any century. "He could see that many of his fellow politicians, his contemporaries, were the same as some of the politicians he read about in that classic book, and therefore he knew exactly how they were going to act in a given situation. That's how he read human beings, and that's why he became a successful politician himself. He based many of his acts and decisions on what he knew of history."

But Waugh is also realistic about how much we change our behavior based on what we learn from history, given that people don't differ much from generation to generation or century to century: "I don't believe that we won't make the same mistakes, because people tend to make the same mistakes over and over again. People say it's just one damned thing after another, but as Churchill put it, it's just the same damned thing over and over."

A disciplined routine is essential to the writing process for Waugh. By keeping to a routine, "the impulses come and the inspiration comes, because you've set in motion all of the requirements that lead to what you would call inspiration." He keeps to a regular schedule, writing at the same time each day. "You start the process by first getting your butt into a chair and ponying up to the typewriter, the computer, or the legal pad—historians write in all kinds of ways. Then all sorts of wonderful things begin to happen. The stuff that you don't even realize you're going to say, you start saying. Things you didn't even think of to put on the page begin to appear on the page." To him, that's where the art and inspiration kick in. He likens his schedule to that of a shopkeeper opening for business whether customers come or not: "I open up shop whether the words come or not. For three hours or longer, I'm writing. My establishment is open. I maintain a pretty strict schedule."

He treats each working day as writing a thousand-word news story, usually finishing at the word processor by late morning or early afternoon. If he needs to do additional research, he does that in the afternoon, along with reading Shakespeare. "I think Shakespeare was the greatest writer in the English language," Waugh says, "so I use him as my guide, hoping to assimilate in some way the kind of verve and style and mastery of the English language that guy had."

Being a Libra, Waugh needs to be neat and organized: "I have to have my ducks together in a line." He takes notes on four-by-six-inch cards by hand, feeling that writing the notes by hand is part of the writing process. Included on the card are the source and the specific page where the information was found, for footnoting purposes. As he takes each note, he knows exactly where it's going to go and how he intends to use it. The projected work is already broken down into chapters, so the cards are filed into their appropriate chapter folders.

He works mainly, as all historians do, from primary sources—first-person accounts, letters, memoirs, personal papers, official records, and newspapers of the time. He uses secondary sources to lead him to the primary stuff. Often after tracking down the primary source, he finds not only what the secondary source used, but also material that it did *not* use that sometimes turns out to be even more apt for his purposes. "All historians do this," he says.

Before beginning to write, Waugh tries to "get the pipeline as full as I can with what I need, enough to start writing, and that's generally quite a bit. I'll start writing a chapter while I'm finishing research on the next chapter, keeping one jump ahead of the sheriff." In that way, he's always ready to start on the following section. "It's really mop-up research I'm doing at this point," he says, "because I've done most of the research before I begin. But I continue searching sources in the afternoon after I spend the morning writing. I work best that way. I never have the research completely done before I start."

The historian often needs to go where the primary sources are housed—the archives at the Library of Congress, the National Archives, universities, historical societies, and local regional library collections. When he did his book on the 1846 West Point class, he spent two weeks at the beginning in the Academy's library, rummaging through its archives.

Tracking down sources can be compared to detective work. "It takes a long time sometimes to get a piece of information. Nothing is inconsequential," he believes. "I think what makes good history is not just the big facts, but the little facts. A little thing that somebody said, a small detail, can make a whole page shine." He spends time looking for those little details, "things that illuminate the human foibles or illuminate passion or illuminate a human condition or a course of events. It's what makes the difference between a piece of writing that is ordinary and one that sings; it makes the difference between fascinating, artful history and dull history."

When he sits down to write a chapter, Waugh breaks his notes into convenient parts and then goes to work on the computer. When he has written his thousand-word news story for the day, all of those notes he pulled out for the day's writing have been used, and "there it all is, rearranged together in narrative form on the four pages I've just written. And so it goes—one day, one word after another until the book is done."

He pays close attention to his documentation, going back frequently to recheck the accuracy of his note-taking and his citations. "That way, particularly for quotes, I can get it precisely right, every word, comma, period, and inflection, exactly as it was in the primary source. I have to keep going back to the horse's mouth. It is the only way I can see to write history that has a hope of being accurate."

The computer is a blessing. "It's great," Waugh says, "because you can get something down and then take parts of that and move it around—sculpt it." Even better is the ease of footnoting. "I don't know how historians used to do footnoting without the word processor," he admits. "This happens automatically on a computer. As soon as I use something from my notes, I immediately throw in a footnote and I've got it. If I put another note before it, they're automatically reordered for me."

Interviewing the historians included in this volume gave Waugh insight into how others work, and their thoughts on what makes for good history. "You've got to love the past," they universally agreed, "you've got to be devoted to truth, you've got to come in with no preconceived ideas, you've got to go where the facts take you. You can't come in with the idea of making a point and then twisting the material to fit your point. You have to have integrity, be naturally inquisitive, and interested in the people you're writing about."

During the interviews, Waugh found a common thread among all these historians—"their devotion to the past and to bringing that past back to the present with integrity." None of them pays attention to political correctness, refusing to change or omit a fact or a quotation because it might offend someone. Their interest is in telling the true story of the past.

Today's historians stand on the shoulders of past historians. "I see the Civil War as being fought twice. It was actually fought during that tremendous, bloody, nation-changing war, but ever since then it has been re-fought by great historians." He believes that "we have all profited from what they have written." He describes himself as standing on the shoulders of past writers such as Bruce Catton (another journalist/historian), Shelby Foote, Allan Nevins, and Carl Sandburg. He is also influenced by today's great historians—James McPherson, James I. (Bud) Robertson, Gary Gallagher, William C. (Jack) Davis, Edwin C. Bearss, and Grady McWhiney, among others. "Now part of the history fraternity myself," Waugh says, "I continue to profit by reading their works." He is always on the lookout for good writing. "It's important to say things not only well and succinctly, but also poetically. I think good historians do that, they try to write something with literary merit."

The historians interviewed for this work uniformly love what they're doing. "I can't wait to get up in the morning and go to work," Waugh says. "Every historian that I know of has the same feeling. This is what they want to do." During the interviews he asked the historians what they might have been had they not become historians. Many of them said they didn't know. "They can't visualize being something else, although some of them started out to be something else, as I did."

"It was stimulating for me to interview all these great historians," Waugh says. "What it amounts to is sort of a collegial discussion with each of them. I start asking questions, and it proceeds just like the writing does, leading down all kinds of avenues. You find yourself getting sidetracked, and the sidetracks are wonderful. I love the interviews because I've been able to tap into how these wonderful historians work, and I get pointers on how I can change my work habits in a useful way."

Waugh believes his own contribution to the field of history may be his impact as a writer. "Perhaps I have been able to show to some degree that how well something is written is as important as how well it is researched. I believe in many cases the writing is viewed by too many historians as a necessary evil, and it doesn't receive the same attention that is paid to the research. That shouldn't be. Style is to some degree as important as substance if you are going to interest a general reader." And that is Waugh's most ardent intent: "I am interested in bringing the great drama of history—the wonderful past—to the general reader. I like to think that to some degree I have made the past sing to us, by the way I have written it." He hopes that his success in doing that may help persuade other historians of the importance of writing a readable, compelling narrative.

Though he came to writing history later in life, Waugh has no qualms about the decision he made to leave his journalistic and political career paths. "I love writing history," he says. "I had no preconceptions. I had no idea if I would succeed or not. I certainly have not harvested a great financial bonanza doing this, but I'm doing what I want to do, something that I think is a service to people. Telling these great stories is a service, in my view." He not only gets to tell the stories on the printed page, but he also visits Civil War organizations to speak to audiences. "If someone asks me to give a talk, I'll do it if I can."

He now sees his mission in life as "the obligation to tell a great story of the past."

⋆ PART 2 ⋆

Special Niches

Although many historians follow a tradition of teaching and writing in an institutional setting, others have eschewed that path to fit their own interests and needs. Sometimes this means that some have chosen to focus on one specialized area outside of an academic setting, whereas others have reached beyond their institutional environs.

Our historians in this section have carved out such special niches for themselves within the historical community. John Tricamo devoted his life to the classroom, preferring the dialogue between teacher and student to the loneliness of writing. For Elizabeth Shown Mills, intrigued by past lives, history is "up close and personal." She has focused her career on generational history and instructing others in this meticulous craft. Lynda Crist's entire career has been with the Jefferson Davis Papers—the demanding job of compiling and editing the Confederate president's huge body of papers—beginning as a clerk/typist as an undergraduate and eventually becoming the director of the project.

Steve Hardin describes himself as "unapologetically a Texas historian," putting Texas's past into its proper historical context. Although his research and writing are focused on the region, Hardin eloquently laments the nationwide state of education today. Another professional whose primary focus is on Texas and the region is Bruce Winders; he is the historian and curator at the Alamo. As a public historian, he sees his job as a way to "make sure that visitors understand the big picture—that it's not just about Texas." Richard Baker is also a public historian with a unique position; in 1974 he set up the Senate Historical Office. Ever since, his office has served "as the information center of the Senate with regards to institutional operations from a historical perspective" for senators and the public alike.

The last profile in this section is of two historians who have often worked as a team. Donald Frazier and Robert Pace's work extends into public history and "entrepreneurial" history. "You don't have to be limited by the boundaries of the profession," maintains Frazier, "you can go beyond that." In doing so, this team has created several special niches for themselves.

John Tricamo

The Historian as Teacher

"I always felt an edge when I went into the classroom. I never felt, oh, this is just another class. There was always that edge."

"It's like watching some of the great actors at work on the stage; you know when they're communicating with the audience or when they're not communicating. That's what it was all about."

When asked to imagine what he might have done with his life had he not become a teacher of history, Tricamo simply says, "I wouldn't know. I just wouldn't know."

WHEN THE TIME CAME FOR HIM TO ATTEND UNIVERSITY, JOHN Tricamo admits, "I wanted history." It all began for him in high school, when he discovered that "history was a story; in fact, it's always been a story for me, and I was just enthused. I just loved history."

After graduating from high school in Brooklyn, he had other things to do: When he graduated in June 1944, he was drafted into the army and sent to Europe, where he joined an infantry outfit in the Seventy-eighth Division. That experience in that theater of the war focused his interest on European history. "After the war," he says, "I was very fortunate to be stationed at Bremen near the North Sea and I had opportunities for furloughs. I went to Brussels, to

Paris, to Rome, to Switzerland, and to Copenhagen," places "just full of history and I loved every bit of it."

In September 1946, Tricamo began his academic career at Fordham University. His parents had always stressed learning, and both encouraged and supported their son's ambition to further his education. His father had left high school after only two months because he needed to work to support the family. "He was bright and sharp and he would always tell me school was most important." Because of the great numbers of returning World War II veterans attending school on the G.I. Bill, it was difficult to get into some of the smaller universities, such as Fordham, but Tricamo's father "had done all the applying the year before. Because of Pop I was able to go."

His early undergraduate years, though, were disappointing. "There were too many people in the classes—the university wasn't really able to handle everybody." But in his last two years he "had some excellent professors who turned me on. I became determined to continue on and be a historian." At that point he focused on European rather than U.S. history: "I've always had this love affair with Europe."

After receiving his undergraduate degree, Tricamo stayed on at Fordham in a two-year master's program. He then went to work for a few years before entering Columbia University for doctoral studies in 1954. At Columbia his attention turned from European to U.S. history, primarily because of two teachers—Dumas Malone, a Jeffersonian historian, who became his doctoral professor; and William Leuchtenburg, "a superb narrative historian and brilliant lecturer on the American period from 1870 onward." David Donald, the great Lincoln scholar, also influenced Tricamo during his doctoral years. Being exposed to these three superb U.S. historians, his concentration turned to U.S. history, with a minor in European history. In 1955, he passed his oral exams.

Tricamo's interest in U.S. history also harked back to his army days, and that guided his choice of topic for his dissertation. He did his basic training at Fort McClellan in Alabama, and when he joined the Seventy-eighth Division most of his friends were Southerners. "They talked about race," Tricamo remembered, "and they apologized in many ways, or tried to explain the racial differences in the South." To better understand his Southern friends, he wrote his doctoral dissertation on Tennessee and the secession movement. He received the doctorate in 1964, after several years of teaching at various schools, doing his research, and writing the dissertation during summer breaks.

The dissertation was the last serious writing Tricamo would do, preferring the excitement of the classroom to the loneliness of research and writing. "I loved the classroom," he said following his retirement. "The students seemed to gravitate toward me. I loved the communication and I loved questions and comments. It was always a dialogue."

Shortly before he passed his doctoral orals, Tricamo began his teaching career at a small Catholic school in Brooklyn, St. Francis College. He spent two and a half years there before moving on to Fort Belvoir, Virginia; St. Vincent's College at Latrobe, Pennsylvania; the University of San Francisco; and the University of Wisconsin, Milwaukee. In 1965, he went to San Francisco State University where he spent the rest of his career. Although publishing is the primary route to advancement in academia, his lack of writing did not hurt Tricamo's upper mobility. When he was soon elevated to full professor, the university "made it clear it was because of my teaching."

His gift and passion for teaching never left him during his long career. "There were times that I'd go into a classroom full of anticipation and unsure of myself—there was that nervousness before you go on the stage. I always felt an edge when I went into the classroom. I never felt, oh, this is just another class. There was always that edge." He likened his teaching to acting on stage. "I remember years ago when I would go to the theater and I would always be amazed by the ability of the actors and actresses. It's all communication. I love it."

In keeping with the theater metaphor, just as an actor would not appear on stage with a script in hand, Tricamo did not use notes when he lectured. Although he did carry his folder of notes into the classroom with him, he never referred to them, but they were not entirely unnoticed: "My students used to make comments about them."

"I thrived on eye contact," he said. "Teaching is the theater, it's a rapport. I've always felt the need of a rapport with the members of the class. It's looking at people, making sure that you're getting your point over." He loved the give and take of the classroom, welcoming questions or comments during the lecture. "It's like watching some of the great actors at work on the stage; you know when they're communicating with the audience or when they're not communicating. That's what it was all about. When the class was over, there was an exhilaration, and also an exhaustion."

Every lecturer has moments when the communication seems to break down. When that happened, Tricamo turned to his students for help. "Folks," he'd say, "I need some comments, some questions, some reactions—and generally I would get it." He believed this was a way of "telling them to get with it, without putting the blame on them. To me it's my show and I'm responsible." He also subjected himself to "a little study on myself; some self-analysis is critical to all of this."

To give his best performance in the classroom, Tricamo gave lecture preparation the same careful attention that a playwright gives to a script. "The first thing I did was to read and take notes, from articles as well as books. It was very important for me to write everything out." All of his notes were handwritten. "I'm computer illiterate," he confesses. "It's kind of my way to sit down and write on paper." He used lined paper to take notes and then organized them in folders by the dates of the events. From the folders, he drew the content of his lectures. "Each semester I would go through my folders, always hoping that I would be adding to them. I was very conscious of changing historiographical themes and trends. History might be just a story or a narrative, but you're always looking for something fresh and new, some new interpretations. I think that's critical to our business. You're also sensitive to the fact that each period, each generation, will interpret and analyze things somewhat differently and you must be aware of how each generation is reflected in the history. Each generation, I think, has its own view—its own emphasis maybe is a better word—of historical problems."

The content of the information he taught did not change much, but the emphasis or the perspective on the subject might change radically. As an example of what he meant, Tricamo cited the issue of slavery. "The U.B. Phillips interpretation of slavery was denounced in my day by people [other historians] like Kenneth Stampp, yet from Phillips I learned so much about personal relationships that existed within the system of slavery; relationships between blacks and whites and between blacks and blacks, and so on."

Although he did not refer to his notes during his lectures, "Maps were critical for me in classes, and I really worked the map. I would always make sure before I started the semester that I had the maps. I can't operate without maps." He found them particularly useful when he lectured about the South. "The South has always been an exercise in geography. The thing that I always loved about the South was that it all depended on where you came from: Were you up country, were you low country, were you from the hill country, and so on. So maps were indispensable for me." Other than maps, the only classroom aids Tricamo used were the blackboard and chalk.

He loved to tell anecdotes. "That's one of the little dangers sometimes," he admits, "because I love stories. Something will come up, like when I was doing military history, and I would fall into a story about some of my own experiences during the war as well as during the occupation. I love stories, but I have to be careful that I don't tell too many stories; I try to finish what I'm supposed to do."

He is a voracious reader. He likes to "futz around in the garden" and interact with his family—he and his wife Joan "have three wonderful children, in their forties, and they're special. And we're lucky with three grandchildren"—"but other than that I'm reading." He subscribes to, and reads, several newspapers regularly: *The New York Times, Financial Times,* and *The Economist.* Then there are the professional journals: *Journal of Southern History, Journal of American History,* and *Mississippi Valley Historical Review.* He also read monographs and biographies, and "pretty much kept up with

the major works in American history all through my teaching days."
Somewhat in keeping with the past, Tricamo doesn't drive a car, so
he uses public transit and he walks a lot. He is such an avid reader,
that he sometimes reads *The New York Times* while he is walking.
"I've gotten in trouble a few times," he admits.

He taught primarily U.S. history, a course on nationalism, a
Southern history class, and U.S. politics, among others. However,
he worked in Europe whenever he could. In the late 1970s, he taught
a military history course that covered Europe and the United States
from 1850 to 1945. "It was a way to get me back into Europe," he
confesses, "which I've always loved."

As he moved toward his retirement in 1993, Tricamo turned his
attention more fully, once again, to European history and World
War II. In 1989, he attended an annual seminar sponsored by Brad-
ley University that met in Germany. He found it fascinating—"I
have just eaten it up, I just love it"—attending all but three from
1989 until 2007. In the early years Germany was still divided into
the German Democratic Republic (East Germany) and the Federal
Republic (West Germany). The organizers were "sympathizers of
the East German regime, so we spent time in East Germany and
we'd always wind up in Berlin and Bonn. Well, the Wall came tum-
bling down, and very soon the seminar, by 1994, was in Berlin and
Prague." Attendance at the seminar allowed Tricamo to travel extensively through Germany.

One year, he was in Berlin for the seminar and spent an entire
day in the German History Museum. "And there it was, all laid
out in this history museum about Germany's relationships with its
Jewish population. It wasn't just about concentration camps; it was
about how the bureaucracy was corrupted. And then it had the last
days of the war, and all the memories kind of came back."

In some ways, he acknowledges, "I'm still living it." In 1980, he
spent a sabbatical leave in Europe. "I did my work in the Imperial
War Museum in London, and then traveled all over Britain and
went to France and visited some of the World War II battlefields."

At Normandy, he confesses, "I started to cry because I was looking at the boys' names that are on the tombstones; they were just a year older than I was."

He believes his greatest contribution to the field of history was as a classroom communicator. His students learned from him, but he also learned from them. "When they came to my office to talk they made me think. For me it's always been an exchange. I knew what our roles were, but students were very important to me."

To be a good teacher, Tricamo believes, "You have to love to be in the classroom. You have to be ready to work and prepare. I can't stress preparation enough. I think it is critical, as is the desire to communicate. You have to try not to be frustrated because sometimes if the students seem indifferent maybe it's because *you're* making mistakes. You have to figure there are days that perhaps you're not coming across and so you try to adjust right in the middle of the class." As a teacher, Tricamo spared no effort to communicate clearly and enthusiastically with his students.

Over the years he had many reminders of how important he had been to his students. One day as he walked along the sidewalk, "a police car pulled up, the policeman got out, and said, 'You probably don't remember me.' He gave me his name and said he had me in class, and he gave me a real handshake."

Often former students offered feedback years later. "I've had phone calls this past year from two students, now retired, who told me wonderful things—that I had taught them to be so devoted and so prepared and how to communicate with students. I hate to say that—it's like bragging. But to me that was so important."

Like the police officer who stopped him, "Every now and then I run into somebody who will remind me who they are, and the experience that they had with me in the classroom. For me it's just been a blessing." Some of his students became his and his wife's friends. "I have a very old friend—over forty years—and he and his wife were students of mine at the University of Wisconsin, Milwaukee, my first year there. They're very successful professionals today. They couldn't be more enthusiastic and more warm in their relationship with us."

When asked to imagine what he might have done with his life had he not become a teacher of history, Tricamo simply says, "I wouldn't know. I just wouldn't know."

John Tricamo passed on, still in love with the past, in 2007.

Elizabeth Shown Mills

FAMILY HISTORIAN

"I have to say I have the past in my bones. There's no other way of putting it. I've always been intrigued by past lives and felt the need to understand them."

"[Grady McWhiney] showed that the truth can give us a clearer understanding about ourselves and our past. And that's the whole point of history."

"Research has to be absolutely exhaustive. You don't reach a conclusion until you are sure you have used every conceivable source that exists."

"To take a name that you just find in a record and make a real person out of that—reconstruct that person, rebuild her life, put her into a family—for me that validates her existence."

"Twenty years ago you wouldn't be interviewing me because twenty years ago genealogy was not taken that seriously within the field of history."

———◆◆———

"I HAVE TO SAY I HAVE THE PAST IN MY BONES," ELIZABETH SHOWN Mills admits. "There's no other way of putting it. I've always been intrigued by past lives and felt the need to understand them."

Mills calls what she does generational history, that is, genealogy with a broad sweep, "the history of families across generations.

There are family-tree climbers and there are genealogists," she says, "just as there are armchair historians and there are real historians." The generational historian follows all the same principles that an academic historian does, "although in reality our standards are a little tougher."

Mills sees a schism between historians and genealogists. "When history developed into a real academic field in the mid- to late-1800s, they had to divorce themselves from the amateurs who were just out there glorifying their own ancestors," she says. "It was the historians' way of protecting their field against the local historian who was also the local genealogist." They adopted scientific principles of research that they applied to history, but the local genealogist and historian did not do that, "so the wall developed." She believes that "the modern historian has handicapped himself or herself by this wall that has been thrown up."

Grady McWhiney was Mills's major professor when she earned her bachelor's degree at the University of Alabama, Tuscaloosa. She recalls having discussions with him about the differences between historians and genealogists. "I remember him so clearly telling me how historians cannot reinvent the wheel; they build upon the work their predecessors have done. That's logical," she admits, "but at the same time genealogists don't operate by that principle." There are many things that are presented in the name of genealogy "by people who don't know what they're doing, so we have to go back and always follow everything to its original source and evaluate that original."

This is particularly true, she says, of information that appears on the Internet. "The family trees, historical abstracts, and databases available online are of highly mixed quality, particularly the 'trees' created by legions of inexperienced researchers. If online genealogical accounts have any scintilla of reliability, they should point to the original records." The web resources most used by genealogists today, Mills says, are images of original records—hundreds of millions of pages from censuses, military and pension files, land grants and surveys, court cases, vital records, and so on—being digitized by commercial firms and the Church of Jesus Christ of Latter-Day Saints, in conjunction with the national archives of several nations.

Born and reared in the Mississippi Delta, Mills says her interest in family history originated with a school assignment to "interview old timers in our family and find out who we were, because that's how people knew who they were back then." She was about ten years old, and she remembers her grandmother's story "about an ancestor, a horse trader who swapped off a fine bay mare one day for a wife who was a Choctaw princess." Of course, she recalls, "half the family was aghast and denied it, but that intrigued me and was the reason I first began to look for my own family." She found all sorts of things that were left out of history books: "It's a whole different history when seen up close and personal."

(As it turned out, that ancestor was not Choctaw, but Creek. Families often claim an incorrect American Indian line because they think they are connected to a nearby Indian village or reservation. "But almost always," Mills says, "in the South when families have an Indian connection, when they are able to document it, they have to take it back several generations further than what the legend says." Mills went back to the Georgia/South Carolina border around the late 1700s.)

Mills began to branch out into the history of other families when her husband's mother asked her to research her family. Her mother-in-law came from the Cane River region of Louisiana. "Her family had been there so long they included practically everybody," Mills says, "and if some weren't family they were all interacting, so you were studying the whole community when you studied any one family that lived along the Cane River."

After she had researched in the region for about three years, the local preservation society asked her to document a historic site that they wanted to put on the National Register. It was Melrose Plantation, allegedly founded by a freed slave, "my first nonfamily project that I worked on." Her husband, historian Gary Mills, joined her on that study. The research report turned out to be a little book that is still sold by the local preservation society and was the first professional writing job she was paid for.

By the time she and her husband finished that project, they discovered "there was not just this one house that the freed-slave family owned, but a dozen of those big-pillared plantation mansion houses." Her husband was finishing his doctorate at Mississippi State, and, looking for a dissertation topic, he chose to return to Cane River for his thesis. "I was mostly working on the family, the genealogical side of it, and Gary was more into the social and economic side for the dissertation he had decided to write." Those years were exciting for them. "We just did so much work together. We were always researching, and I was working on something or he was working on something, and there was a lot of doing it together and hashing over of ideas and it became really hard to separate one from the other." Although so much of their work intertwined, "I began to publish some things on my own, and then he published on his own, and it just grew."

Mills had a checkered higher education. She first enrolled in college when she was barely sixteen and finished at the age of thirty-six. "I married at eighteen and dropped out to pursue the Ph. T. (Putting Hubby Through) while bearing and raising three children." During that time, Mills "grabbed classes on a catch-as-catch-can basis wherever Gary attended or taught." She completed the coursework for a degree in business before switching to history. By the time she finished she had attended Delta State University, Mississippi State University, McNeese State University, and the University of Alabama.

Along the way, Mills studied under two teachers who made an impact on her choice of career. Her first history professor, William LaForge, "believed you should see the human side of history, and I was impressed with that." Then in 1976, her husband took a position at the University of Alabama, Tuscaloosa, where Mills met McWhiney. "He became my mentor, my role model, and everything else. I was really impressed by how he approached history honestly, and he showed by example why the truth of history needs telling, even when the world doesn't want to hear it. He showed that the truth can give us a clearer understanding about ourselves and our past. And that's the whole point of history."

While her husband focused on the Cane River community for his doctoral dissertation, Elizabeth used all of the colonial Natchitoches outpost for her senior honor's thesis in history. Identifying over two thousand settlers in that northwest quadrant of Louisiana, she tracked each to the family origin in France, Spain, Canada, or Mexico. She followed them wherever they went in the colonies to reconstruct their lives, and then reconstituted the families they produced. The thesis studied the social, economic, and family patterns of the colonial Louisiana frontier.

"It was a fascinating study," Mills remembers. "One of the things I found was that over half the white population of that part of Louisiana at the time of the Louisiana Purchase had Native American ancestry, and 25 percent of them had slave ancestry—albeit Indian slaves rather than African. Some were rooted in native Louisiana tribes like the Chitimachas, but most were from the western plains where they were captured by the Spanish and sold into Louisiana. Many French males without wives later married the Native American women whom they had purchased. Their children were then accepted into the white population."

At the time of this interview, Mills had published over five hundred articles on family and social history, as well as biography and literature, for a variety of magazines, journals, and professional publications. She likens the pain of writing to that of childbirth: "There's no other way a woman is going to get a kid all her own without going through that pain. Writing is sort of like that, but when you've got something you want to say, that's the only way you can do it."

In addition to the hundreds of articles she has written, Mills has also published books. Her first volumes were edited translations of colonial Natchitoches records, church and civil, from the original French and Spanish documents. Those works have been widely used across the decades by borderland historians. She is best known today for two groundbreaking guides to historical sources in general. The first of these, *Evidence! Citation & Analysis for the Family Historian,* is a little handbook she wrote to guide genealogists in the use of historical materials.

Although guides to scholarly citation have long existed, Mills explains, "*Evidence!* focused on the nuts and bolts of original records that the standard guides don't cover." For example, if a writer cites a will, "readers can't assume it's in the local courthouse. Even if you refer to one in the local courthouse, are you referring to the record clerk's copy or are you referring to the original will that's in a probate packet, or are you referring to a twentieth-century copy of a seventeenth-century will that somebody transcribed because it was illegible?" That's why it is so important to genealogists to go back to the original: "Every one of those copies has errors that have been created in that copying process."

The "wee little" *Evidence!* has since been mightily expanded. It's sequel, *Evidence Explained: Citing History Sources from Artifacts to Cyberspace,* is an 885-page manual that the *Library Journal* named the best reference book of 2007. It also takes the subject beyond the genealogical community into academia, where it has already been adopted as a textbook at several major universities. As its title implies, the work seriously tackles the subject of historical evidence— how it is created, where it is found, and how it is analyzed.

"Traditional citation guides," Mills explains, "simply demonstrate the kind of concise citations that publishers prefer. Researchers do need that help, but they also need guidance in the use of that material." In *Evidence Explained,* Mills provides those citation models, more than 1,100 of them for mostly unpublished original record types found in the archives of twelve western nations. But she also helps users understand the kind of information they need to capture for each type of source so they can make informed decisions about the reliability of that source's information.

For another major book, *Professional Genealogy,* Mills brought together and edited the essays of twenty-four writers, herself included. Alone or paired with *Evidence Explained,* "ProGen" as this book is widely known, has also become a classroom textbook used in both degree and professional certificate programs.

One of Mills's more unusual accomplishments for a professional genealogist has been the publication of a novel, *Isle of Canes*. It began as an offshoot of the Melrose Plantation historical site documentation project that she and her husband worked on. Gary did his dissertation on a socioeconomic study of the community, but many things that they turned up couldn't be worked into his book. Some of it, Mills explains, "was family history or tradition that you could find enough evidence for to suggest that this is likely true, but yet you didn't have the evidence to prove that it *was* true." She believed "there was a bigger story there to be told, and that's what I wanted to do." She worked on the novel at the same time Gary wrote his dissertation.

Mills found that the fictional approach helped her develop insight. "That was a real challenge," she admits, "because my background is not the background of that society. To try to put myself into the skin of these people that are so totally different from me was a challenge." She tried to portray them honestly "within the context of the records without violating historical or genealogical accuracy." She also strived to "present what their society was like, the experiences they went through, the effect it had on human lives."

The premise of the story made it a hard sell. "The whole concept of many women who had been born in slavery breaking free of those chains and then turning right around and buying and enslaving others is an unpopular thesis," Mills admits, and that is what her major character, Coincoin, had done. It took thirty years to find a publisher, finally publishing with Ancestry, a company that "appreciates the truth of family stories."

The *Historical Novels Review* reacted favorably to the book, validating her ability to write a work of fiction. She received an invitation to address the International Historical Novel Society on "how to go about reconstructing a historical character for a novel—how to find the records, how to piece them together, and how to interpret them." The success of her venture into writing fiction has whetted her appetite for more, and she has plans to write one based on another true story she turned up in her research.

Mills works at home, at a huge U-shaped desk that is "right in front of the window so I can look out at the azaleas and the dogwoods and life going by on the street." Although she prefers silence while she works, if there are other distractions in the house or nearby, she will play classical music that has sounds of nature inserted: "They're just marvelous for relaxing, almost like being able to go out in your yard and absorb nature while you're writing."

When she is researching, Mills takes notes on a laptop when possible. It makes it less likely to make mistakes in transcribing hand notes. Some places afford even better ways of gathering information. The Family History Library in Salt Lake City is a technologically advanced facility, and she can simply press a key and a digital copy will be made right onto her disk. She brings that digital copy home and prints it out. "It's a lot easier than standing in line at the photocopy machine." However, you can't just click and go. "You've still got to thoroughly study what you're discovering there. You can't just collect documents and wait until you get home to analyze and see what you've got because there may be pieces of information within a document that will send you off in a different direction." When she returns home, Mills prints out and integrates the information she has gathered at an archive. All of the notes go into the file folders that she works from as she writes.

Mills starts her writing with an outline—"You need some basic structure"—but it serves as a beginning only; "with a research project things often take on a life of their own." She tries to do all of her research before she starts writing, "but when you get in the middle of something, you always need something else and you've got to go work on it."

Her day begins with thinking things through. "I get my best ideas right as I'm waking up," she says, "and if I've got a good idea going it can take me a long time to get out of bed." She gets up anytime between 6 and 9 A.M., works through e-mail, professional matters, and other normal everyday stuff until about mid-afternoon. "I'm pretty active professionally, and there are a lot of causes that I care about that I work with, and so it's usually about 3 P.M. before I get down to a real day's work." She finds it less distracting to work at night: "When the rest of the world settles down, you can get a lot more done without the interruptions." She usually writes between late afternoon and 2 A.M. and finds she does not tire if she's engrossed in what she's doing. "Once I get up a good head of steam I don't like to quit." Writer's block is quickly cured with a "bag of cookies or a bowl of popcorn."

"Those who work at the microhistory level routinely deal with contradictory material," Mills says. She emphasizes two things when she's teaching research methodology. "First, research has to be absolutely exhaustive. You don't reach a conclusion until you are sure you have used every conceivable source that exists. Second, you always go back to the original, or as close to it as you can get." Then the researcher must try to evaluate the conditions under which the source was created—"internal conditions, external conditions, maybe do more research into the context politically or economically, or the laws that applied at that particular time so you can be sure that you interpret each document correctly." After all of that, and you have "a firm grasp on what was going on at that time, then you can make an informed judgment about what the most reliable source is."

Mills finds research more fun than writing because "that's the ongoing discovery." Writing is a chore, "but it's got to be done. It does not do any good to do research if you don't then report your findings."

Mills says she often has exciting breakthroughs. To her, "every discovery of the identity of an obscure person who has been lost to history is a breakthrough. To take a name that you just find in a record and make a real person out of that—reconstruct that person, rebuild her life, put her into a family—for me that validates her existence. To try to understand history without understanding the families that are at the core of everything is like confronting a robot and pretending that you find a pulse on it." She firmly believes that "everybody in history is a somebody. To try to study George Washington or George Washington Carver without understanding the needs of those common men and women who propelled the George

Washingtons and the George Washington Carvers to do what they did" doesn't give her a real understanding of history. "Knowing the kinship puts all aspects of history into a totally different light."

Outside of her field, Mills reads whatever strikes her fancy. In her reading pile at the time of this interview she had Bryan Sykes's *Seven Daughters of Eve,* which deals with mitochondrial DNA; Marylynn Salmon's *Women and the Law of Property in Early America;* David Lieberman's *Get Anyone to Do Anything and Never Feel Powerless Again;* and an issue of *Before and After: How to Design Cool Stuff* because she designs her own books. "Every little thing that you do fertilizes your brain and you never know when it will call up an 'aha!' connection, so I like to read different types of things."

Mills believes that to be a good historian, one must possess three qualities: "Thoroughness, candor that can't be silenced, and a curiosity that can't be quenched." She refuses to "sacrifice truth on the altar of political correctness."

Revisionism can be a problem for historians if it is done "just for the sake of following some political or ideological dogma." However, Mills believes all history is subject to revision "because it's our own effort to interpret what we have found, to make sense out of what we have found, and as we find more things it sheds different light on it."

An example of putting things into their proper context occurred while Mills was researching the family she portrayed in *Isle of Canes.* The French father of Coincoin's half-African children made a will in which he declared, "I am a bachelor and I have no children." Many have declared him "heartless, and that's the logical conclusion we would draw using our modern mind-set," Mills says. "But if you go back and look at the law that existed at that time and place, if he had acknowledged those children as his own, the law would have forbidden him to leave them anything at all." As it was, by falsely declaring himself childless, "he left them quite a bit in his will, as much as the law would allow him to leave people who were not his siblings." Under the law he had to leave two-thirds to his siblings because he was not married at the time he wrote the will, but the other one-third he could do with as he pleased. He bequeathed all of that third to Coincoin and their children.

Mills spent sixteen years editing the peer-reviewed *National Genealogical Society Quarterly*. It was "a learning experience in human nature, and how to go back to people and explain the problems that you've encountered with their submission while keeping a good working relationship." She believes that "editing is an experience that everyone should have, but it's not one that I wanted to do for the rest of my life."

Besides writing and editing, Mills teaches seminars and institutes internationally, including forums at the National Archives for fifteen years and Samford University in Birmingham, Alabama, for thirty. Her students are adults who want to learn how to research history—"methodology for research, how to analyze evidence, how to interpret materials." She finds it exciting. "They're all eager. They want to learn and they're being exposed to something from a different angle. It's really a pleasure to work with them."

She learns from them, too. Most of them are not professional genealogists. Her class at the Samford Institute of Genealogy and Historical Research "is a sort of rite of passage for those who want to be professional genealogists and are very serious about it." But most of her students are professionals in other fields who are researching their own family, and "they have all of these different quirks that they've not been able to find within the historical literature. It opens up your mind to different things that need exploring."

Mills believes she has contributed to the field of history in two ways. First, "I hope that I have helped traditional historians better understand and appreciate the value of family history and the complexity of family history," she says. "I have days when I get really, really discouraged over prospects, but then obviously there are some inroads." She cites this interview as an inroad: "Twenty years ago you wouldn't be interviewing me because twenty years ago genealogy was not taken that seriously within the field of history." She believes "I have made some contribution in helping historians realize that family history is history in microcosm, it's history up close and personal, and it's a fundamental building block to all the broad interpretations historians want to do."

Second, Mills believes that her greatest contribution in the field of family history is the "methodology that I've tried to develop and teach for doing research on obscure people, the things that historians aren't getting into. I think the extent to which I've been able to elevate the professional and the scholarly standards in the field of family history is an important contribution."

Asked if she can imagine having spent her life doing something else, Mills says, "No, I cannot even conceive of anything else. I think I have been very blessed in life to be able to do what I enjoy doing—studying individual families and using them as building blocks to put together a community and see the social structure that exists there."

Lynda Crist

CONSERVATOR OF A LEGACY

"We have always had...all kinds of people who are interested in Davis, from schoolchildren on up through the most senior scholars who spend hours, days, months here."

"His personal library was pillaged during the war and a lot of things were carried off, destroyed, or just lost forever."

For serious scholars, using the website is "like having a little library on their desktop."

"I'm happiest when I'm down in the stacks or prowling around manuscript collections looking for material."

"I think what he said is what he meant, and that's very inspiring to me."

"In science they care about what was published yesterday, but for historians you have to go way back."

"You need to think about that person in his or her day before you start coming to conclusions; be careful of presentism."

Lynda Crist has spent her entire distinguished career working on the editing and publishing of the voluminous Jefferson Davis Papers at Rice University in Houston, Texas. "I feel like a relic myself, these days," she admits, "I've been here so long. It's been very gratifying to me. I love it, I love the work."

Crist grew up in Houston and earned both her undergraduate and master's degrees at Rice. Although she had always liked history and English, her father, an engineer, encouraged her to pursue a science, so she had enrolled as a physics major. To earn extra money as an undergraduate, she took a part-time position as file clerk/typist with the Davis project, and that was life-changing. "I just kind of fell into the work and switched to U.S. history."

In the early 1960s, Frank Vandiver, the noted Civil War scholar on the faculty at Rice, and the historian Allan Nevins were both working on Davis material at the Huntington Library in California. They met there, and in conversation they discovered that each had found a number of Davis manuscripts that were not in the 1923 edition of Davis's papers. Because it was the Civil War centennial, they thought it would be a good idea to do a supplementary edition. They found so much that Vandiver originally envisioned fifty volumes, "but we cut that back to twenty-five, and now it's fifteen," Crist says. Vandiver "managed to get an office from Rice and some financial support," and that's how the project came to be housed at Rice. Nevins and Bruce Catton were on the charter advisory editorial board. "We've had a lot of stellar names, thanks to Frank, who supported this effort," says Crist.

As a graduate student, Crist continued to work for the Davis project and for *The Journal of Southern History* in the offices next door to earn her graduate stipend. She also worked for one year as a grader and tutorial leader and as a research assistant for Vandiver for a couple of his books. Then in the early 1970s, the Davis project offered her a job as an assistant, which she accepted.

She worked for a few years under editor James T. McIntosh before deciding that she really needed to get a doctorate if she wanted to make a career of documentary editing. The University of Tennessee, where the Andrew Johnson Papers are housed, offered her the best situation, and she worked on the Johnson Papers while earning her degree. "It was an incredible learning experience!" she remembers. They were further along than the Davis project at that point, and "an amazing woman named Pat Clark was kind of the indispensable person of the project, the associate editor and office manager," Crist says. "She was one of my great mentors in editing." Crist graduated from Tennessee with a doctorate in U.S. history.

Throughout her schooling several people influenced Crist in her final choice of career—first of all her mother, "a great reader," who read to Lynda and her sister "from the beginning." Crist remembers of her mother that "education was always very high on her list because she had not had the chance to go to college, but always wanted to." In high school, Crist had "an amazing English teacher, and he almost convinced me to major in English." But she also had "an incredibly good high school history teacher, Kathryn Timme," with whom she remained in touch. "I have to say that she was probably my role model as a wonderful teacher and a teacher of writing in history."

When she enrolled at Rice, Crist found "several really excellent undergraduate history teachers who also inspired me to write history." Besides Vandiver, Crist admired Sanford Higginbotham, a professor of early U.S. history and the editor of *The Journal of Southern History;* Charles Garside, who she believes "was probably the best classroom teacher I've ever had anywhere"; and Ira Gruber, "who was just an amazing historian and writer, and a fabulous writing teacher."

With her new doctorate, Crist returned to Rice and the Davis project, where she has been ever since. The university "shelters us and gives us office space and university benefits for the staff members," access to interlibrary loan services, and "vital things like that." She believes that the project "could not exist except in a research library," and that Rice is an ideal home. "They've been just wonderful. The university and library services here are excellent and that's really what any documentary project most requires." The project is defined by the university as a research center, and the staff is considered professional staff, much like the library staff. "In fact, we really are more like an archive than an academic department," Crist says. There are two full-time editors, Crist and Suzanne Scott Gibbs, plus graduate student interns, usually doctoral candidates in Southern history.

The biggest challenge facing the project was finding all of Davis's papers. He had no collection of presidential papers in the Library of Congress as so many of the U.S. presidents have. They spent nearly seven years "just canvassing, looking for his papers, and they still continue to drift in," Crist says. Much was lost—"his personal library was pillaged during the war and a lot of things were carried off, destroyed, or just lost forever." Frequently, "things are in the marketplace with autograph dealers, in catalogs, and so forth." Much of his work is in private hands, Crist says, and she believes that the people who have them would probably be willing to help if they knew about the project. "But it's impossible to reach every household in the country that might have Davis letters stuck in a stamp album or an attic."

The search began long before computers and e-mail. Letters went out to "every public library and every university in this country, and many in England, asking if there were any Davis documents in their collections." Haskell Monroe, the first editor of the papers, visited the repositories of some of the larger collections and made checklists of the Davis materials, copying whatever they had. Many items were microfilmed for them, particularly at the National Archives. For fifteen years, the project employed a contract researcher who produced some 105 reels of microfilmed Davis materials from "many, many record groups in the archives."

The Davis Papers project allows open access to its files, unlike many documentary projects. "We have always had scholar researchers, not just academics, but all kinds of people who are interested in Davis," says Crist, "from schoolchildren on up through the most senior scholars who spend hours, days, months here." It gratifies Crist to read books that are published by an author who has done research in the Davis Paper files—to "see how the material is being used and how it fits into the whole work in general."

The project's website has saved a tremendous amount of time because many questions, especially those from schoolchildren, can be answered there. For serious scholars, using the website is "like having a little library on their desktop. It really saves them a lot of time traveling everywhere." Not all of the letters are printed in full, but "they have a very good idea of where the big collections are, and if they have a specific research interest they often get in touch with us, and, thanks to our electronic databases, we're able to send them a list of documents and where those documents are so they can either travel or contact those repositories on their own."

Funding for the project can be harrowing. Cuts under Ronald Reagan's administration reduced their full-time staff from three to two people, and they have never recovered that third position. In 2004, the George W. Bush administration "zeroed out" the federal agency that channeled most of their funds. "That was a very scary time," Crist remembers, but funding was eventually restored. The project also receives an annual grant from Mississippi, Davis's home state. "The hand-to-mouth existence gets a little stressful," Crist admits. "We might not be here this time next year, or just one of us might be here, or both of us might be here on a very short schedule, half-time or something like that." The uncertainty "makes it hard to attract and keep people."

Volume twelve, the first postwar volume, has recently been published. There are two more projected volumes dealing with the postwar, and then a planned fifteenth volume that will be a cumulative index and bibliography. When they are completed, all of the documents become the property of Rice. The hope is that there will be a "nice Confederate research center here because we have so much ancillary material on the war, not just Davis documents. That would be a wonderful legacy in addition to the printed books."

The work setup has been in place since 1968. "That's incredibly rare on this campus," says Crist, "for somebody to occupy the same office space for that long." They have three "really substantial rooms" in the library: a file room accessible only through Crist's office where all of the documents are kept, along with a safe that holds several original Davis letters; Crist's office, which contains most of the project's library and office files; and a larger workroom for the assistant editor, the graduate student interns, and visiting researchers.

A quiet atmosphere is important during work time. "I often tell people that we live a kind of monk-like existence up here," Crist says. "We're just busy all day at our computers or down in the stacks or down in the microfilm room." Their collections of government documents and micro-materials are heavily used, as are the micro-filmed newspapers. "Every desk has a computer and a microfilm reader; they're our essential stock-in-trade." There is also a library of about three thousand volumes composed of Crist's books, the project's books, and items checked out of the university library. "We try to keep a good working library up here just for convenience."

The work is intense. "We go over and over and over documents in the three years it takes to get a volume out," Crist explains. "We proofread them in teams, out loud; every document is proofread at least three times before it's ready to go into the book." Many documents are not annotated, but are entered in full in the book.

In selecting items for annotation, Crist and her team concentrate on documents that Davis himself wrote, and that "carry the story along chronologically; and those that are particularly revealing of Davis's thought processes, his personality, his judgment, what he's doing during the time period covered by the volume." The annotations identify people, places, and events that have not been identified in previous volumes.

The project has always included Davis's wife's letters, too. Varina "was an amazing woman, who had a really hard life," says Crist. Marital discord, the late arrival of children from the union, and the loss of several of their children made life difficult. The project has a database of just her correspondence, along with the databases of her husband's material. Many of her letters to other people are used in annotation.

The research subjects that have to be dealt with "are just all over the lot" because of the nature of the correspondence. "Every footnote is a little mini-essay, whether it's a biographical sketch of a well-known person or a really obscure person." Topics range widely. In volume twelve alone, they included: the McLane-Ocampo Treaty of Transit and Commerce with Mexico in pre-Civil War times; the insurance business, because Davis was an insurance company president during this period; the Panic of 1873, which ruined the insurance business; the flooding of the Mississippi River because it impinged on Davis's management of his brother's estate; constitutional legal history for his treason trial that never happened; European research because he lived in Europe for nearly a year during the time covered in volume twelve and met "all kinds of interesting people in England and Scotland and Ireland and Wales." The list can go on and on. "It's just really a hodgepodge of material," Crist says.

Crist and the assistant editor divide up the writing either chronologically or by topic. For volume twelve, former assistant editor Brady Hutchison chose the earlier material from the prison years and everything that had to do with the trial because he had a year of law school and was very keen on legal history. "I did the European material and the insurance business," Crist explains, "and we both worked on the plantation management questions."

Crist admits that she enjoys both the research and the writing. "I *love* the research part; I'm happiest when I'm down in the stacks or prowling around manuscript collections looking for material. But I like the writing, too, because it's just so much fun to see it all come together."

All researchers, including the editors, use three-by-five slips of paper, dating from the 1960s forward, which are filed in an old library catalog unit that was "scavenged from the library when they started getting rid of all their card catalogs." There are also "lots of checklists from all the document repositories in big loose-leaf binders, and then the research files of xeroxed materials of all sorts."

Crist keeps regular office hours, but finds almost every day is different. She works best in the morning, coming in early and leaving about 4:30 in the afternoon, rarely taking work home. However, she has "been known to take indexing home with me, volume indexes, just so I can have a long period of quiet." The project does its own indexing—"we insist on it." At one point Louisiana State University Press, which publishes the volumes, hired someone to do the indexing; the project immediately realized that was not a good idea. "Actually it's something I really enjoy," Crist admits. "I don't know if it shows what a strange little mind I have, or whether because it's the last thing to be done on the volume and I'm just so ready for that volume to be over and get on to the next."

Crist appreciates the Louisiana State University Press forcing them into a deadline for each volume. "At some point," she says, "you just have to stop. You're never going to find *everything,* and at some point you just have to submit the book so they can get it on the schedule." The press needs to set its production schedules, its advertising, and so forth, and it needs to have an estimate within a few months of publication so it can plan ahead. Because the books are "very complicated and very expensive to produce," the press can't afford to publish one every year. On the other hand, "we have to produce the books regularly or we don't get funding." That forces the project to move along. "I guess otherwise we could sit around and work on a volume until the end of time," Crist says, "looking for this and that."

"There's always plenty to do around here," she says. "If you can't quite get it together to write the footnote, you just go on to the next one, or do some additional research downstairs, or just turn to the e-mail and try to answer some of the research queries."

There have been some exciting finds for the project. One that Crist remembers in particular was the discovery of two large books of original telegrams from the Civil War period, owned by an art gallery in Shreveport, Louisiana. She visited the gallery and copied the Davis items, almost all new material, not found even in the *Official Records.* The material "will not change the course of history," Crist admits, "but that was fun to find."

Having spent her career with Jefferson Davis, Crist believes he "was a straight arrow." Although she did not always agree with what he stood for or had to say, "I think what he said is what he meant, and that's very inspiring to me." He was straightforward, and "truly a Southern gentleman." Crist admits he did "misremember things to his own benefit occasionally," but "in general, I think he was a really fine person."

He was, though, lacking in writing skills. His two-volume memoir of the war is "deadly! It's absolutely deadly. We recommend it for insomniacs. It's just so terribly long and tedious." Varina was a much better writer than her husband: "Her memoirs are quite wonderful; they're really a lot of fun."

Crist believes curiosity and clarity of expression are the two top talents required of any historian. "You have to really be a little bull-dog about research," she says, "keep at it and keep thinking about it and go back to it, and just remain very persistent in tracking down information, and be willing to leave your desk and your computer to go out and find it." A science colleague asked why she needed the library, since everything is now online. But it isn't, Crist points out. "In science they care about what was published yesterday, but for historians you have to go way back."

Using the Internet can have its pitfalls. "You have to really drill into the graduate students that you need to be absolutely certain of what you're citing, whom you're citing, from the Internet," Crist says. That's why it was so important for the project to get its website up and running. "It is vast, but we really wanted to have a place with good, accurate information on Davis, something people could rely on."

Political correctness has played little part in compiling the Davis Papers. Crist believes that "Davis is probably one of history's least politically correct persons." But, she warns, "You need to think about that person in his or her day before you start coming to conclusions; be careful of presentism"—viewing the past through the lens of the present. Terminology has remained consistent throughout the volumes. "We started out in volume one using the term 'black' for a person of color, and we have stuck to it. The same thing with Indians, whom we do not call Native Americans because none of our documents called them that." The only bow to political correctness is that there is now an index entry for women, which was not in the previous volumes. "People want to know what women were thinking, what they were doing, which ones were writing to Davis, to whom he wrote."

The importance of the project cannot be overestimated. Most important, Crist says, is "having the documents out there in their complete form, history in its purest form, as I like to say." Second in importance, she believes, is the index, followed by the annotation. The indexes are excellent, she says, and can help researchers "find very specific information about Davis and his colleagues and his family and his times."

Crist takes pride in her contribution to the field of history. "It's wonderful," she admits, "just to have your name in print now and then—and my mother loves it, too." But more than that, Crist knows she has "participated in something really permanent and lasting, and something that is obviously so useful to so many people." No one anticipated just how widely the Davis Papers would be used, "that it wouldn't just be about Jefferson Davis, but it would be used for so many other topics that people find interesting in the nineteenth century."

Her position as editor of the Davis Papers brings with it other obligations. She is often called on as a speaker: "There's always a heavy call around Davis's birthday in the first part of June—everybody wants a little speech," she says. She also reads grant proposals for agencies and book manuscripts for university presses, and the project gets involved in preservation of Davis-related sites "because we often have information they need—we're very supportive of that kind of work."

If she had not spent her career on the Jefferson Davis Papers, Crist believes she would have spent her life as a librarian or an archivist. "I've always been surrounded by that kind of material and those kind of folks who are just very congenial to me and seem to suit my temperament and personality." In retirement, she plans to "volunteer to work in a library or a bookstore or something like that." She has also taught English as a second language and thinks that might be something else she would do more of in retirement.

But for now there is Jefferson Davis and the job of preserving his legacy.

Stephen L. Hardin

REGIONAL HISTORIAN,
SELF-PROCLAIMED

It was an epiphany to realize that what he was "good at was not fighting battles, it was studying battles."

"A book is not the place to reveal *all* you know; a book is the place to craft *what* you know."

"If you can't delight people, if you can't hook them in some way, it's going to be difficult to instruct them."

"I don't think that as historians it is our job to judge people who lived in the past, but rather to understand and explain them."

STEPHEN L. HARDIN GREW UP IN THE 1950S AND 1960S IN McKinney, Texas. "History was in the air in those days," he recalls, "and as a boy growing up in Texas, it was hard not to be aware of the past." During that era, Walt Disney and Fess Parker had the nation caught up in the Davy Crockett craze. "Like a lot of kids my age, I had the coonskin cap, the moccasins, the little canteen, the little rifle, and somewhere my mother has a picture of a five- or six-year-old me in full Davy Crockett regalia." And then in 1960 came the John Wayne Alamo movie: "I think John Wayne probably ignited a spark that hasn't gone out to this day, so I owe him and Fess Parker an enormous debt."

But Hardin was slow to adopt history as his life's work. When he entered college, he planned to be a career Air Force officer. He matriculated to Southwest Texas (since renamed Texas State), where he earned his undergraduate and his master's degrees, because they had an Air Force ROTC program. But with "woefully inadequate" math skills, it became apparent that he "wasn't pilot material." He also discovered that "the more I spent time with military types, the more I realized that I didn't enjoy the military as much as I did reading and studying about the battles." It was an epiphany to realize that what he was "good at was not *fighting* battles, it was *studying* battles."

After dropping his plans for the Air Force, Hardin had to choose another career path. English and history both beckoned, and he double-majored for his bachelor's degree. An English professor, Edgar Laird, ironically, helped steer him away from English to history by pointing out that every paper Hardin wrote for his English courses "dealt with the historical elements in the literature." The first scholarly paper he ever presented in public "compared the archaeological record to the Old English poem *Beowulf,* to see if *Beowulf* accurately reflected the arms and armor of the seventh century. And, of course, it did." His interest in Geoffrey Chaucer was "always about descriptions of the armor." His favorite Chaucer character is the knight in *The Canterbury Tales.*

When working on his master's degree, Hardin focused on history; his thesis, written under James Pohl, studied the weapons and tactics of the Texas Revolution. Having now made an "investment in this research area," he jumped at the opportunity to attend Texas Christian University (TCU) to study military history under Grady McWhiney. But when he arrived there, he found much more than just McWhiney's expertise. It was 1985, a time that was a "Golden Age" for TCU. "The stars were in some sort of alignment, because during the years I was there, I could study with Grady McWhiney, Don Worcester, and Ben Proctor. Worcester is a master stylist; McWhiney taught us the importance of organization; and Proctor emphasized and drilled us and drilled us and drilled us until we mastered scholarly citations. I brought something away from each one of those men, and, of course, you need all three skills to produce a work of scholarship."

Hardin believes that the mastery of proper form is "what separates the professional historian from the lay historian." He is always puzzled by the many people who call themselves historians, but when asked where they earned their degree, they admit that they're avocational historians. Hardin's response to that is, "Well, I myself am an avocational brain surgeon." He believes that "if you start looking at the elements that separate a trained historian from a lay historian, the assumption is that we, the professional historians, don't expect you to take our word for it. We cite our sources, and I think we would all rather not have to deal with that because it's burdensome [messing with footnotes and bibliography] but it's important."

Hardin firmly believes that "attention to scholarly detail, professional citations, and an approachable style do not have to be mutually exclusive." He cites McWhiney as an example: "While his books certainly dealt with scholarly concepts, his style was very approachable and that's something he always emphasized and I took to heart." And it works. Hardin's doctoral dissertation, written under McWhiney's supervision, became the basis for his *Texian Iliad: A Military History of the Texas Revolution,* a book that has sold remarkably well since its publication in 1994. His studies at TCU, Hardin says, prepared him to write for the "guy down the street," not the "guy down the hall," as so many academics do today.

Besides those already mentioned, Hardin gives the greater credit in the choice of his life's career to his father. Each night, at bedtime, his father made up Davy Crockett stories. "None of these comported in any way, shape, or form to history," Hardin recalls. "Dad would just make up these stories." In them, "Davy rode a horse called Old Paint because Dad liked paint horses." Hardin vividly remembers a story that featured a grizzly bear sneaking up on a sleeping Davy Crockett. Old Paint broke loose from his hobble and kicked the bear in the mouth, breaking one of its teeth. "The bear ran off into the woods howling—and Dad would throw in the sound effects." They also went to history movies together and discussed them afterward.

"As I got older I realized that his interest in history and the movies had a lot to do with planting a seed for me. I think that's the best thing parents can do—help their children discover what it is they're interested in, encourage them in that, and then step back and let them fly."

Hardin's work has focused on regional military history. "Fortunately," he says, "we've had a lot of battles. I may spend the rest of my career writing about the battles we fought in Texas, and still not cover them all." As far as "limiting" himself to regional history, he always remembers something Pohl said to him: "Remember, Steve, Herodotus was also a local historian."

Hardin has an "investment" in Texas history. "I know Texas, I know where the archives are," he says. "I can't reinvent the wheel every time; I can't go back and learn the sources, and I think most academic historians are like that. I think they stake out an area, and they have an investment in it." Hardin is close to his sources, he's interested in Texas, and as he travels "across the landscape of Texas, I'm so acutely aware of the history that's around me. I'm still that little boy to some degree—it's in the air." That's why, he says, "I'm unapologetically a regional historian."

When researching, Hardin takes notes in longhand then types them on the computer and prints them out on full sheets of paper; one note, one thought, per page. All of those notes go into one big folder until it's time to organize the book into chapters. That's when he decides where each piece of information fits, and at that time it goes into a specific chapter folder.

When writing, information that Hardin has gathered during his research is used judiciously. "My constant standard is if it doesn't advance the narrative, it doesn't get in. I'm aware of cluttering up the narrative, and I do not want to clutter up the narrative with bits and pieces of extraneous information." He recalls one of the most instructive things McWhiney ever told him: "A historian needs to know what to leave out." He believes that whatever success his books have enjoyed, it's "as much for what I've cut out as for what I put in." Hardin's maxim is, "A book is not the place to reveal *all* you know; a book is the place to craft *what* you know."

When he is ready to write, Hardin tries to "start with an episode and go from the specific to the general." Each chapter begins by centering on a human activity, "like a person riding into town, or someone being hanged, because people want to read about other people." Once that "human event" is down, he lets his source material "direct how the chapter is going to evolve."

When Hardin began writing, he wrote on a legal pad. He admits that to this day "I'm a two-finger typer... [but] a pretty *good* two-finger typer." So today he writes on a computer, a blessing to him since he is a "compulsive editor." He sees writing as a lot like sculpting. "Your rough draft is something that sort of looks like a head, and then in your second draft you're working on the nose and the eyes, and it's beginning to look more and more like a person. But with each successive draft, it becomes leaner and leaner until finally it's readable." He believes that "all writing is rewriting." Getting something down is the hard part; once it's down you can craft it.

In graduate school, Hardin recalls, "I did a lot of writing in my underwear." Suffering from insomnia, he regularly woke up at 3 A.M. He talked about it with Worcester, a fellow sufferer, who said to him, "Hell, put it to work." So he did. Much of *Texian Iliad,* he figures, was probably written at three o'clock in the morning in his underwear. But insomnia doesn't appear generally to be a real problem for him. "I seem to get most of my work done late at night," he says. "When I'm really cranking, I've written all night."

Hardin doesn't keep to a regular writing schedule. "I could write every day, and I should write every day, but I don't." He does, however, always have a book in mind. At the time of this interview he's had a fourteen-chapter book in the works "for a long time" for which he has completed the research and written two chapters. "But I've gotten to the point where I don't want to write a book on spec [speculation], I don't want to write a book that somebody hasn't expressed an interest in publishing." On the other hand, "I haven't done my work, either, because I really haven't shopped it out." Rather than procrastination, Hardin refers to this as resistance. "Here I am finding reasons for not finishing this book, and they may be perfectly justifiable reasons, but that's still resistance."

Hardin believes that aspect of human nature—resistance—is inherently evil, that "it keeps us from being the best we can be." He cites a book by Steven Pressfield, *The War of Art,* which posits that the creative person in whatever field has that enemy resistance. Pressfield argues that the "writing is not hard; sitting down to write is hard," and offers suggestions for overcoming such reluctance. "One of the great tactics for overcoming resistance," Hardin believes, "is having fear and a deadline." His first job at Victoria College did not require that he write articles and books. In fact, when he was interviewed for the position, he asked if he would "get any brownie points for my publishing." The response was, "Well, we don't mind that." The dean explained to him that Victoria College was a teaching institution, and Hardin could publish all he liked, but it wouldn't count toward a higher salary or enter into the working of tenure or promotion. "It was just a nonissue," Hardin recalls. "They promised me that, and they kept that promise faithfully."

On occasions when he must write, even if he doesn't feel motivated, he says, "I just gut it through. You just have to get something down and you can come back and fix it later." Often, he says, "writers can get a little precious—going to cocktail parties and talking about what you're going to write is not writing; researching is not writing; making note cards is not writing; writing is writing, and writing is work." Hardin knows it's time to stop writing for the day when he reaches exhaustion. "When I start messing up, I know that it's time to stop; when it starts being crap. I'd rather stop than to have to rewrite extensively."

Before beginning a day's writing, Hardin reads the entire chapter he's working on up to the point where he left off. "That will give me a sense of where I am," he says. Sometimes when he's exhausted and calling it quits for the day, "I will write the next topic sentence to give myself a prompt for when I come back. I know what I want to say next at three o'clock in the morning, but I might forget that by the time I get back to the computer."

During his research Hardin has experienced "transcendent moments." One such moment came when he found himself holding a book that had belonged to Stephen F. Austin. "That was an 'Oh, wow,' sort of moment." On another occasion he found "a box that held the buttons from Confederate general and Texas Ranger Ben McCulloch's jacket, and the bullet that killed him." They had been sent to McCulloch's mother from Elkhorn Tavern with a note written on the battlefield. "I got shivers down my spine!"

"Things like that"—holding a letter by Austin or Sam Houston or William Barret Travis—Hardin says, "are tangible links with the past. So many times history is so intangible and we're straining to make it relevant and tangible, but when you can touch it and feel it that makes it real for me and impresses upon me that these are not characters in fiction, these were real people and they've left evidence of their presence." Hardin feels privileged to spend his life with that evidence. "I've become very jealous and protective of that evidence," he says, "and if I go into an archive and I don't think they're taking care of it properly, I get cranky."

Reading is one of Hardin's favorite pastimes. At the time of this interview, he had nearly finished Patrick O'Brian's twenty-volume series of Aubrey/Maturin sea stories—every one of which he has in hardback. "I am a believer in hardback books," he says. "When I have a choice, I will always buy a book in hardback."

Hardin is always on the lookout for ideas he can use. "When I see a phrase or a sentence that I think is elegant, or a nice way the language is used, I enter it into my computer in what I call 'interesting constructions.'" Then if he is stuck and doesn't know how to proceed or how to phrase something, he will go back to his 'interesting constructions,' find one that seems apt, and plug it into what he is doing—without plagiarizing. He can "almost always find a way to do that."

Hardin believes a good historian must have the "characteristics that define any artist, and that is a deep and abiding fascination with people. I don't think a misanthrope could ever be a good historian." Because history is about people, he tries to make his "courses revolve around people, and through people I introduce the ideas. Chaucer said that you have to delight to instruct, that that was his job. I always try to remember that in my teaching and in my writing: that if you can't delight people, if you can't hook them in some way, it's going to be difficult to instruct them." It's not a sure-fire approach, though. "Sometimes it works, sometimes it doesn't, and sometimes it works beyond your wildest dreams."

Political correctness does not factor into Hardin's work. If he felt any pressure to bring political correctness to his writing or teaching, he says, "It would be a point of pride to resist it." He believes you can say anything you want or need to say, as long as it is done respect-fully. "I don't think that as historians it is our job to judge people who lived in the past, but rather to understand and explain them."

Revisionism, Hardin says, comes with the territory. "I'm always trying to say something that no one else has said. Whenever you do that, you revise the historical record and when you revise the historical record you are, by definition, a revisionist.... I thought that was what all historians were supposed to do." That's the purpose of writing history: "How can you make an original contribution to knowledge without being a revisionist?" Hardin believes the term *revisionist* has taken on a new meaning and that when most people use that term today they mean "a cynical, anti-American historian." He thinks these people could just as easily say "a bad historian, or a biased historian, or a historian who is not properly trained, and I don't think that's what any of us are about."

One of Hardin's more unique experiences as a historian was working as a historical advisor on the John Lee Hancock film, *The Alamo,* produced in 2004. When he met with Hancock, the direc-tor made it clear that the movie would "be as historically accurate as possible, but it had to be cinematically appealing." One of the first things Hardin and Alan Huffines, another historical advisor and Alamo expert, worked on was the script. They found that the lines for the characters sounded modern, so they spent a day editing the language to a period vernacular. "That's one of the things that I'm proud of," he says. "When you listen to the movie, these people aren't speaking the same way that people speak today. I think that lends some fidelity to the movie."

During the actual filming, Hardin and Huffines watched the takes, trying to catch mistakes "with a historian's eye." He remembers in particular an occasion when he suggested that the actor change his tone of voice when addressing a slave from one of "gruff boss" to one of "condescension," an attitude particularly resented by slaves. In the end, Hardin says, "I thought the delivery on that scene was so much more interesting and had so much more historical fidelity."

They also worked with the actors, who were as concerned as the director to get it right. About the actors, Hardin says, "I saw nothing but dedication and hard work. We started filming when the sun was up, and we stopped filming when the sun went down. That made for some very, very long days, and people left exhausted. There were even some night shots that ran from five o'clock in the evening to six the next morning. "It's damned hard work and I wouldn't want to do it full-time." In all, he found the whole experience "tremendously exciting."

But this also led him to an appalling discovery about the state of education in the United States. In discussing the film when it opened, a nineteen-year-old relative asked what the movie was about. The young lady was "a native Texan, a product of Texas public schools, and was at the time attending a Texas community college" where she was a good student. "When you teach Texas history for a living," Hardin laments, "it's those moments that make you want to go shower with a toaster.... If *she* didn't know what the Alamo was about, what chance did the kids in Peoria have?" Her ignorance, he says, "might suggest the reason our film bombed among the vital seventeen-to-twenty-five demographic."

Hardin finds teaching challenging, finding that too often students "are going through the motions, they're not really concerned if they're actually learning anything." He blames the public schools for this attitude. "I believe that there is a dark, dirty secret in this country that permeates the entire education system—very little learning is taking place, and everybody knows it, and the implied contract is, okay, kids, here's the deal: I will pretend to teach and you will pretend to learn, and at the end of the process I will get a paycheck and you will get a diploma and this will be our little secret."

He admits that many teachers work hard, "but I think there is a systemic problem with American education wherein we have substituted the joy of learning for an academic, bureaucratic process, and everybody is just going through the motions." At one time, each generation was better educated than the preceding generation. Hardin believes that peaked in the 1960s, "and ever since then we have been *less* educated than the generation before. We're going backwards in a period of increased international competition."

This state of affairs "does not bode well for us as a society," Hardin warns. "For years," he says, "we have forecast the enormous social cost attached to growing cultural ignorance, and now the future is here and our citizens are so ignorant that they can no longer appreciate what was once a staple of the Hollywood studio system, the historical epic. Our young people are too ignorant to know what it's about."

It's true that today we live in what we call the Information Age, but that information comes in "little 'info bites' without some sort of context." Without that context, he says, "it's just information, it doesn't transcend to the next step, which becomes knowledge. Where do you fit the information unless you have a knowledge base?" Without the knowledge base, "you can't transcend to the next step and take that knowledge and apply it to your own life and your own relationships, whereupon it becomes wisdom." Hardin believes that too many kids today are "a long way from getting wisdom because they haven't even gotten to knowledge." He fears that our society is telling the children that accessing information is enough. "Well, it's not enough. That's why so many of our young people are adrift. They don't have knowledge, they don't have wisdom. They can access the information, but that's not going to help them get through rough times in a marriage or build character."

Hardin admits that he has aired some opinions that people might not like hearing, "and normally they will not thank you for telling them." He is reminded of an old Jewish folk-saying: "Tell the truth and run!"

He believes his unique contribution to the field of history is his *Texian Iliad*. He wanted to write a book that took the focus off of the Alamo and pointed it to the larger picture of the entire War for Texas Independence. "I've often said that Texans 'Remember the Alamo' to the exclusion of everything else in their history," he says, "and I wanted people after having read this book to come away with an understanding that a lot more went on than just the Alamo. You really can't understand that event out of context, without knowing what came before and what came after."

His dream of being an airman still lingers, but not as a pilot in this era. "I would have enjoyed being a fighter pilot in World War I, and maybe even World War II, but not the jets of today." He recalls a high-ranking Saudi fighter pilot during the first Gulf War reporting how he shot down four or five Iraqi jets—"I saw a blip on the radar screen and fired my rockets." That's not Hardin's idea of a dream job. "They're technocrats today, and I've never regretted not going there."

He had also toyed with the idea of being a lawyer, but only if it was like it is on television—"going into the courtroom and arguing and pitting your brains and your knowledge against someone else's brains and knowledge." But having talked with lawyers, he discovered that most times the job is "long and boring." He admits, "I think I like the idealized notion of being a lawyer far more than I would have liked the reality of it."

Reality—truth about the past—is what Hardin has insistently sought, and found, in the history in the air all around him in his region of the world.

In 2009, Hardin joined the faculty at McMurry University where he continues to advance the cause of Texas history.

Bruce Winders

Keeper of the Alamo

"[I] had the feeling that I was the preeminent historian in the field of Mexican War studies, but the problem was that there was no field of Mexican War studies."

"If you have a project that's exciting and something you really want to do, then you'll find the time to do it."

To be objective about your subject "may mean that you have to recognize what your own biases are and be up-front about that."

"I CAN HONESTLY NEVER REMEMBER A TIME WHEN I DIDN'T HAVE a sense of history," Bruce Winders says. "I grew up in a family that really valued reading, valued history, and growing up in the late 1950s and early 1960s, there was a real glorification of American history in the popular culture."

Winders remembers both of his parents being great readers. His father "loved literature," while his mother avidly read mysteries, historical fiction, and historical narratives. "It just rubbed off on me," he says. His father served in the Air Force in Europe during World War II, and Winders remembers friends of his father visiting and telling stories of their military experiences. "It reinforced in my mind that historical things had taken place, and I was interested in them." Further reinforcement came from family trips to historical sites.

Because his father was in the Air Force, Winders moved frequently during his childhood due to his father's new assignments. He was born in South Dakota, but when he was about a year old the family moved to Colorado Springs. When he was four or five he recalls living in a house from which they could see Pike's Peak. "I wanted to know why it was called Pike's Peak, who was this Pike guy?" For a time they lived in St. John's, Newfoundland, "right on the ocean, and there were icebergs and I got interested in naval affairs and sailing ships." Then it was back to Colorado Springs until he was about nine years old, when they moved to Kentucky. Thus, Winders had variety in his formative years. "Most kids my age would just read about something historical," he says, "but I had the opportunity to travel and see these things."

When the family moved to Kentucky, an uncle ten years his senior, John Michael Bourne, joined them. Bourne was a college student studying history and art history, who brought books home and allowed his nephew to read them; Winders recalls in particular Robert Utley's book on the Battle of Wounded Knee. "So here I was, probably still in junior high," Winders says, "reading all these college survey books that he brought home. It broadened my sense of history and my interest."

The high school Winders attended was in a rural setting. Strapped for money, it had expanded into World War II Quonset huts instead of buildings, "which," he says, "shows that it's not how much money you put into the facilities, and not the physical settings, but it's what you bring to it." Winders believes that the ultimate responsibility for learning is on the student: "You have to be an avid reader, you have to have an interest, you have to be aware that there's more to the world than just you and your tiny little setting."

As much as he loved history, Winders avoided it as a career when he entered Murray State University in western Kentucky; he thought all you could do with it was to teach, and extreme shyness made that idea "horrifying." So he turned to geology, another subject that stirred him, particularly historical geology. With his new-won degree, he headed for Fort Worth, Texas, in 1978, where he worked in a soil-testing laboratory "and found that a life in a geoscience field was going to be pretty boring." Before long, the bottom fell out of the building industry, and he lost the job.

At this point, he reevaluated his career path. Shortly after arriving in Texas he had joined a Civil War reenactment group, an activity that forced him to deal with his shyness: "We went into schools and talked to teachers and students," Winders says. "That's what gave me the idea that I would like to do this for a living." The thought of it was no longer horrifying. Having overcome the idea that he couldn't teach—and having "had a taste of what my life would be like if I didn't teach—sometimes a negative experience can be a great motivating factor"—he decided to give teaching a shot.

He taught earth science for two years in Arlington, Texas, bouncing around from school to school as the population in the area shifted. Looking to make his job more secure, he returned to school—the University of Texas at Arlington (UTA)—to add history to his certification. That same fall he finally achieved what he really wanted—to teach history. Within a couple of years he earned his master's degree and became the head of the history department at a junior high school.

To attract the interest and attention of his students, Winders brought his reenacting and living history techniques into the classroom. He soon became "sort of a local star in the Arlington school system," and stories about him began appearing in newspapers.

An interview with one particular journalist would have a profound impact on his life years later. In 1985, Donald Frazier, at that time an undergraduate communications student earning money as a reporter, contacted him about doing a story on reenacting. Winders invited him to a reenactment in Louisiana. "It was one of those moments that was important for both of us," Winders says, "because I think it reinforced his love of history, and it put me in contact with somebody who would later become an important influence in my life."

Five years later, in 1990, after one of the vice principals of his school was shot in the school parking lot, Winders again questioned what he really wanted to do. He discovered that Frazier had changed his mind about his career path and was working on a degree in history at Texas Christian University (TCU). Frazier suggested that Winders do the same. "So I did. I left teaching and went to TCU."

Winders's master's thesis had been on Mississippi volunteers and the Mexican War. That choice was dictated to some degree by the "fine Mexican War collection" at UTA, and by his love for the Civil War. "It was a direct tie to the Civil War," he says, "only it was fourteen years before." The thesis combined two of his interests—the Civil War and his "real affinity for the southwest. This was where those two themes crossed."

When he arrived at TCU, Winders began to study for a doctoral degree in history under Grady McWhiney. He found the professor more than willing to work with him on the Mexican War. Because Winders already had a background in that subject, he wanted to continue in it, "with the idea that at some point I would make the crossover back to the Civil War." For his dissertation, Winders began what would become the published book, *Mr. Polk's Army: Politics, Patronage, and the American Military in the Mexican War.* He began by writing unit histories of Mexican War troops. "The armies were small enough that you could identify every single regiment and write a thumbnail sketch," he says. The book was already under contract while he was still at TCU, "so I was able to graduate with a bona fide book in production."

That, however, did not lead immediately to a job. Like so many of his fellow graduate students, he spent a year or two sending out resumés and interviewing for college-level positions, with no luck. Then another former TCU student told Winders of an opening for a historian/curator at the Alamo in San Antonio, Texas. He was uniquely qualified for the position: He had his doctorate, his Mexican War studies, his experience in education, and during his time at UTA, he had taken several classes dealing with archives and knew the principles of collection. "That combination did it for me," he says. In May 1996, he was hired.

Winders says he doesn't have a "typical day or week" at the Alamo. He supervises a staff of about fourteen people: an education coordinator, a museum technician, an assistant curator, and guides. In addition, there is a volunteer staff of about twenty. Part of his job is to oversee the collections, making certain that they are physically secure. His public relations duties include talking to outside groups, writing short articles on the Alamo for various publications, maintaining the Alamo web page, and creating special educational events at the Alamo. Those events are often living-history based, and he develops programs for authors and publishers to interact with the public at the Alamo.

He is "on call" for visitors with questions and conducts tours for the general public and for VIPs. "By being where I am," he says, "I've been in contact with statesmen and actors and other notable people. It's interesting because it's just a different audience." He also serves as the head of the education department, which runs in-service courses for public school teachers and helps prepare teaching materials for classroom use. At the time of this interview, he was also working on a major new permanent exhibit for the Alamo, one that would present a fresh approach to the Alamo and to southwestern history. "We wanted to make sure that visitors understand the big picture," he says, "that it's not just about Texas." The exhibit was titled *The Alamo: A Story Bigger than Texas.*

"Every day," Winders says, "I may be doing one of those things full-time, or I may be doing three different things."

Besides his many duties at the Alamo, Winders finds time to write. "I think if you read a lot you reach a point where you begin thinking you could do that," he says. "[Writing] was just something I'd always wanted to do; I never really had a fear of it." While he was teaching in the public schools, he had started writing his own textbook. He attributes his affinity for writing, in part, to his upbringing. He was "raised by a World War II veteran who believed there was no such word as *can't.* I guess I got to where I actually internalized that because I've never said I really can't do that, only that I just haven't done that yet."

He also comes from a family of writers; one of his sisters teaches literature, and when his father retired to civilian life he wrote a column for local newspapers. "So," Winders says, "it was just one of those things where I always believed I was going to write; it was just a matter of when I was going to start doing it."

With the publication of *Mr. Polk's Army*, Winders "had the feeling that I was the preeminent historian in the field of Mexican War studies, but the problem was that there was no field of Mexican War studies." Winders and Frazier, together with a few other historians, teamed up to produce an encyclopedia of the Mexican War, and then Scholarly Resources, a publishing house, asked Winders to write a book on the war. He told them he would prefer to do a book that would put the Mexican War into a broader context. The publisher agreed and that book became *Crisis of the Southwest*.

"What I like about writing," Winders says, "is that you have an idea of what you're doing as you go into a project, but as you progress you find out where the gaps in your knowledge are and that spawns the questioning process and pushes you into further research." For Winders, that led to a broader understanding of the time period. It also led to a young readers' book on Davy Crockett "because I wanted to see if I could write a children's book. I could and I did," he says. He also did a book on the story of the shrine, *Sacrificed at the Alamo*.

His job does not dictate what he writes about, but he specializes in learning about the era and the region, and he tends to "take topics that leapfrog off of one another." One of his directors told him that if he needed time to write, he should just take it, "because it's important for you to do that." Winders believes that "if you're going to be the historian for a public institution like the Alamo, you have to be an active historian; you can't rest on your laurels. You have to be perceived by the historic community as a player, to be somebody who is actively researching and writing." He sees that as an integral part of the job, "so therefore I make it happen."

Winders is always on the lookout for things that fit into the next project he has in mind. He earmarks useful sources to revisit, "continually expanding my awareness of what the sources are and where they are and doing the groundwork in preparation for writing." During the research phase he makes notes that are organized by topic or theme on the computer. When he starts writing, he pulls those notes up on the computer. He also has "pretty extensive files of copied materials" that he refers to as he writes. He tries to have all of his research done before he begins writing. "Once you're writing," he says, "that encourages you to keep writing. If you have to break away to go find something, it gets you out of the mood and it's easier to put it off."

When he begins to write, Winders decides how many chapters will be required. The organization and outlining for the book happens in his head. "The books that I have written recently essentially were organized in my head and then they just came out of there, although I had a paper trail." When he starts a chapter, he goes back to his notes "and pulls from those."

Winders does not follow a regular writing schedule; he does it in his spare time—on weekends, at night, or during a week's vacation that he schedules just to write. When his vacation week is coming up, he prepares ahead of time "so that when it arrives I can just step right into it." He tries to avoid distractions. "When I write, I write; when I'm not writing, I'm doing the thinking and the researching," he says. He marvels at the people who wrote "back in the age of typewriters and carbon paper. You *really* had to want to write, you *really* had to devote yourself to it, because physically it was just harder to do." Writing is easier today with computers, but, he warns, "That doesn't mean that better things are always coming out."

Winders believes the hardest part about writing is getting started, "but once I start, then I get encouraged and I'm ready to do it." During a writing day he writes until about four o'clock in the afternoon, and then again from eight until midnight. He does not tire easily. "I get really excited about it and I want to do it. I'm actually disappointed if I have to stop. I don't want to be interrupted." If he does become weary, "I rest for a few hours, then I'm ready to go back and write again."

He takes on projects only if he really believes in them. He has turned down things that he could not get enthusiastic about. "If you have a project that's exciting and something you really want to do, then you'll find the time to do it." And he finds deadlines "wonderful": "I need them sometimes to give me that extra push. They give me a time frame to work with."

Winders has found his reading habits have changed over the years. He used to read "World War II history, mythology, westerns— I read really about everything." But since he got his degree, he doesn't read as much as he used to, and he doesn't read for entertainment as he once did: "I have the feeling that if I'm reading, I should be reading something historical that I can use." On occasion, though, he will reread the classics and books that earlier influenced him, such as "Jack London and Robert Louis Stevenson. It's like visiting old friends." Now he reads them to figure out what made their writing so effective.

Winders believes one of his strong points is "having a pretty broad knowledge of this time period, early nineteenth century U.S. and Mexico." Another strength "is that I'm not arrogant enough to think that I know everything."

He likes to think of himself as an academic doing public history. "I find that what helps me is having had that public school experience where I dealt with really complicated concepts and had to craft an explanation that a layperson understands." You have to recognize that there's a broad audience for history, Winders says, and "you really have to put it in terms that a broader audience is going to understand and find relevant to them."

A good historian, Winders believes, has to have a natural curiosity; "you have to want to know how that happened, why that happened, who is that person." And you have to be objective about your subject. "That may mean that you have to recognize what your own biases are and be up-front about that."

A historian needs to bring the past alive. "History is about people, so the people you're writing about have to be made real. You do that by writing as if it's a play or a story with historical figures that come to life. Along with that, things have to be explained in a comprehensible way, a way in which the public is going to understand, as you create a narrative."

And history has to have some relevance for the audience; they need to be able to relate the past to their own life experiences. Winders cites as an example his presentation on the Texas Revolution. "I explain it as an immigration policy that was out of control. Mexico invited these people into Texas, so legally there was a gate for them to come through, and they became naturalized Mexican citizens. But then there was also illegal immigration. What a lot of people will then pick up on is that we have a situation like that today that is just reversed." For himself, Winders has broken history down into themes—immigration, the nature of government, economics, art, technology, labor, and so on—that he uses to help himself sort things out. "You have to be able to explain it to yourself so it makes sense to you."

Political correctness does not order Winders's life at the Alamo. He says, "I believe it's more important to be correct than it is to be politically correct." The narrative visitors receive at the Alamo is "based on the evidence." Some people view the story of the Alamo as "a fight of brave Texans against despotic Mexicans." But when you look at the historic record, "you find that it's a really complicated event." On the other hand, some visitors believe "this is just a naked land grab by those white guys who came down to steal land from Mexico." Winders does not try to avoid controversial issues. "Rather than run away from it, I try to come up with an answer for it."

Recently, Winders says, there has been a change in the general field of Texas and southwestern history, with much more emphasis on incorporating Mexican history and a Mexican point of view. "You have to understand that Texas in 1835 was part of Mexico, you have to know what the Mexican political system was, who the political figures were, what was happening in Mexico. It doesn't mean that you have to identify with the attitudes of Mexicans at the time, but you certainly have to understand what they were." And you need to know who the important and influential players were in both the United States and in Mexico.

Winders believes that, unfortunately, the latest movie about the Alamo (2004) is a missed opportunity. "On one level," he says, "you want to say this is the best Alamo movie that's ever been made, and then you want to say, but can't we do better?" People of his generation often point to the 1950s and 1960s history-themed movies as their path to an interest in history, "so the pop culture aspect of history is something that's very powerful." He thinks "historians would be well-served to find a way to incorporate the interest that develops from movies and to use it as a hook to talk about the actual events and people."

Winders believes that *Mr. Polk's Army* may be his most important contribution to the field of history; not only is it used as a reading for U.S. military history classes, but it also introduced a new approach to the study of armies. But in the long run, he hopes that his major contribution "will be the interpretation that I've been able to build about the Texas Revolution, the Republic of Texas, and the War with Mexico as one historical time period, rather than a series of isolated incidents." As the Hispanic population of the United States grows larger, he says, this time period is important in understanding how this territory changed hands and what's happening with it now. "These are things that shape human activities, either as individuals or as societies, and that's part of interpreting history."

Winders remembers lessons he learned from McWhiney. "He had a very gentlemanly approach to history. It was scholarly, it was not mean-spirited or adversarial." McWhiney pushed his students to write "so people could read what we wrote, so people would *want* to read what we wrote." Winders believes historians have a responsibility to make people understand the importance of their craft to society. "I'm afraid that we're in the process of losing the history of what made the United States successful and unique," he laments. "There needs to be a concentrated effort to recreate an accepted narrative that incorporates different interpretations and different opinions, but doesn't take that adversarial approach. It doesn't have to glorify our history, but it also shouldn't denigrate what this country has done and the position it holds in the history of the world. It's hard sometimes being a historian and keeping your political views out of your work, but you have to do that as much as you can."

Winders is happy with his calling and wouldn't change it if he could. "History was always going to be a major part of my life," he says, "and I was just fortunate enough to be able to make it a professional part."

Richard Allan Baker

The Luckiest Historian in the World

"I was sort of rocked in the cradle of the American Revolution."

"What do you say about freedom in four hundred words?"

"We expect there will be at least a million visitors each year [to the Capitol's new visitor's center] . . . and one of the great satisfactions of this job is to be able to reach such a huge audience."

"Nobody these days seems to be terribly interested in the history of great white men."

"I am the luckiest person in the world, the luckiest historian I know."

"I WAS SORT OF ROCKED IN THE CRADLE OF THE AMERICAN Revolution," says Richard Allan Baker, who grew up in Melrose, Massachusetts, just outside of Boston.

From an early age everything conspired to encourage Baker's interest in history. His parents took him on Sunday trips to Lexington and Concord and to Paul Revere's home in Boston. They gave him books written by Esther Forbes, a Pulitzer Prize-winning biographer of Paul Revere. On school field trips, he visited early eighteenth-century homes in Melrose. He recognized how different life was in the past: "There was a disconnect," he remembers, "and I had to try to figure all of this out."

While still in elementary school Baker spent much of his free time in the public library. There he found "a wonderful series of biographies of the great men and women of early America, and that just fanned the flames." He visited the library every Saturday to view a film, then "loaded up on books, carried them home, read them all, and then carried them back the next week. That had an enormous impact on me."

All of these activities "opened new vistas and new worlds," he says, "just as any other educational activity would do at that age, particularly in history. I thought I really would like to learn a lot more about that when the time comes."

In high school, Baker had "a gifted teacher of American history" who had the students memorize facts and dates. He found that, along with Latin, "difficult at the time, but down the road both courses provided some major benchmarks in my life, some reference point."

When he matriculated to the University of Massachusetts at Amherst, Baker started as a business major. His father was in business, and "he was the closest model I had." The program required two years of liberal arts before focusing on a major. At the beginning of his junior year when he started taking business management courses, he found he "really longed for the history I'd been exposed to those first two years, so I switched my major to history halfway through my junior year." That meant staying for an extra semester, "but that was really no hardship at all; it was a joy." At that point he hadn't decided where this was going to lead, but he "found it very satisfying and very broadening and enriching."

Following graduation, Baker spent two years in the army. After his discharge, he had to choose a career and thought he might like to teach history. He attended Michigan State University for three semesters, earning a master's degree in history. From there he took a position in a small college near Middletown, Connecticut, where he was the "entire history department," teaching both European and U.S. history.

In 1965, Baker decided he needed a doctorate if he was to "move along in academic circles," and entered a program in eighteenth-century French history at the University of Connecticut, attending evenings and weekends. Soon, though, he concluded that there "wasn't exactly a huge demand for that." So he decided to "merge my interest in history with librarianship." He had a lofty goal: "to become the director of the Boston Athenaeum, or some such large cultural institution." Columbia University accepted him into its school of library service, "one of the best in the country at the time," and he spent the next year-and-a-half earning his master's degree in library science.

Following graduation, he won a place in an internship program at the Library of Congress. That six-month program's purpose was to train the library's future managers, and it accepted alumni from major library schools around the country. Baker "happened to be the guy from Columbia." This led, in a roundabout way, to his life's work.

In 1968, after six months of a "very intensive" internship, he accepted a job at the Legislative Reference Service at the Library, specializing in U.S. history. Then, in late 1969, a call came to the Reference Service from the Secretary of the Senate and the majority leader's office requesting someone with training in history and library science to help them set up a curatorial program for the Senate. "I thought, what the heck, that will get me back to my first love, history, and it was a great way to blend history and the archival component of library service." It was a temporary position, lasting from late 1969 until mid-1970—"just long enough to help them set up that program."

The curatorial program had been initiated by Senate Majority Leader Mike Mansfield (D-MT), a former history teacher. Mansfield was convinced that the Senate, as an institution, needed to inventory what they had as a way to "know our cultural heritage, in terms of paintings, furniture, and ultimately historical documentation."

Baker worked to set up that program and then went to work at a new public policy publication, *National Journal,* as director of information services. He remained there for five years before getting another call from Majority Leader Mansfield's office. The Senate had decided to create a permanent Senate Historical Office, and Mansfield wanted Baker to apply for the job. "I did," Baker says, "I got it, and had the unprecedented good fortune to be told to set up the office any way I liked." He began with a staff of five, which has since grown to nine, including seven historians.

With his new responsibilities, Baker believed he needed a doctoral degree. At the University of Maryland, where he went to get it, he specialized in twentieth-century political history. For his dissertation under Walter Rundell, he chose a recently deceased senator, Clinton P. Anderson of New Mexico, "who left a rich collection of papers that I had the good fortune of stumbling across—1,100 boxes of papers, conveniently located at the Library of Congress." His objective was to understand how a senator's office worked by reading "the documentation of his service over a long period of time." Because the papers were so voluminous, he focused on Anderson's interest in the conservation of natural resources. After receiving his doctorate, Baker revised the dissertation, and it was published by the University of New Mexico Press.

Baker now focused all of his attention on the Senate Historical Office. The office is the information center of the Senate, dealing with questions about institutional operations from a historical perspective. "The Senate is a profoundly precedent-focused, traditionally conservative institution," Baker explains. "If the leadership of the Senate can find a precedent for an action, then it saves having to explain a new way of handling an old problem."

For example, he says, in the impeachment trial of President Bill Clinton, "they were very happy to borrow as much as they could from the precedents of the Andrew Johnson impeachment trial 130 years earlier." His office needed to supply the senators with information on what the relations between the Senate and the House should be—how much the Senate should be looking over the shoulder of the House while it carried out its part of the process—and how the Senate should gear up for the trial. Should the House vote to impeach, the Senate could then move quickly to carry out its responsibilities, rather than take several months to get up to speed. At the same time, not wanting to seem to presume the outcome in the House, Baker's office worked as part of a "nonvisible team of historians, lawyers, and administrative staff to prepare a matrix on what needed to be done, who was going to do what, and how had it been done in the past."

Baker's staff also responds to requests for information from the public. At one time, they produced a newsletter that circulated to about one thousand recipients. Now, with a website in place, they get "tens of thousands of hits in a week." They frequently work with the media, supplying historical background for stories "in as balanced a way as possible." Many of those questions can be answered on the website, and now when reporters call "they only want 5 percent of the story because they have already gotten the other 95 percent from our website." That makes the staff's job easier, and "we can be more focused in our answers."

There can be a fine line between history and politics, but for over thirty years, Baker says, "I must say it has been very easy to stay on the history side of that somewhat ill-defined line." The Historical Office, by its nature, works closely with the leaders of the Senate from both parties. "I've found that among the one hundred sena-tors, those who really care about the institution's history are almost by job definition the leaders. They have to know what other models of behavior of leadership exist. They may not choose those models, but they at least want to know what the range of historical practice and experience has been." Those who are not among the leadership "are generally more focused on their states and their predecessors in the Senate."

The late Senator Robert Byrd of West Virginia was one of the se-nior senators with whom Baker has worked closely. One quiet Friday afternoon in 1980, Byrd's granddaughter and her school class visited the Senate Chamber gallery to watch the Senate in session. With no immediately pressing business before the body, Byrd launched into a speech about the history of the Senate and its chamber. The follow-ing week, the same teacher was coming back with another class, and

Byrd wanted to vary his presentation. He needed help doing that, so he called on Baker.

That was the start of a ten-year partnership during which they wrote thirty-page essays on a particular topic or a chronological period in the Senate's history, which Byrd delivered as floor speeches. Baker believes that Byrd, who was the longest serving member, was beginning to see himself as the "Father of the Senate." There had always been someone who served as a father figure to "educate the younger senators and to maintain the constitutional prerogatives of the Senate and to be the guardian of all that." In 1977, when he became the Senate majority leader, "Senator Byrd moved into that role very quickly."

In 1989, the Senate celebrated its bicentennial. By then, Byrd had accumulated one hundred historical lectures. Aware that senators, staff, and members of the general public were cutting them out of the *Congressional Record* for future reference, the Senate decided to publish the essays in two volumes. One would be devoted to the Senate's chronological history, whereas the other would include topical essays such as "The Senate in Literature and Film" and "Impeachment Trial in the Senate." This project ultimately yielded two more volumes. One of them is forty-six classic speeches, from Daniel Webster in 1830 to Byrd, and the other is a book of lists, statistics, and other records from the Senate's history.

Baker's time as the head of the historical office is taken up, about sixty/forty, answering requests for information and with projects generated on his own volition. One of those of his own making has been an administrative history of the Senate: How did it pay its bills? How did it operate from day one in terms of office space and financial management? Who were the key administrators? How did they share—or compete—for power? "We hope," Baker says, "that it will have a long life of helping the institution understand itself and helping people who want to do research on how the Senate has operated."

Another self-started project is a history of the Senate rules. One of the first things the first Senate accomplished was creating the Rules of the Senate. "Being a very precedent-conscious institution," Baker says, "it did not create them out of whole cloth." Instead, Thomas Jefferson's Rules of the Continental Congress of 1776 were reshaped and served as the foundation for the Senate. However, Baker says, "The Senate operates not so much on its Rules, but on the exceptions to the Rules—on the precedents." On occasion the Rules will be changed "when there is a lot of pressure—and that pressure is where the storytelling comes in." Over a two hundred-year period there have been plenty of "pressure" stories that have ignited some fire-fights and some insights that are vital to understanding the Senate.

Yet another project that recently brought Baker particular satisfaction was the development of the new Capitol visitors' center, a massive addition that is three stories deep and contains two-thirds of the space of the existing Capitol. Baker and his staff sat down "with a blank piece of paper and one of the best museum-design firms in the country, Ralph Appelbaum Associates in New York," to decide what to put in the center to tell the story of the Capitol building and the House and the Senate.

For five years they helped draft the script for the exhibit and for the films being shown in its three theaters. "It has been very difficult," Baker says. "You can't write long, convoluted, explanations; you've got to keep it simple." A chronological exhibit on one side of the display is organized into six major areas. The other side illustrates national aspirations—freedom, common defense, unity, knowledge, general welfare—offering "an opportunity to display original documents that people otherwise would never get to see, documents that are stored away in the Library of Congress and the National Archives." The documents will be displayed in six-month rotations.

The real challenge, Baker says, was writing the text. "What do you say about freedom in four hundred words?" Finally satisfied with what they had written, the designers said, "That's too many words; let's do two hundred words." That still did not satisfy the designers; they wanted it cut to one hundred words. Frustrated, Baker protested, "Why not just put the word *freedom* up there and show the document, letting the individual captions for the documents tell the story?" But in the end, "the museum designers won, and the results are less than one hundred words." Baker does have some consolation, however: "They're not bad because we were the ones who ultimately got to say what those words would be."

And there is further fulfillment. "We expect there will be at least a million visitors each year, if not two million, and one of the great satisfactions of this job is to be able to reach such a huge audience, discussing something as fundamental to American lives as the Congress of the United States."

Baker has also written a series of Historical Minutes. In 1987, Republican Senator Bob Dole wanted to start each daily session of the Senate "reminding his colleagues about something related to the history of the Senate." These "minutes"—three hundred little talks of about two hundred words—Dole put together as the *Senate Historical Almanac*. Then in 1997, Senator Tom Daschle invited Baker to attend the Democratic caucus luncheons held every Tuesday to deliver a little nugget of history that the senators might find interesting. "So since 1997," he says, "I've been getting up there every Tuesday with four hundred words." At the time of this interview, he had delivered about 250 of them. They have been posted on the Senate website and published as *200 Notable Days: Senate Stories, 1787–2002*.

One of Baker's more memorable Historical Minutes concerned a senator from North Dakota, "Wild Bill" Langer, who served from 1941 until his death in 1959. When he first arrived at the Senate, members were reluctant to seat him because of complaints from his home state about his unethical behavior while governor. The Senate conducted a year-long investigation, producing a 4,200-page report that concluded that Langer "should not be seated because he did not have the moral character to be a United States Senator. Immediately his defenders wanted to know where in the Constitution it mentioned moral character." Langer was seated. His other claim to fame is that he was the last senator to have his funeral in the Senate chamber.

Baker has found that the academic historical arena has changed over the years. "Nobody these days seems to be terribly interested in the history of great white men," he says. In the past, his office had close interactions with university history departments, but "the political historians have pretty much left those departments; the old-timers have retired and their jobs are being subdivided into two jobs taught by adjunct professors of social or cultural history." This has shifted the focus of what he does toward a broader audience—"the media, the general public, the constituency here in the Capitol Hill community."

Although Baker would like to write another book of his own, that has been relegated to his retirement years. "I would be draining away my energies from my work," he says. So his writing for the historical office is job related, and he writes almost exclusively in his office. If there is a pressing deadline, he will work at home. "Sometimes I do my best writing at home, on a quiet Sunday morning or even Saturday morning, just to have two or three solid hours without the telephone ringing." He works best in the morning. "If I have a writing problem that I'm trying to fix and I look at it in the afternoon, I can waste hours and not fix it," he admits, "and then the next morning the solution is there. It may not be perfect, but it's better."

The difficulty is that his mornings are often interrupted—"I'm at the beck and call of a very wide audience. Sometimes I've actually made notes about how a morning, which is the best time for me to write, can just fall apart with an administrative problem or a call from the Senate floor or a press call, or what have you." Baker believes that anyone working in his office must enjoy fitting things in between interruptions. "I think that somebody who spent an entire lifetime in a cloister would go mad here."

The Senate Historical Office handles massive files. There is a file on "every one of the more than 1,900 people who has ever served in the Senate," including a visual likeness of all but fifty of them. They draw information from around the country. "Every time I appear on C-SPAN," he says, "we get calls from people who have collections of papers from ancestors who served in the Senate." Historical newspaper databases on the Internet add to the information at their fingertips.

As Senate historians, Baker and his staff "pull from this previously inaccessible source material, primary source documents, and then make something of them. We can begin to weave and see the fabric and the pattern emerging." They are uniquely positioned to do this. "Nobody else is really in a position from an institutional perspective to do that, nobody is paid to care the way we are." He believes that "the long-term result will be a much deeper understanding of this institution and its basic rhythms."

Most of Baker's research material is nearby. His office has custodial care of fifty thousand linear feet of Senate records at the National Archives. One of the things that he is most proud of is that he persuaded the National Archives to "care about the records of Congress under its custody." Until the early 1980s there were "maybe two people" looking after all of the records of Congress, and they discouraged researchers from using the papers. One of the first things his office accomplished was the opening of most Senate records more than twenty years old. In 1985, the National Archives split off from the General Services Administration; Baker's office played a role in educating the appropriate Senate committees and officials to the benefits of that action. Now a staff of twenty people, rather than discouraging researchers, helps them penetrate "this large and sometimes opaque collection of records of Congress."

Besides the resources in the National Archives, the Senate Library—"the best legislative reference library in the world"—is just a five-minute walk from the office, and he and his staff have full access and borrowing privileges at the Library of Congress. "How can a historian be any happier than that?" he asks.

One of the Historical Office publications that Baker is proudest of is the journals of Montgomery Meigs, the army's quartermaster general during and after the Civil War. The Library of Congress had Meigs's shorthand journal covering the years 1853 to 1872. Because the shorthand was devised by Meigs himself, although based on the Isaac Pittman system, they hired someone to translate it. Each month Baker received 30 pages of translation, totaling, finally, 1,800 pages. Approximately 50 percent of these were edited and turned into a 900-page book with footnotes and a detailed cast of characters.

As it turned out, nine hundred pages is too long. "But it was so good!" Baker says, and he "was too wedded to the project." A four hundred-page book, he believes, would have been more reasonable. "The problem is that when you did that," he says, "you took out all the color and the fire and the human dimension." Unfortunately, the book was published the week before the terrorist attacks in New York City and Washington, D.C., on September 11, 2001. It got "totally lost" in the chaos that followed. The "great plans" for book talks and C-SPAN programs "didn't happen." It did win a prize from the Society for History in the Federal Government in 2001, which Baker found "very nice, but I still would like to have seen it go farther."

A good historian, Baker believes, must have "an inquiring mind, certainly diligence, tenacity in going after missing information, a sense of order, and certainly a literary style—music to the speech." The best way to know if your writing has rhythm, he says, is to "stand up and read what you've written," as he does on a weekly basis at the Democratic caucus luncheons.

Baker views the setting up of the Senate Historical Office as his major contribution to the field of history. "I take pride in that," he says. "But I would give a lot of credit to the institution; it's a place that nurtures history and respects it, that cultivates it."

Baker's job differs from working in a university in a number of ways. The three senior historians on staff are paid at the rate of full professors at private universities, but they work year-round, and they don't get sabbaticals. On the rare occasions of a vacancy, they advertise in the *Chronicle of Higher Education,* a publication for the university community. Some who respond say that they don't like the idea of "being a nine-to-five employee as opposed to the flexibility, the softness, of the academic schedule," Baker says. "So somebody who has been in that world for a very long time just wouldn't work out here."

There is nothing in this world that Baker would rather do. "I know how lucky I am," he says. "It's wonderful to be paid to do what you love doing, and there aren't many people who can honestly say that. I am the luckiest person in the world, the luckiest historian I know, for sure."

Baker retired in 2009 after three and a half decades as the U.S. Senate Historian and is working on his history of Senate rules and customs.

Donald S. Frazier
and **Robert F. Pace**

Kindred Souls

"I really believe that to be a good writer you have
to be passionate about your subject." — *Pace*

"I was the big-picture context
guy, and he was the big massive-amounts-of-information
guy." — *Frazier*

"You don't have to be limited by the boundaries of the profession; you can go beyond
that." — *Pace*

"To try to go back and inject
the present day into the past is
intellectually dishonest and disingenuous." — *Frazier*

"Somebody says, 'Hey Don, I found a source that
may adjust the way you look at something.' That's
intellectually honest criticism, and for a moment
there is this communion among fellow travelers
that we're all seeking the truth." — *Frazier*

"I've learned that learning is a process.... You see these wild-eyed
freshmen walking in the door and four or five years later see them
walking out the door as qualified historians." — *Pace*

D ONALD S. FRAZIER AND ROBERT F. PACE ENJOY A UNIQUE
collaborative partnership. It started, Frazier says, on "day two

of graduate school." Pace agrees: "I was about to say the same thing," he says. "We hit it off pretty quickly—kindred souls."

Neither of them can explain the chemistry. "We're not exactly two peas in a pod," says Pace. Frazier jumps in with, "That's right, because when I met you, you were a big-time lefty Democrat and you were pretty sure I was a Nazi." They had different ideas of what they expected their careers to be. Frazier "comes in with this kind of real idea of what it is to be a scholar, a writer—he's absolutely confident of that," Pace recalls. "I come in absolutely confident about what being a teacher is going to look like."

Although they both grew up in Texas, they took different paths to that first meeting. Pace's father grew up in South Carolina and Florida, and every summer the family traveled back East to visit relatives. Each year they drove a different route, stopping to visit historical sites along the way. Both of his parents talked about the places they visited as being part of "our" story. "That was always very interesting to me," Pace recalls, "so the idea of the story being *our* story was always there for me." However, he didn't "really connect" with those ideas then "like I should have."

Academically, Pace's interest in history blossomed in college. He remembers "a moment in a college history class where I had a good professor, Light Cummins, at Austin College in Sherman, Texas. I was taking a class on the Civil War from him, and he inspired me to read good history. I read Bruce Catton's *Stillness at Appomattox* and I just had this epiphany moment." In talking with Cummins about the book, and thinking back to the family vacations, "I suddenly saw that all of this was one big exciting story that *is* our story. I was nineteen years old and suddenly this all came together."

In Cummins's class, "I started to see connections and I took more classes, and ultimately decided to major in history." Cummins convinced him to go to graduate school. "I hadn't intended to do that; it was not until my senior year that he told me I would be a really good historian and a really good professor." Pace thought about it, and "as I rolled that around in my head, it sounded good to me."

For his bachelor's honor's thesis at Austin College, Pace wrote on Texas Methodists. At the time he was a Methodist—his father is a Methodist minister—although now he says he is a "proto-Methodist—I'm Episcopalian." To work on his master's degree, Pace chose Texas Christian University in Fort Worth. He planned to study Southern history "because the Methodists had split in 1845 over slavery and I thought that was interesting and decided to look deeper into the South."

Grady McWhiney taught Southern history at TCU. Although Pace was familiar with McWhiney's work—*Attack and Die,* in particular—he did not at first realize he was the same person. When he cited McWhiney in his thesis, Pace had misspelled his name, leaving out the W; throughout, it was Grady McHiney. It was not until a week after meeting him that Pace realized this was the same guy whose book he had been citing and name he had been misspelling.

For his master's thesis at TCU, Pace did a statistical analysis of the intensity of slave labor on antebellum plantations, concluding that it was "not that intense compared to a variety of things." When he presented the paper at his first historical conference, Pace had a rude awakening. "I stood up there just as naïve as could be, feeling just wonderful that I had proven something historically and statistically—I had now proven that slave labor wasn't that intense."

He might just as well have said the Civil War wasn't bloody. "There were lots and lots of people, all of them yelling at *me.* People started standing up, asking, who do you think you are? You racist this, and you racist that! I'm just sitting there thinking, I'm not racist at all! Look at the evidence; the evidence shows this! I remember looking to the back of the room, and both Grady and Don were putting their heads down, knowing that I had to go through this on my own. It was baptism by fire for sure, and it was important, it was good, and it was shaping to see that, okay, maybe it's not just about the evidence. If you're going to tell a story that people won't like, you've got to be prepared."

That experience made Pace decide "that that would not be my doctoral dissertation; I wanted to do something else." Instead, he did a statistical analysis of Southern agriculture from 1850 to 1880, an offshoot of McWhiney's work in *Cracker Culture*. Pace admits that "It's not sexy stuff; it's not shooting and killing, but it's stuff I thought was important."

Fresh out of graduate school, doctorate in hand, Pace was hired at Longwood College in Farmville, Virginia. He taught there "for a great seven years," while he continued working on expanding his dissertation with an eye to publication. While he continued researching, others in his graduating class, writing on more exciting subjects, were being published, and Pace felt discouraged.

He was sidetracked, providentially, from his work on agriculture by another project brought to him by McWhiney. McWhiney and a colleague, Warner Moore, had been editing for publication a massive journal kept from 1843 to 1877 by plantation owner James Mallory. Moore had passed away, and McWhiney was too busy with other things to devote the time needed to complete it. Pace took on the project and spent the first four years after graduate school "just doing intensive research on that and getting the footnotes together." When it was published, Pace was credited as one of the three editors.

Meanwhile, he had found a collection of letters that excited him more than agriculture, but he felt an obligation to finish what he had started and to see it published. One day, talking to Frazier about how tired he was of the subject, Frazier asked him why he had to get it published. "Well," replied Pace, "because you're supposed to get it published." Frazier then asked why he had written it in the first place. "Well, it was my dissertation and I had to do it to get a degree." Frazier asked if he got his degree. Pace said yeah, and Frazier said, "Then move on." Pace felt a huge burden lift from his shoulders: "It was this freeing moment in my life!" he recalls. "I didn't have to research agriculture ever again if I didn't want to!"

Pace turned his attention to the letters that had excited him, a collection written by college students in the Old South. That became his passion. "I really believe that to be a good writer you have to be passionate about your subject," he says. "You could be *interested* in the subject and get away with it, but it's going to come through in your writing that you're not passionate about it. I never really had a passion for agriculture. Agriculture got me my doctorate, and that's how I had to look at it." In 2004, he published a book about his real passion—*Halls of Honor: College Men in the Old South.*

Frazier came to academic history by a more circuitous route. "My father was a windshield historian," he says, "—he was a windshield everything." As they drove along, his father would point out the windshield and say, "'See that pile of rocks over there, well, back in blah, blah, blah such and such happened'; then he'd point to another hill and say, 'See how there's all sorts of interesting veins of igneous rock in there with the sedimentary, well, that probably used to be an undersea volcanic vent.' I could watch the clouds go by and Dad would talk about the cloud formations and what sort of weather pattern they represented. It was like driving through the world's largest classroom with my dad."

As the youngest of ten children, Frazier also learned history from his siblings. His brother Rob introduced him to war games. "We played with lead soldiers, and boy, that was cool because all of a sudden it's not just about words on pages, it's about three-dimensional soldiers shooting at each other with a rules system that's based on trying to model the realities of the situation back then. I found that absolutely engaging."

Frazier read voraciously. He remembers the first book he ever bought with his own money, *The Golden Book of the Civil War,* with "cool maps that showed soldiers going across three-dimensional terrain." He was an eclectic reader. He read his way through the *World Book Encyclopedia* and *The American Heritage Illustrated Encyclopedia of American History* while "everybody else was out playing football." He wore the spine off of the Civil War and the War of 1812 volumes of *American Heritage.* "If it had *war* in the title, I pretty much read it all."

With his passion for the past, Frazier wanted to teach history, but his older siblings talked him out of it, pointing out that "there's no money in education. What you need to do is go to college and study business." So he headed off to the University of Texas at Arlington

(UTA) where, he says, "I got a degree, although I don't think I got an education." Finding business per se "kind of gray and soulless," he instead graduated with a degree in communications—radio, television, film management, and sales—"a kind of business degree with an arts edge to it," he says. He knew how to make radio and television documentaries, "how to splice stuff together and come up with a product." Meanwhile, throughout his undergraduate years he worked as a reporter for the Fort Worth *Star-Telegram*. "I really thought I was going to be a newspaperman, as misguided as that is," he says.

"Anyhow," Frazier says, "I was not really trying to get an education, I was trying to get a degree." After graduation, however, he found that the newspaper business was not very welcoming. So he went to work for General Dynamics (which became Lockheed-Martin), where he figured he could go "and make the world safe for F-16s." He wrote technical publications, and his life became ordered by the buzzer: "I got there at 7:30 before the buzzer went off, went to lunch by the buzzer, left by the buzzer—total control, and boy, I hated it! It was a vast ocean with endless horizons and that's all I had to look forward to." He found he had a lot of time on his hands, lots of time to "think about what I really wanted to be doing with my life."

During his undergraduate studies at UTA, Frazier had had a "very strong minor in history. Any elective I could take, I took in history." Now he had no doubt in his mind that his life was going to be in the past. "I had figured out that if I wasn't doing something I was passionate about, my life would just be long and tedious." He decided to go to graduate school and chose TCU because it was on his drive home and because a graduate of the university had spoken highly of Grady McWhiney.

Frazier met with McWhiney, who agreed to take him on. The topic he chose to focus on was the Sibley-Green Confederate invasion of New Mexico. He had come across that subject, "I'm embarrassed to say, while I was on my honeymoon in New Orleans and ran across a book, *Battle in Bayou Country*. Now it's embarrassing that I'm in New Orleans with my new wife and I'm looking for Civil War books, but I was." The book was about a brigade of Texans who went to New Mexico during the Civil War, an eye-opener for Frazier, "because I never knew anything was going on in New Mexico."

He originally intended to do a muster-in to muster-out history of the brigade, "but through learning and growing, I began to figure out that history is not just about telling the sequence of events but talking about the significance, where it fits in context, and textualizing human events." In the end, his master's thesis was about the Confederate invasion of New Mexico, and his doctoral dissertation was what that invasion meant. That work became his first book, *Blood and Treasure*.

Although he had had some work published while he was still in graduate school, Frazier found it difficult to land a job in academia. He had a one-year position at TCU teaching history survey courses, and while in graduate school he had started a map-drawing company. The map business was "pretty steady, and getting steadier," so he thought perhaps he would "have to start a historical services kind of thing, maybe do documentaries and maps and stuff like that."

But an academic job did come through. McMurry University in Abilene, Texas, hired him for a one-year position that turned out to be permanent. "What I saw at McMurry was a great place to stretch and do a lot of different, really interesting things. I set my eyes toward the West and emigrated out here from the great metroplex."

It was at McMurry that the collaboration between Pace and Frazier moved to a new level. In graduate school they discovered that their different approaches to information complemented each other. "Robert's got this great ability to take in and process massive amounts of information," Frazier says, "so he would do that and he would kind of relay that information at collaborative study events. Then I would try to place all that information into some sort of context. I was the big-picture context guy, and he was the big massive-amounts-of-information guy. That's the kind of the team we made up as study partners." Pace recalls an instance when "we were studying for a military history minor field exam and I took J.F.C. Fuller's three-volume history of the world and synopsized it for the group, and then Don taught me what it all meant."

The study group included other McWhiney graduate students. "Grady's people were seen to be kind of a mafia," Frazier recalls, "kind of a clique." On seminar nights, McWhiney took them out for dinner before the three-hour seminar. This was typical operating procedure for the professor. "He just gave us total access at all times," says Pace. McWhiney's students thought that was the way it was in all graduate schools until they talked with people in their profession who had entirely different experiences—having to schedule appointments with their professors three weeks ahead of time, and then the one-on-one time was limited. "I'd never heard anything like that!" Pace says. "I thought your major professor meant they got inside your soul and you got inside theirs, and you really had this collaborative thing going on."

In 1996, McWhiney suffered a stroke, and it looked like he might not be around much longer. Having no children or siblings, he had never decided how to dispose of his estate after his death. Frazier, Pace, and another of his former students visited him and discussed setting up a foundation that would become the beneficiary of his estate. McWhiney liked the idea, and the Grady McWhiney Research Foundation was born.

Frazier, executive director of the Foundation, persuaded McMurry University to give over part of its new library addition for McWhiney's massive research collection and to house the Foundation offices. Busy now with business affairs that the Foundation required, in addition to his teaching duties, Frazier needed Pace's skills and support. So he went about luring Pace to Abilene.

Frazier had to convince not only the university administration, but also Pace. Pace had two options—remain at Longwood, where he was very happy, and "have a very traditional academic experience— continue to be well-loved and well-received," or move to McMurry, where he saw "an opportunity to really build something. Whatever it was, it was guaranteed that there was going to be nothing traditional about it; wherever it went, it was going to be exciting and different and sometimes scary." In 1999, Pace moved his family to Abilene, where he became the Foundation's vice president and chief operating officer, and taught history.

And there the collaboration begun in graduate school moved into high gear. They both taught in the history department, where they shared a vision of what a good department ought to be. They came up with a course sequence in which students got Pace first as sophomores and juniors, and he taught them the technical skills they need: "I teach them the spiritual importance of footnotes, and they're just rolling their eyes," Pace says. The following semester Frazier gets them and "puts the art on them." His attitude is "footnotes, schmootnotes—get them right, but first communicate." And they do get them right, Pace points out, because "they've already had me."

The first book they collaborated on was *Frontier Texas*. It grew out of research they had done for a new museum opening in Abilene. They ended up with huge amounts of background information for the exhibitors and the script writers that the museum visitors would never see. Pace thought it would a good idea to put the information together in a book that people could purchase at the museum—"take it home and the experience continues."

At first they thought they would just put it together like an encyclopedia, but then realized that it would not be comprehensive. They decided there had to be a narrative: "That's Grady," Pace says. "Grady always told us you've got to tell a story." The problem was that they wanted to have it available when the museum opened in April, it was already November, and they really wouldn't have time to write until the semester ended. It took them just "eighty days from the first word on paper to book on the shelf." It didn't hurt that by then the Foundation had its own publishing business.

Pace wrote the narrative, "dragging stuff out of the corpus of the research that we had already done." When he had finished each chapter, he e-mailed it to Frazier, who "made it sing." Frazier added things that "I had forgotten or hadn't even thought about and he'd say, 'You know, you kind of skipped over this whole thing,' or 'I think this would weave in here beautifully,' and then he would write four pages on this and weave it in and then he'd send it back to me." By then, Pace would have the next chapter finished.

Sometimes, Pace says, they were going to include something that Frazier knew a lot more about, so he would just indicate where it would fit in and leave it for Frazier to write. "I don't want to give the impression that I wrote the whole thing," Pace says. "That was not how it worked. I got the first words down." "He did the foundation and the framing and the roofing," says Frazier. "I might have done some sheetrock work and laid some carpet."

Although their offices were next door to one another, they did everything electronically, e-mailing back and forth. Frazier wrote right onto Pace's draft. "We cannot look at this thing and say this is my paragraph and that's your paragraph," says Pace, "because even within paragraphs he would change this sentence, and vice versa." Pace admits that they have different writing styles, and they had to make adjustments. "Don is much more of what I would call a newspaper writer—short sentences, action-packed. I use more adjectives and commas, and I usually have longer paragraphs."

It all comes down to trust, Frazier says. "Robert trusts me to take his work and put in stuff that would only make it better." Pace admits that there were times that he was not so sure about the changes his partner made. "Don has a way with words, and occasionally he will put in flights of metaphorical fancy that you're kind of going, 'Oh my, let me get out that encyclopedia that *he's* read cover to cover but the rest of us haven't.'" But he doesn't recall ever changing anything back to the original. "Usually I trust it," he says. "I like the way Don writes, I like the way Don communicates, and I think it's good, entertaining, interesting history."

Another project they have collaborated on is a windshield history—a hangover from Frazier's upbringing: two CDs designed to be used traveling by car from Abilene to Fort Worth or vice versa. On this project the pace and content of the story were critical—the narrative had to match the listener's location along the road: "You want to be talking about Mineral Wells when the driver is going through Mineral Wells," Frazier says. "Right," says Pace, "so you can't spend forty-five minutes on Mineral Wells," because, Frazier finishes the thought, "by that time you're in Albany." Once again, Pace mined the information, put it together, and fleshed it out, then sent it to Frazier who filled in "a lot of the more jazzy things."

The research habits of the two men are as wildly different as their writing styles. Pace is methodical. "I do all the research first, think about it, organize it, put it together—it's a process," he says. Whenever possible, he takes notes on the computer; if he can't do that, he enters them into the computer when he gets back to his office. The notes are carefully organized into topics, a new page for each source, with the entire footnote reference on the page. He then prints out a hard copy—"in case the computer blows up." As he writes, he pulls out the hard-copy material he'll be using that day, stacks it on his desk, finds the information he wants from it, and cuts and pastes it into his narrative from his electronic file. As he uses each source, he tosses the hard copy. "When the stack is gone I know I've reached the end," he says.

Frazier, on the other hand, is "researching and writing in sort of a rolling campaign." Pace describes the scene in Frazier's office when he's writing: "He has seven books open and laying all around him, and other books in a stack with little notes in them. It would drive me nuts, but he has the ability to pull it together and make it work."

When he travels to an archive for research purposes, "I hit it hard and I hit it fast—copy it all and sort it out when I get back to the house," Frazier says. But he also likes to "think about the humanity behind it, kind of listen for the muse—what am I hearing, what am I listening to."

Frazier likes to find unused sources. "I don't like to work plowed ground; I like to break the fields out fresh if I can." He tries to figure out where sources might be, where letters or diaries might have ended up. "I kind of like that sleuthing part of it." He also likes to "travel the ground. I like to go to places that I'm writing about and actually look at it, and smell the breeze, feel the sod beneath my feet, and I start to get a feel for it. I want to get inside my topics almost at a DNA level; I want to understand it from the human perspective."

Both men find it difficult to write in their offices during the day when, besides teaching, they're busy with the history department and also with running the Foundation, which has grown far beyond its original vision. Some years ago they took on the Buffalo Gap Historic Village, a group of historic Texas buildings open daily to visitors and a venue for special events. At the village, they have a bed-and-breakfast available to tourists. In addition, the Foundation now has two publishing companies whose operations they direct. During the day, "There's a constant stream of people in and out."

"If we didn't have a Foundation and we weren't doing all these sorts of entrepreneurial enterprises," Frazier says, "we could work up here in our offices because we'd be like most sleepy academics. Nobody would come to bother us because we wouldn't be all that interesting, we wouldn't be all that useful. We'd just be back in our offices and if a student wandered by we'd say, 'Look, my office hours are posted—go away.' But that's not the kind of place we run, and that's not the kind of work we do."

All of this can be distracting, and Pace admits to being easily distracted. His office has no windows. "If I had windows in my office, I'd never get anything done. A bird would fly by and I'd look at it, then I'd muse about the bird, I'd wonder what kind of bird it was," ("...wonder where it was hatched," interjects Frazier), "wonder what kind of day the bird had, and suddenly thirty minutes would go by and I've contemplated this bird." Any time he has ever had windows in his office, he has immediately put blinds up—"only then can I maybe get some things done." On the other hand, he says, "Don has the window—and binoculars."

When writing, Pace tends to do it in the late afternoon and far into the night, until one or two o'clock in the morning, when there are no distractions. Frazier writes in the morning, reads during the day, and writes again at night until ten or eleven, mostly at home. When he's teaching, he organizes his week so that on writing days he writes and on teaching days he also administrates. "I know that my time blocks are going to be five minutes over here, twenty minutes over here, and you can write an e-mail or you can respond to a letter or you can return a phone call in five, ten, twenty minutes. But you cannot understand what General Nathaniel P. Banks is thinking in twenty minutes; you have to sit there and cook on that for hours."

"What I've discovered is that when I'm writing, and I'm in the zone, I'm in 1863," says Frazier. "If the phone rings, don't expect me to be making any sense because I am communing with the dead, and I really am in the zone." When he is so immersed in writing, footnotes become a distraction, so he just leaves "something that will remind me mentally about where that information came from so I can go back when I'm in a technical mode and rebuild that footnote."

While Frazier communes with the dead, Pace communes with his footnotes. For him, "they're not just technical. When I'm writing the footnote, I don't see it as the technical aside that's in the way of my writing; I see it as this kind of spiritual combination of now I'm here and now I get to tell where it came from, and there's a connection between this footnote and these words and it's all part of the same whole." For Frazier, "coming from a journalism background, the sources are just the sources and who cares?" says Pace.

With all of their responsibilities and the many and varied problems that need to be dealt with on a daily basis, they make an effective team. "If somebody is looking for me to make a decision on an issue, my response is always if you can't find me, ask Robert because he'll answer the exact same way, I guarantee it." They enjoy a genuine union of minds. "There are a lot of times when we find each other finishing each other's sentences," Frazier says. "It's a pretty consistent world view."

They have another collaborative research/writing project on the burner—"a large, comprehensive investigation about how America does history—all the ways, from the History Channel to reenactors to how history is taught academically, where it fits into the curriculum in public schools, how Hollywood treats it," says Frazier. "It's a huge project," Pace puts in, "so we're going to have to figure out how to do it."

They also collaborate in Frazier's cartography business. "I started having such a high volume of business that I needed some backup, and Robert said, 'Well, I'll learn how to do these maps.' So he learned how to do maps and we've been sharing jobs right and left." Together they did the three hundred maps in the *Dictionary of American History,* a major milestone publication.

The two men consider themselves history entrepreneurs, selling history in whatever form they can imagine—movies, documentaries, CDs, museums, publishing companies—"there are so many different things that in some way reflect the nature of how history is done in the modern world—and we're participants," Pace says. "Don had that attitude from the moment I met him. You don't have to be limited by the boundaries of the profession; you can go beyond that. That's how we run the Foundation, that's how we teach our students, and that's how we look for new projects." Frazier adds, "Part of what I try to teach my kids here is fearlessness, because so often there is a need to have a sort of comfort zone that limits your thinking." Frazier's educational background—"a business degree with an arts edge"—enables him to envision projects outside the "boundaries of the profession," and gives him the know-how to accomplish those projects.

As close as they are professionally, they still pursue individual interests. Pace is interested in Episcopal church issues "that's got *nothing* to do with me," Frazier says, while Frazier is currently working solo on a Texas-in-the-Civil War project for another museum.

Frazier believes curiosity and imagination are required for a good historian. Pace agrees, but adds, "I think also the ability to answer the who-cares question, to take it beyond one damned fact after another." Historians too often don't give their subject relevance. "They take some really important stuff," Frazier laments, "and then they start breaking it down into little tiny esoteric discussions so that they can all impress each other, and they quit talking to the people who are out there and who are the ones who are going to be determining the fate of the study of history."

Pace believes history "has to answer a question. Now, what the question is depends on where you're coming from, but it has to be a question that anybody would think to ask at one point or another. It has to be a broad question about what it means to be human." Frazier agrees: "The universal thread for history is that this is a human story." They believe history should have some practical applications. "A lot of people study history just for the fun of it," says Frazier, "but we actually think that it informs the present day as well, and it ought to."

Pace sees "highly trained, immaculately trained, historians who are focusing more and more on less and less." On the other hand, he continues, "You have people who are passionate about history and who are writing and doing stuff that's interesting, but they're not trained or they don't have the ability and so you end up with a lot of things that aren't well done. It's sad that those who are trained are abandoning it to those who aren't."

The two men have definite thoughts on political correctness. To Frazier, it means "that you're going to go out of your way in making extraordinary efforts to come up with a feel-good sequence for a feel-good story without asking the hard questions." He points out that the controversy is as old as history: "Herodotus thought there ought to be a moral in it, and Thucydides said no, just lay it out there and let people consider it." He agrees with Thucydides: "You need to just throw it out there and consider it and sometimes history is going to make you mad or it's going to make you sad or it's going to make you happy or it's going to make you feel triumphant, and it is what it is. To try to go back and inject the present day into the past is intellectually dishonest and disingenuous."

Pace is concerned about "those who will use the excuse of anti-political correctness to justify actual hatred or discrimination." He admits that it's true that over the span of the profession "there have been large sweeps of it where groups have been left out of the historical record—women, minorities, etc." It is important, he believes, for historians to complete the record, but the "problem comes when the profession then takes it so far that if you're not doing something related to filling in the holes, then you're not a part of the profession."

Pace cites the time when he and Frazier prepared a panel discussion for the Southern Historical Association meeting in New Orleans several years ago. His paper dealt with the socioeconomic effects of the Civil War on southern Louisiana, and Frazier's studied the military aspects of the area. Their panel was turned down. "That's when I said political correctness has gone too far," Pace says, "when the Southern Historical Association is meeting in New Orleans and will not do a panel on the Civil War in southern Louisiana."

In looking over the program for that meeting, Pace noted that 94 percent of the presentations had *race, gender,* or *class* in the title. "If the role of the historian is to be curious, is to be passionate, and is to answer the who-cares question, the what-does-this-all-mean question, then you're once again limiting things if you're then trying to put on top of that some overlay that it has to be about race, it has to be about gender, or class, and you have to be mad at somebody."

The issue of revisionism is important to them. "I think each succeeding generation is going to have different insights," says Pace. "It's intellectually dishonest to try to impose a modern mind-set on the past, but by the same token each succeeding generation can have a new way of looking at things." Frazier agrees. "As the Earth spins on its axis through space there's a greater accumulation of human experience," he says, "and so for me, history is by nature revisionist. History is not written in stone, it's written in Jello®; you're always going to find new evidence."

And what about others' reactions to their work? Pace does not react well to criticism of his work: "I bristle," he admits. "But I realize there's nothing I can do about a negative review, all I can do is the best I can do, and beyond that, I'm happy to spar with people if they want." Frazier accepts valid criticism but becomes annoyed with invalid criticism. For example, one reviewer of *Blood and Treasure* blasted the book because it had no index. "Well," Frazier says, "my wife did the index, I'm looking at the book and it has an index in the back, so either he got a defective copy or he couldn't find his way to the back of the book." Frazier's favorite kind of criticism is "when somebody says, 'Hey, Don, I found a source that may adjust the way you look at something.' That's intellectually honest criticism, and for a moment there is this communion among fellow travelers that we're all seeking the truth."

When considering his contributions to the field of history, Pace begins modestly, saying, "It's small. I haven't moved any closer to the sun, but I think that I have really expounded and expanded on the nature of the code of honor in the South as depicted in these college students [in *Halls of Honor*], and I don't think anyone can ever again write about colleges or higher education in the South without having read my work. It's the same with this whole honor ethic—it's incomplete unless you have referenced me. That's not huge."

But Frazier quickly jumps in. "I think that you're overlooking some things, Robert. You're looking only at your traditional academic projects, but we don't play that game." He points out that "we impact 18,000 people a year by the way we run Buffalo Gap Historic Village and the interpretation we put on it. We're putting 60,000 books in the marketplace with the publishing companies. We have students in the classroom, many of whom leave changed human beings because of the mentoring that you do. In the grand scheme of things, how people react to our books is just a little cul-de-sac, a little pod, of an otherwise fairly large contribution that you make as a human being, and you're making it through history."

On his individual projects, Frazier says he's proud "that with *Blood and Treasure* I recovered some history for some people." He loves it when "somebody shows up with a well-thumbed copy of the book" and that person says "you were talking about my grandpa and now I understand a little more about me, or you're talking about my town and now I understand more about my community." Frazier says, "I have a great face for radio, so I don't think I'll be the darling of the History Channel. My career has taken me to a small teaching college, a liberal arts college, so I'm not going to have a vast array of graduate students that I can crow about, but I think in the final analysis what I'm doing is important."

They have learned from their students. "I've learned that learning is a process," says Pace, "particularly in a small school like this where you see these wild-eyed freshmen walking in the door and four or five years later see them walking out the door as qualified historians." Frazier believes his students have taught him that "everybody's got their own history, they've got their own place in the universe, and they've got their own suite of wants, needs, and desires." They have helped him define his career: "I see my role on Earth as helping them achieve what their ambitions are." And, adds Pace, "to open windows and doors that they may not have even known were there."

Frazier has also learned that teaching is not only about the classroom. "That's one of the great joys about having a publishing company, the Village, going to Europe with groups of students to study battlefields—sometimes you teach them things like you need to show up at the van at 8 A.M. with your traps together. It's those sorts of lessons students teach you. If you're just going to impact your students for three hours a week in one-hour blocks of time, then I think you're missing a big chunk of what it is to be an educator."

When a new student approached McWhiney about working with him, he had a standard procedure he followed: Go home and think about anything else in this world that you'd rather do than this. If anything else presented itself, he would advise the student to do that instead because history was not worth it unless it was what you really wanted to do. By the time Frazier received that suggestion, he had already tried other avenues and knew that history was the path he wanted to follow through life. Pace at one time had contemplated the ministry, and for a time rigorously pursued that path, but in the end he decided on history.

In talking about history, it is clear that both of these historians, separately and together, have a passion for what they do. It goes beyond the classroom and their writing and their collaborating. They are indeed kindred souls and history entrepreneurs.

Since this interview Pace has left McMurry University to study for the ministry.

· PART 3 ·

THE CIVIL WAR

MANY HISTORIANS HAVE DEVOTED THEIR CAREERS TO STUDYING THE American Civil War (1861–1865) and the years leading up to and following that tragic passage in our history. The historians included in this section have focused exclusively or primarily on the Civil War era.

Growing up in a town named after a Confederate general sparked Anne Bailey's interest in the war, an interest that has continued through her professional life. Her work embraces studies of the role played in the war by various ethnic groups, military campaigns, and her favorite—Confederate cavalry.

Steven E. Woodworth describes himself as "a storyteller masquerading as a historian." As with many of our interviewees, he aims to make the narrative flow smoothly and tell an exciting story; unlike most historians, he enjoys writing more than researching.

Growing up in a family of educators steeped in history, and just thirty miles from the Shiloh battlefield, Charles Roland came virtually predestined to his vocation. Focusing primarily on the Civil War, Roland believes that "both the present and future are greatly influenced by the past, and that the better we know the past...the better our society will be." He is another rare historian who prefers writing to research.

Gary Gallagher knew at an early age that he wanted to teach Civil War history. By the time he was a junior in high school, he already owned 250 books on the war. He sees a huge divide in the history of the Civil War between those interested only in its military side, and those who focus on its societal and political aspects. Part of his mission is to bring those two camps together. He has written several books, but the form he prefers is the essay. Besides writing his own essays, he has edited and published several collections of those written by other scholars.

William C. (Jack) Davis, too, knew at an early age that he wanted to teach history. However, he has spent most of his career outside of an academic setting. A prolific writer and editor, Davis prefers the research. "Research," he explains, "is like having a party; writing is like the clean-up afterwards." He is gifted at pursuing new avenues of research, sometimes in little-known and seldom-used public archives and at other times tracking down information in private family collections.

As the great-grandson of a Confederate soldier and growing up in Danville, Virginia, the last capital of the Confederacy, James I. (Bud) Robertson came by his interest in the Civil War honestly. Robertson has had a varied career: He was Executive Director of the United States Civil War Centennial Commission in the 1960s; he has been a football referee, officiating at nine major college bowl games; and he teaches a legendarily large Civil War class. He calls himself a "people's historian," interested in writing for the general public and for children. He strives to keep the human element, the emotion, in history.

James M. McPherson came to the Civil War a bit later than most of the historians in this section; it wasn't until he was in graduate school that he decided to focus on the Civil War era. He sees the theme of his career as the "centrality of the Civil War to all of American experience, and how and why that is the case."

Deciding even later than McPherson to focus on the Civil War, Carol Reardon was a graduate student in biology when she saw the error of her ways and switched to Civil War history. She believes that her gender has worked to her advantage, getting her important appointments earlier in her career than many of her male colleagues because she often is the "diversity" that political correctness demanded. Of course, groundbreaking work in both the Civil War and in Vietnam War history fully qualified her for success.

These are our historians whose life work has been dominated by the Civil War, who have by their good works enriched our knowledge and understanding of it.

Anne J. Bailey

CAVALRY SPECIALIST

"Learning the value of constructive criticism is important to success."

"Our goal as historians is to write a story that will appeal to the general reader."

"We have to make history interesting or we lose our audience."

———◦◆◦———

ANNE J. BAILEY EXPLAINS HERSELF IN THIS FASHION: "I WAS BORN in a town with an unusual name—Cleburne, Texas—and I wondered where that name came from." It wasn't just a typical name for a town, and when she discovered, in third or fourth grade, that it was named after Confederate general Patrick Cleburne, she says, "I had to find out about the Civil War."

That triggered an early interest in history in general, further nurtured in high school, where she had "two excellent history teachers," one in U.S. history, the other in European history. "Both told stories and made history interesting," she remembers. Her fascination was nurtured further during her undergraduate years in college when she volunteered at the Layland Museum in Cleburne to research Civil War soldiers from Johnson County. There was a personal tie in all this—"My paternal great-grandfather served from this county and died in 1864."

By the time she matriculated at the University of Texas, Arlington (UTA), Bailey "knew exactly what I wanted to do"—major in history and "write a dissertation on the Civil War units that I had been researching for so long, or at least the cavalry brigade that one of the companies came from." She wanted to be a military historian. From the beginning, she planned to work straight through to a doctorate: "It never occurred to me to stop at any point; I just thought of it as a seven-year program from the very start."

After earning her undergraduate degree from UTA, Bailey moved to Texas Christian University (TCU) for her master's and doctorate study because "TCU offered more opportunities for graduate students." When she first arrived there, there was no Civil War professor in the history department, so for her master's degree she wrote a thesis on antebellum Texas history under Don Worcester.

When she finished that, Grady McWhiney had joined the TCU faculty. Here at last was her mentor. Now she could focus her doctoral studies on the Civil War. She found McWhiney "a perfect southern gentleman, absolutely—as nice and hard working and as concerned about his graduate students as you could ask for." Like other of McWhiney's students, "I didn't realize until I was long out of graduate school that I had been very fortunate, because I know that my experience was not typical. Many people have graduate advisors who barely pay attention to them, and then just drop them as soon as they finish."

But not McWhiney. Bailey credits him with teaching her "how to be a professional and how to treat other people and particularly how to treat students with respect. He gave all of his students a sense of how we should mentor our own graduate students."

She also credits McWhiney with teaching her how to write. She recalls him telling his students, "You're not a born writer, unless you're a Hemingway." He stressed that writing "is a learned craft, and if you don't practice it all the time, if you stray away from writing for several months, then when you come back to writing you're going to be rusty. It's like any other skill—you have to practice it constantly so that you're always on top of it. It's an art, and like any art must be consistently practiced."

She has come to believe that "it is possible to learn to write even if you think when you begin that you're not very good; if you truly aren't a natural writer, you can improve if you work at it and take advice."

She believes learning the value of criticism is critical to success and that "the most important thing is to accept advice and to listen to what people say. I tell this to my students, because when they start on a master's or Ph.D. program, most of them can't write well and they become discouraged. They have very few technical skills coming out of undergraduate programs. They begin a master's program and they still don't know how to form a thought into an article or a book."

Bailey says that she didn't understand the technical side of writing when she started her graduate work. McWhiney taught her about "topic sentences, transitions, introductions, and conclusions. Grady had the skill to improve my technique and analytical ability without discouraging me in the process." She was his graduate assistant for the first two years he was at TCU. He was working on a book and he had her sort his notes by topic, helping her to understand what a topic sentence was, "and that a paragraph would be about one topic. That sounds so simple to say," she says, "but I really had no concept of how to do it properly." As she watched him work, Bailey "tried to duplicate everything he did."

When it was time to write her dissertation, McWhiney told her to write it as a book, not a dissertation. She did, and when it was submitted to a press, it was published as *Between the Enemy and Texas: Parsons's Texas Cavalry in the Civil War.* "Very little was changed because he had already helped me put it into a form that was very readable."

Since then Bailey has branched out into other writing projects, but they tend to build off of one another. Her second book, *Texans in the Confederate Cavalry,* expanded the dissertation to include other Confederate cavalry from Texas. From that she turned her attention to African Americans enlisted in the Union armies, some of whom fought the Confederate cavalry along the Mississippi River, and she has written several articles about African American soldiers.

Parsons's brigade included German-American Texans and American Indians, and she has done work on both of those ethnic groups. When she took a job at Georgia College and State University in Milledgeville, she branched out into the Georgia campaign, where a number of African American soldiers enlisted in the northern part of the state. "It seems like one topic leads to another," she says.

Being "one of a handful of academics" who study German Texans and African Americans from the lower South, Bailey has written several chapters in various books that have been published on those subjects. She finds these anthology contributions easy, "because I have the research, usually, left over from a book I've published, so it's just a matter of pulling it together and casting it a different way."

Bailey does all of her writing on a computer. Word processors became widely available while she was researching her doctoral dissertation, and McWhiney, who had been using an army-surplus Wang word processor for several years, encouraged her to buy one. "The ability to edit and change directions easily was one of the reasons why my doctoral dissertation was so much better than my master's thesis," she says. "I think the old way, where you wrote by hand and then typed it on a typewriter, lessened the motivation to make alterations. Since I started using computers, my writing has improved 100 percent." Now she wouldn't be without one. "I compose on the computer; I don't even think any other way. I can't do anything in longhand. I don't know how I ever did it before."

When she is collecting information, Bailey uses half sheets of paper for notes. She puts one thought or one quote or one citation on each sheet—the McWhiney way—then sorts them into chapters. When she's ready to write, she arranges the notes into the order that she plans to tell the story. "I'm very fortunate because the Civil War is basically chronological... there's no question where you start if you're writing a narrative, or where you're going, or how it's going to end." She believes that "our goal as historians is to write a story that will appeal to the general reader. We have to make history interesting or we lose our audience." The writing includes analysis along with the narrative, but it "needs to be woven into the story." Bailey uses the words of the participants to carry the story—"It makes writing easy because the people are saying it for you."

Her mornings are consumed in editorial work. She edits the *Georgia Historical Quarterly* and is a former book review editor for *Civil War History*. She also edits the newsletter of the Society of Civil War Historians and serves on a number of boards for various professional organizations. "These are the kind of tasks where I don't have to compose or think or organize my own thoughts," Bailey says. "My own writing I enjoy doing, and I like to do it at my leisure." She does most of her writing in the early and mid-afternoon. "My theory has always been that at five o'clock I'm through. I like working in the yard, so I've always had this five o'clock bell and I'm done."

She says research "comes whenever I have free time; there's no real set time. I just do it when I can work it in." She likes to have most of the research completed, however, before she starts writing, adding to it if she finds something missing as she goes along. But basically, before writing begins, "I have my facts and my quotations carefully placed in the order I plan to use them." Bailey's favorite part of the whole process is the research—"finding information and the thrill of searching through collections, looking for new items."

When she finishes a day's writing, Bailey puts it away for two or three weeks. "I think a lot about what I want to do," she says, "so I don't have to look at where I stopped the day before." When she comes back to it, "to reread it and think about how to improve it," she has a new perspective. "Setting work aside is very helpful because when you return to it, the words flow better. It's like reading something that's not your own work, and is very helpful for making needed revisions."

Bailey occasionally struggles with procrastination—"Don't we all?"—especially when it comes down to finishing touches and cleaning up a manuscript. "Finishing is not as challenging or rewarding as creating," she says. "There's not the fun of finding exciting items. It's just correcting the grammar, so I tend to put it off." Writer's block is not an issue for her. She thinks she probably has it, "but I wouldn't recognize it. History is not like creating fiction," she says, "where you have to be creative from the beginning. In writing history you can always fall back on the words of someone else. The kind of writer's block that you would have as a fiction writer is different."

Political correctness plays little part in Bailey's thinking or work. "With a period piece," she says, "you're using direct quotes, so there's no question of political correctness if you're placing it in the context of the 1860s. It's just not an issue."

She doesn't consider herself a revisionist historian, although on one occasion a reporter for a newspaper accused her of being just that. In a presentation she made at the Georgia Historical Society in Savannah, Bailey said that Sherman had not burned everything in his path. "Clearly," Bailey says, "this person didn't know what a revisionist historian was, but my version of Sherman was not what they wanted to hear"—not what they believed about him—"so I became a revisionist historian."

Bailey frequently speaks to groups. When she is addressing other academics, she reads her presentation because it must have pinpoint accuracy, but when speaking to groups such as a Civil War Round Table or a Sons of Confederate Veterans Camp, she can be more informal and speak without a manuscript or notes. "It has to be a topic I know really well and I'm really comfortable with," she says, "and I can be more open for questions and conversations."

By the nature of her associations, Bailey is thrown together often with other historians. These frequent contacts are important to her. She has always found a warm reception within the Civil War community, and she also credits McWhiney with much of that. When she began her career, "Grady was regarded as a fine historian, so when I was with him I was always accepted." In the early 1980s "it was not easy for a woman to be a success in military history," she says. "I never had any problems, and I think it was because everyone respected Grady so much that they just accepted me as an adjunct to him. I don't think that road would have been nearly as easy if I had tried to break into military history on my own without him paving the way for me."

The Society of Civil War Historians is especially important to her: "The members have been wonderful because Civil War historians are a great group of people." Jerry L. Russell, late director of the Civil War Round Table Associates, suggested to McWhiney in 1985 that there should be a formal association of Civil War scholars. Together, Russell and McWhiney planned the first session of the newly founded organization at the Southern Historical Society meeting in Houston that year, and the group has flourished. "It's a growing organization," Bailey says, "but we all know one another and are very supportive in sharing information."

Bailey believes that "if I've done anything worthwhile it's been what I've done on Parsons's Texas cavalry brigade, because that was not a topic that had been looked at before." She finds satisfaction in the fact that "readers still write or e-mail me and say they picked up my book on Parsons's brigade and they had a relative in one of the regiments. I always feel good that although nobody else in the world cares, this relative does. I enjoy that." Several books later, that first work is still her favorite. "I enjoyed the research because everything with that book was new, it was all original." Again, "it was the researching in family papers and diaries that I enjoyed." Since then, she says, most of her work has been "more secondary—it's not like I was the trailblazer." Along the same lines, though, she has recently edited and published the Parsons's Brigade order book, which "had never seen the light of day," making it accessible to other researchers.

Bailey has no idea what she would have done with her life other than history. She always knew what she wanted and went after it. She unceasingly credits McWhiney with the joy and success she has found in her chosen field. "Grady's one of a kind," she says, "just an absolute jewel. I think we often fail to give credit to those people who have helped our careers along the road to success. Grady was equally giving with all of his graduate students and all he asked was for us to work as hard to succeed as he had done." And that she has done, living up to her mentor's expectations and hopes for her. Her gratitude is boundless: "I wouldn't be where I am today without him."

Steven E. Woodworth

PROLIFIC STORYTELLER

Woodworth knew history could be interesting: "I had read Bruce Catton, Barbara Tuchman, Cornelius Ryan, and Walter Lord."

"Am I as good a writer, is the prose that I compose at a keyboard as good as what I would compose writing longhand?"

"I'm a storyteller masquerading as historian."

———————◆◆◆———————

STEVEN WOODWORTH SAYS HE WAS BORN INTO HISTORY. AT A time before fathers were welcome in the delivery room, his father, waiting in an anteroom, "actually read several chapters in a history book while I was being born."

Woodworth's pastor-father was soon sharing his strong interest in history with his son. Woodworth recalls "bugging him to read to me and he would read me history books." That was before he was able to read himself, "so it was before I was six or seven years old." Some of the things his father read were children's books, stories "of pioneers and patriots, and little biographies and stories about Daniel Boone and things like that." But he also recalls that when he was still quite small his father read to him "Lt. Haskell's account of the Battle of Gettysburg, and Bruce Catton's *Civil War,* and other history books that I still enjoy today."

Although he had an early and precocious bent for history, Woodworth "didn't realize for a long time that that's what I wanted to do vocationally." He began to think seriously about it in high school, and by the time he entered college he knew he wanted a doctorate and to teach history at the college level.

Born in Ohio and raised in Illinois, Woodworth did his undergraduate work at Southern Illinois University in Carbondale. Despite his undergraduate history classes, the majority of which "bored me half out of my skull," he persisted in his desire to make history his calling. He knew that history could be interesting: "I had read Bruce Catton, Barbara Tuchman, Cornelius Ryan, and Walter Lord."

After earning his undergraduate degree, Woodworth went straight to a doctorate, without ever getting a master's degree. John Simon, the late editor of the U. S. Grant Papers, was one of his professors at Southern Illinois. When he told Simon that he wanted to go to graduate school for history, Simon tried to dissuade him. "He said there aren't any jobs, that 99 percent of the people are not going to get jobs." But Woodworth says, "I was just completely stubborn and could not be deterred. I thought well, 99 percent are not going to get jobs, but I'll be the one who does. Kind of cocky, I guess."

At Rice University in Houston, Texas, Woodworth wrote his dissertation under Ira Gruber. Gruber suggested he write on the Confederate president and his relationships with his generals. That became Woodworth's first book, *Jefferson Davis and His Generals*. This became a common method of choosing subjects to write about—other people suggesting them.

"It's been almost serendipitous, almost accidental," he says. "I have a lot of interests and it seems like I keep running into people who suggest topics to me." *Davis and Lee at War* grew out of the first book. Anne Bailey suggested what became *Six Armies in Tennessee*. His book on the religious world of Civil War soldiers, *While God Is Marching On*, "came about one day while touring Perryville battlefield with Mark Grimsley and Brooks Simpson, both Civil War historians." At the Shiloh battlefield several years later, Simpson suggested he write a book on the Army of the Tennessee, which led to *Nothing but Victory: The Army of the Tennessee, 1861–1865*.

He followed all that advice, "so that's how they've come about."

Woodworth wrote his first book in ballpoint pen on notebook paper, "but that was the last one I did that way," he says; now, he "wouldn't be without a computer." But something about the change has nagged and haunted him. He wonders, "Am I as good a writer, is the prose that I compose at a keyboard as good as what I would compose writing longhand?" It's a question he will never answer because he isn't likely to give up his computer.

While researching, Woodworth writes his notes on four-by-six-inch cards, which are filed in boxes. As he writes each note, he puts the date of the event in the corner of the card. When it is time to write, he organizes them chronologically, then reads through them to start getting the story in his mind—"what's this going to look like, how's this going to flow"—and then he begins discarding note cards. "It's like you turn the vacuum cleaner in reverse—you were gathering notes, you were sucking in every bit of information, and then it goes in reverse and now the thing is to get rid of note cards." As he makes the first pass through the cards, "the sculpture begins to emerge from the block of stone," and he can eliminate those notes that are not useful.

As he begins to write, Woodworth pulls out, for example, a month's worth of note cards. He reads them again, "sharpening my concept of how the story is going to flow." At this point he is discarding still more cards until he gets down to those he thinks *will* be useful. Then the writing begins.

He begins his day early, rising about 4:30 A.M., getting about six hours of sleep—"although I probably run better on seven. I start to get even more forgetful than usual." After a cup of coffee, he sits down at the computer and begins the day's writing. Almost all of his writing is done at home while listening to instrumental music. "You can't have lyrics," he says—"what I'm writing is the lyrics." A good day of writing, he believes, produces at least two thousand words; on one occasion he managed seven thousand in one day.

Woodworth likes to have all of his research in hand before he begins writing, occasionally adding to it if it "becomes apparent that I need some more information about a particular topic." Research, he believes, can bring on a real high—"when you find things, when you're at a manuscript repository and you bring out a new file box and open it up and you wonder what's going to be in there and it turns out to be something very good." But as much as he likes researching, he enjoys writing more.

Woodworth uses both primary and secondary sources. "Primary sources are more important," he says, "but often secondary sources can give you context." He finds secondary sources particularly useful for their footnotes, which he can track down and often "find even more stuff than [the author] had." His use of both types of sources "tends to be back and forth between the primaries for a bit and then to the secondaries, and then back to the primaries, and so forth."

Recently Woodworth has been thinking about taking a break from the Civil War to do a book on the 1840s. "You've got the dual stories of expansionism and the breakdown of the political system, which become entangled with one another. Here is the political system sort of coming to age, not necessarily in a completely good way, but here it is, nonetheless. And then here's this expansion, almost as though the camera shows one car coming down one street and then cuts away to another car coming on a cross street, and BOOM! They run into each other. I think it would be a lot of fun, and there are a lot of good stories to tell"—stories about the Mexican War, the California Trail, and "the Donner party and folks eating one another."

It would be a great story, and Woodworth loves to tell stories. "I'd say that I'm a storyteller masquerading as historian," he says. "I prefer to do narrative history—tell a story—and I'm not as prone to do analytic history."

Besides reading for information and pleasure, Woodworth also listens to recorded books. "I think reading and listening to very good writing helps us to write better," he says. Recently he listened again to Shelby Foote's three-volume history of the Civil War "to try to improve my own writing style."

Writer's block poses little difficulty for Woodworth. Procrastination can be a problem, but not in the way one would expect for a writer. "What gets procrastinated more are things I really hate doing, like balancing a checkbook; I'd rather go to the dentist and have an extraction," he says. When faced with a task he wants to avoid, he finds "it's always easier to sit down and write a few more words." His sort of procrastination may actually increase his writing production, although it is already prolific enough.

On occasion, all historians find conflicting material in their research. When this happens, Woodworth first tries to see if perhaps the differing information can be "harmonized, that they could both be true. If you bear in mind the different perspectives of the people that were writing them—one saw it from this angle, and the other from that angle—then maybe both could be true; or things could happen at different times." For example, on a Civil War battlefield, even though witnesses are reporting the same event, their time can be off by as much as one or two hours. When he can't harmonize accounts, he tries to figure out if someone had an axe to grind, or who wrote closer to the event, or look at "what interest a given witness might have had in saying what he said. It's always more credible if it looks like he had no possible interest in fabricating or fudging the story that he told."

Before beginning a day's writing, Woodworth reads over the last few pages he wrote in the previous session. He does some rewriting, but "probably less than I used to do." He has found that with experience, "I tend to get it the way I want it more the first time," although there will always be some revision.

Woodworth teaches at Texas Christian University (TCU) in Fort Worth, Texas. He juggles the research and writing and teaching by "separating days." On the two or three days that he spends at TCU, he usually does not write. Instead, he focuses on "getting the syllabus ready and all the class-related things." He meets with classes (both undergraduate and graduate), keeps his office hours, and usually lunches with some of his graduate students.

He finds that they sometimes give him new ideas or insights. "Conversation with them is very beneficial to both of us," he says. For his part, he offers suggestions for thesis subjects to work on: "I kind of help them figure out what it is about the Civil War that they want to write and where the opportunities lie to write about that topic."

Along with his researching, writing, and teaching, Woodworth and his wife homeschool their seven children. Usually his wife teaches the younger ones while he works with the two older boys, who have their own desks in his office. "That's good for them because I need it relatively quiet to get *my* work done, and so they can't be fooling around. It works well," he says.

Although Simon had tried to discourage him from a degree in history, citing the scarcity of jobs, Woodworth's cockiness paid off. The weekend he graduated with his doctorate, he was hired by Bartlesville Wesleyan College in Oklahoma (now Oklahoma Wesleyan University), where he taught for two years before moving to Toccoa Falls College in Georgia for eight years. Although he liked it there, it couldn't offer him the salary he needed to support his growing family, so he began looking elsewhere. "I thought it would be relatively easy to get a tenure track assistant professorship since by that time I had a couple of books published and I had won some prizes, and I thought, well, an assistant professorship shouldn't be too hard to get. Well, it was hard!" He says forty-three institutions turned him down before his stubborness paid off and he was hired at TCU.

To be a good historian, Woodworth believes, "good writing skills are important, a lot of patience is necessary, a lot of persistence, some degree of understanding of people and how they work." He says aptitude is important, too. "You notice aptitude most when you don't have it—like me trying to play any sport."

Woodworth has little patience with political correctness, which he finds is "rampant in academia." He isn't sure what it means anymore, "because I guess what passes for 'politically incorrect' seems to be mostly crude and offensive. On the other hand, I think the original meaning of political correctness was a sort of a leftist-feminist party line that was imposed and that you weren't supposed to say things contrary to that." He finds himself in a minority among academic historians in that he is conservative—"politically, culturally, socially, and religiously—so that makes me unusual in the field."

Historians today, he believes, only value studies that focus on race, class, or gender, and how oppression has flowed along those lines. He labels that neo-Marxism. In classical Marxism, he says, "you have Marx saying that what makes history go is class oppression; the driving force of history and what shapes it and gives it its flow and direction and sets its course is the class struggle between the oppressors and the oppressed." Neo-Marxism says that "what gives history its flow and its course and its shape is not just class struggle, but also gender and race struggle. People who have money oppress people who don't, people who are white oppress people who aren't, and people who are male heterosexuals oppress people who aren't."

Woodworth believes this approach has skewed the study of history. "If you do a study and the result is that in this particular thing race didn't make much difference, class didn't make much difference, gender didn't make much difference, then you don't have any significant results—your study was a failure because you really didn't turn up anything significant. But if you can construe this study in some way that race, class, and gender are important, then you have an exciting, significant, interesting, groundbreaking study."

The permeation of this attitude throughout the field of history, he says, forces graduate students, who will soon be looking for scarce jobs, to toe the line. If they are seen to be conservative, "that will mark them and they won't get hired and they won't get promoted."

Woodworth believes in revisionism, and that it "can go in any number of directions." For example, he says, "It can be someone writing that George Washington was really homosexual or something, or it could be someone writing something not actually brand new; for example, James Powell brings out clearly in *F.D.R.'s Follies* that the New Deal actually prolonged and worsened the Depression." The operative question for him is, "Is it true? And if it is, so be it."

Another example Woodworth points to is the question of Davy Crockett's death at the Alamo: was he captured alive and then killed, or did he die fighting? "In talking with some historians, it seems to me that they're not particularly concerned about what is true, and what bugs me is when I feel that their concern is not so much what is actually true, as it is that they *want* Crockett to appear less heroic. They don't want Crockett to have died fighting. Things like that bother me."

Associations with other historians are important to Woodworth. Most often, he says, they are informal associations, friendships with other individual historians. Through his overall editing of a series of books for Scholarly Resources, he has been closely involved with many historians. "I've made a lot of friends," he says, "and found a lot of very nice people that I've enjoyed meeting."

Woodworth believes that his unique contribution to the field of history thus far would be "making history interesting and accessible," that he has shown "that it really is a story." He also feels that his "rejection of the race, class, gender paradigm" is also an important contribution. Of his publications, *Jefferson Davis and His Generals* has probably been the most successful and influential thus far," but he sees *While God Is Marching On* as the most important subject he has addressed.

Some of his work has "drawn a lot of fire." His first book, a "semi-rehabilitation of Braxton Bragg" was criticized, and his views on religion during the Civil War "have taken fire from both conservatives and liberals." Woodworth takes it in stride: "I don't particularly enjoy criticism, but a certain amount of it is unavoidable and just has to be endured."

Woodworth says the one book he regrets doing is the one on the battle of Gettysburg, although he enjoyed writing it. He believes that Gettysburg "is viewed as important because it has already been viewed as important. People write books about it because so many books *have* been written about it. People go to visit it because so many other people go and visit it. It has become sort of a feedback loop." He believes "There are a ridiculous number of Gettysburg books published every year."

When asked if he can imagine having spent his life doing something other than history, Woodworth recalls that as a child he thought he might go into archeology or paleontology. "But I didn't go that direction—the road not taken, as Robert Frost wrote." And that has made all the difference—for himself and for the field of history.

Charles P. Roland

Synthesizer of the Past

Professor Simkins said, "My, Charlie, that's a magnificent sentence! What the hell does it mean?"

"I've always loved words. I love words and I just enjoy putting them together, and polishing, rewriting, and polishing."

"The better we know the past, and the more accurately we study it, the better our society will be."

C HARLES P. ROLAND AND HISTORY GO WAY BACK. HIS grandfather, a teacher, ran a private high school in West Tennessee, and "from infancy on up I heard him talk about history." His father, too, loved the past. A polymath, he taught history, along with "a little of everything," at a junior college. When his father retired on his ninetieth birthday, the records showed that he had taught twenty-seven different courses, including mathematics, calculus, chemistry, physics, "and what have you." But he was primarily a history teacher.

Aside from the teachers in the family sparking his interest, he grew up just thirty miles from the Shiloh battlefield. "There's no way of counting how many times I've been over that battlefield," he says. "From the time I was a little boy I developed a burning interest in that battle, and the interest spread from that to the whole Civil War."

By the time he hit college, Roland knew he wanted to major in history. He spent the first two years at Freed-Hardeman Junior College, where his father taught all those courses, and attended Vanderbilt for his last two years. There he encountered "very outstanding scholars and professors": William C. Binkley, who specialized in frontier history; and Frank Owlsley, "probably the best-known scholar in Southern history at that time." Roland particularly bonded with Owlsley's course on Sectionalism and Conflict: "I thought that was a great course. I became deeply involved then as a history major."

With his undergraduate degree, Roland for a time taught history at Alamo High School in Tennessee. Meanwhile, he had passed a civil service examination, and in 1940, after two years of teaching, he was called to Washington, D.C., to work for the National Park Service (NPS). He delivered "little lectures" at various sites, including the Lincoln Memorial, the Washington Monument, Lee Mansion, and Ford's Theater. His early lectures were "canned." Dissatisfied with those, he soon added research of his own and "enriched my presentations."

He held the job with the NPS for about a year and a half before being drafted into the army on January 15, 1942. He served in Europe during World War II as a combat infantry captain, returning home in December of 1945. When he came back to the United States, he also returned to his NPS job for a little over a year. "They didn't have any office space for me," he recalls, "so they put me in a plush little office in the newly finished Jefferson Memorial. Except for Thomas Jefferson's towering statue, I was literally the first occupant of the Jefferson Memorial."

Roland began taking graduate courses at George Washington University under the G.I. Bill while he continued to work for the NPS half-time at half-pay. He took courses through the summer of 1946 and enrolled for the fall semester. While at home in Tennessee for the Christmas break, he ran into an old friend who was attending

Louisiana State University (LSU), who persuaded him to transfer. "So I went back to Washington, finished the semester at George Washington, resigned the Park Service job, flew to Baton Rouge, and walked in and enrolled for graduate work at LSU."

He walked cold into the history department and told the secretary why he was there. She asked if he had been accepted to the graduate school. "No, I didn't know anything about that," Roland said. She said then he should talk to the department chairman. She waved him into the chairman's office; "I walked in and found this tall, handsome man that I would have taken to be an advanced graduate student, sitting at an old-fashioned upright typewriter," Roland recalls. "He wheeled around in his chair, thrust out one hand, and said, 'I'm Bell Wiley, chairman of the history department.'" Wiley looked over Roland's Vanderbilt transcript, and "before I left that meeting, he offered me a job as his graduate researcher."

Roland had never heard of Wiley. His *The Life of Johnny Reb* had been published in 1943, while Roland was in the army, and "I didn't know anything about it." Wiley was currently working on *The Life of Billy Yank,* and that is what Roland spent his time researching. "That's how I was first introduced to primary source research," he remembers, "because he had me going through the *Official Records of the Rebellion,* and I'd never heard of them, and a lot of other stuff." The excitement of that time is still with him: "This was a tremendous experience!"

When Roland completed his master's, Wiley left LSU for Emory University. But the legendary Francis Butler Simkins took Wiley's place at LSU, and Roland also worked under T. Harry Williams. "I couldn't have gone anywhere in the United States and found three professors that good in my particular field," he says.

Although "they had *vastly* different personalities," Roland became close personal friends with each of them. He and Wiley had been born and raised about forty miles apart in west Tennessee. That created a bond between them, "and the more we talked about it, the stronger the bond became. He would play a key role in every job I ever got."

He remembers Williams "loved nothing more than to be in a shouting argument with a graduate student, and, of course, there were a whole bunch of us that had just come back, veterans who had been officers in World War II, so we supplied the arguments and we just had a tremendous amount of fun."

Simkins "was the world's greatest eccentric." Whenever Roland turned in a chapter of his dissertation, Simkins would invite him to sit with him under the oak trees on campus "and read your opus." As Roland read, Simkins would close his eyes and seem to be sound asleep, "but every now and then he'd pop up and say, 'My, Charlie, that's a magnificent sentence! What the hell does it mean?' I would explain what it meant and he'd say, 'Well, you know you're going to have a lot of people reading this (of course, I didn't know that at all!) and not many of them are going to be up to reading these magnificent sentences." Roland found that in "that eccentric and gentle way, he would kind of tone me down and I would write in plainer English."

Roland graduated with his doctoral degree just as the Korean War began. "I'm in the reserves," he says, "and they were hot on my trail as a veteran combat infantry captain." He had already been ordered up for a physical examination when Wiley changed the course of Roland's military career. Wiley's friend, Dr. Kent Greenfield, was the chief historian of the army and had contacted Wiley, looking for "some young person with advanced training in history, preferably with a Ph.D. degree, and who was in the reserves with a commission of at least the rank of captain and could be brought back into uniform and assigned to him as his administrative and editorial assistant." The qualifications exactly matched Roland's, and he was taken on. He spent a year and a half at the Office of the Chief of Military History, today's Army Center of Military History. The project he worked on was the history of the U.S. Army in World War II, which eventually became "a monumental study of fifty-five volumes, called the Green Book series because it came out in green covers from the Government Printing Office." Roland considers his time there "the equivalent of a high-level postdoctoral experience with a very distinguished historian. I learned an awful lot there."

All this time, Roland knew he wanted to teach. "I knew that's what I was really cut out for, to be a teacher." Tulane University accommodated that desire, hiring him to teach the U.S. survey and the Louisiana history courses, which expanded into the Civil War and history of the South. He taught at Tulane for eighteen years, beginning in 1952, before moving to the University of Kentucky, where he taught for another eighteen. During those thirty-six years, he produced eighteen doctoral students, nine at each institution.

During his long career, Roland has found that the subjects to write on "just sort of fall into my lap." His doctoral dissertation, *Louisiana Sugar Plantations during the American Civil War,* came from a list of topics suggested to him by Wiley when he was looking for a subject for his master's thesis. When he went to Tulane, a colleague told him that the university library held the leading extant collection of Confederate General Albert Sidney Johnston's personal papers. That immediately sparked Roland's interest, given his familiarity with the Battle of Shiloh and Johnston's death there. "Well," he says, "I was over there right away browsing around in the Johnston papers." Twelve years later he published *Albert Sidney Johnston: Soldier of Three Republics,* still the standard Johnston biography.

Another subject that fell into his lap was *The Confederacy.* At a meeting of the Southern Historical Association, a colleague was talking with Daniel Boorstin, editor of the series *The Chicago History of American Civilization,* who mentioned that he needed someone to write on the Confederacy. His colleague pointed to Roland, who was sitting nearby, and said, "There's your man!"

Another book he particularly relished writing was *Reflections on Lee.* In a roundabout way, that book grew out of a 1961 symposium organized by Grady McWhiney at Northwestern University in Evanston, Illinois. "It was Northwestern University's bow to the Civil War centennial," Roland remembers. "They decided to have this conference with four distinguished historians, and Grady smuggled me in." The other historians who read papers were Bruce Catton, Harry Williams, and David Donald, "all three of whom had either already received or would receive a Pulitzer Prize. And there was little Charlie Roland; I was really a dwarf among those three."

Dwarf he may have been, but his paper on Lee, published in the volume that came out of that symposium—*Grant, Lee, Lincoln and the Radicals*—was impressive enough that he was offered a contract to expand it into a book.

At one point Roland moved away from the Civil War. He wrote *The Improbable Era: The South Since World War II,* and when he went to Kentucky he "met and became fascinated by perhaps the most colorful political figure in Kentucky history, Albert Benjamin 'Happy' Chandler." He decided to do a biography of Chandler, spent years interviewing him and all of his associates, his political supporters and enemies, and wrote about 20 percent of the biography when "I suddenly just burned out on it." By then Roland was close to retirement, and he foresaw its entirety being consumed by this project. He turned the biography over to a former graduate student.

Roland's interest in the Civil War was rekindled by an invitation to teach for a year as a visiting professor of military history at the Army War College, where one of the courses he taught was the Civil War. Reinforcing this new interest, he was approached by an agent from a publishing company to write a brief history of the Civil War, which eventually came out as *An American Iliad: The Story of the Civil War.* He was also receiving many invitations to lecture on the war. "All of those things kind of came together to draw me back into the Civil War," he says.

When writing, Roland "did all of my work by fits and starts, in the most disorganized way possible. I cannot, I simply am incapable of, organizing notes into neat categories the way I think most historians work. I just have to read stuff, make notes, and kind of jumble them together and read them and reread them and come up with what I guess Professor Simkins would have called an impressionistic picture of it, and then write it down."

Roland likes to write standing up: "It seems to free me in some way." He writes one paragraph at a time. In the old days, if he wanted to rearrange the paragraphs, he would cut and paste. "My floor would be covered with versions of paragraphs that I'd just wadded up and thrown away and started over again." But not now. "I have become an addict of the computer. You can type anything you want to in there, no matter how silly, how crazy, how spontaneous, and if you don't like it you can change it. The word processor was made for me!"

In his earlier days, most of his writing was done in the afternoon and evening because he usually taught in the morning. Before starting the day's writing he reviews the previous pages and revises as he does so: "I don't leave a paragraph until I've written it and rewritten it and worked it pretty much into the shape in which I want it." To get his writing day started, he sometimes will go as far back as the previous week's work "to get my running start for the day." As he revises, Roland reads his material aloud. "I've decided that I'm a very aural person. I really need to *hear* it."

His research, Roland says, "didn't really follow much of a pattern." The exception was when he went through the Johnston Papers, where he "just started at the beginning and worked my way through them chronologically, making notes, and stacking up note cards on my desk." After a year or two, he would go through them and "arrange them on my desk, and when I ran out of desk space I'd put them on the floor, into sort of crude topics." He never used file folders for them, he just stacked them all over.

He took his Johnston notes on five-by-eight index cards by hand. Because "a life is lived chronologically," the cards were pretty much arranged that way. Eventually they made their way into 8½-by-11-inch manila envelopes, which he labeled—"they became my file folders," he says.

For his other books, he drew from his lecture notes. As he prepared to teach various courses, he took notes on things he read and put them into file folders. "Years later," he says, "when I sit down to write, all I've got to do is go and pick up those file folders and start writing." He does need to do some additional research, "but the basis of it comes out of those lecture notes."

Roland claims to be "one of the world's greatest procrastinators." But he says, "once I get into it I can pretty well keep going." He reminds himself of an essay he read long ago by Jacques Barzun, a dean at Columbia University, who said that you can take notes for the rest of your life. At a certain point, you need to stop researching and start writing with whatever you have in hand, filling in as necessary. "That was a great piece of advice," Roland says. "The day after I read that essay, I started writing the Johnston biography."

He believes writing may be more difficult than researching, but he finds it more pleasurable. "I never did really enjoy the research all that much," he says, although "there were moments of exhilaration" when he found something that he had been looking for in an unexpected place. "But generally," he says, "I found the research really hard work; you're just sitting there reading and jotting down notes."

He finds writing so pleasurable because "I've always loved words. I love words and I just enjoy putting them together, and polishing, rewriting, and polishing." He believes this came to him in part from listening to good speakers—"my own father, my grandfather, the ministers at the little Church of Christ college." Some of them, including his father, "were very eloquent speakers, had great vocabularies." Another influential source was reading and hearing "innumerable quotations over a period of many years from the King James Bible. That's about as strong as language gets to be," he says.

He also credits Simkins with influencing his writing style. He recalls that on one of his exam papers Simkins commented, "You have one of the qualities of a fine writer—you know how to say a lot in a few words." That made him think about compression being a valuable part of writing. "I began then consciously to try to condense, and make my writing more compact." Simkins also encouraged his students to read great literature. Roland read Gibbon, Prescott, and Macaulay, "and I started reflecting on what seemed to me to be particularly striking passages." Before he began writing his book on the Confederacy, he read Thucydides's *History of the Peloponnesian War,* "and I think that all of those things kind of went together to mold my writing style." He still reads outside of his field, including novels. "If it's well-written, it appeals to me," he says.

Roland believes a good historian must have a strong personality and be deeply dedicated to the discipline of history. A historian must believe that knowing history is important, that it's the "central part of the glue that holds a society together." Both the present and the future are greatly influenced by the past, "and the better we know the past, and the more accurately we study it, the better our society will be."

As with most frontline historians, political correctness has little influence on Roland. "I am *very* much averse to the kind of political correctness that actually alters not only words, but alters conclusions." Too often, he says, "we revisit the history of the past in terms of the present." For example, he says that a lot of the brutalities to slaves were also perpetrated on nonslaves—indentured servants, soldiers, students, and others. "So to fix on the whipping of slaves, and to take that completely out of the context of that day and time, I think is not history; I think it's a terrible distortion of history."

He doesn't consider himself a revisionist, although some of the things he's done could be considered revisionist "in that it runs against what was written fifty years before." He believes revisionism can become presentism. For example, on Harry Truman's decision to use the atomic bomb, some writers take it "completely out of the context of the time" and berate Truman for that decision. "I think that's wrong," he says, "that's nonhistory to do it that way. Revisionism of that kind becomes present-day propaganda."

Association with other historians has always been important to Roland, especially the Southern Historical Association. He went to all its meetings, met and chatted with people, "and it helped to get me offers to go places." He served on various committees, and eventually became president of the association. "All of that experience I consider to have been a very important part of my career."

Roland believes that his unique contribution to the field of history is his ability to synthesize "vast amounts of material into a compact, manageable corpus," as he did in several of his books. That is particularly true of *American Iliad,* his compact synthesis of the

Civil War. His lifetime as a historian gave him "the perspective of having read and reflected on vast amounts of material that couldn't be put into a single volume."

If he had to choose another career, Roland thinks he might have enjoyed being a journalist—the writer coming out in him. And some of his friends urged him to go to law school instead of graduate school when he left the army at the end of World War II. "When I look back on my decision now, I see that I would have been far more affluent today if I'd gone to law school," he says, "but I would not change that decision."

Gary Gallagher

MASTER OF THE ESSAY

Photo by Dan Addison

"There isn't *an* answer to anything in history. It's very complicated and can be murky and maddening."

"There are few things in my life that have been as satisfying as just wandering the stacks of a really wonderful library."

"I get great satisfaction from finishing a piece of writing that seems to get my point across the way I want to get it across."

"It's absolutely critical that you play it straight with the evidence, even if it just *kills* you to have to abandon some notion that you had about something."

———◆◆◆———

GARY GALLAGHER CAN CLEARLY PINPOINT WHEN HE BECAME interested in the Civil War. When he was nine years old, he got a subscription to *National Geographic* magazine, which ran a couple of articles in anticipation of the Centennial. "I was captivated by the images of the battlefields and by the text," he recalls. In 1960, he bought a copy of the *American Heritage Picture History of the Civil War*, "and that was it for me, that was the real start." It put him on the path of a lifetime Civil War bibliophile: "I probably had 250 books on the Civil War by the time I was a junior in high school."

He was so well-read on the war that one of his high school teachers enlisted him to teach the section on the Civil War. "I knew by then that I probably wanted to teach about the Civil War as my life work," he says. He read Bruce Catton, Douglas Southall Freeman, and others, and "followed their footnotes to lots of firsthand accounts." In addition to books, he had good teachers in college, particularly Norma Lois Peterson whose interest was the Civil War. He also remembers another undergraduate professor who did not specialize in the war, "but who loved books and nourished my bibliophilic tendencies."

In graduate school, he studied under Barnes F. Lathrop at the University of Texas (UT), who trained many graduate students, including Frank Vandiver and Stephen Oates. Another influential professor was George B. Forgie, a Lincoln specialist. "He's a great undergraduate teacher; I learned a lot about teaching from him, and from Lewis Ludlow Gould, who is a Gilded Age and Progressive Era political historian at Texas."

Gallagher was born in Los Angeles but grew up on a farm in southern Colorado. He attended "public country schools, where they had multiple grades and just a few teachers," then went to Alamosa High School. For his undergraduate degree he enrolled at "a little teacher's college in Alamosa, a normal school that turned into a teacher's college and then into a liberal arts institution called Adams State College." He then matriculated to UT for his master's and doctoral degrees.

For his doctoral dissertation, his advisors assigned him the presidential election of 1852. "But my heart was never in it," he says. He was so turned off that he dropped out of graduate school, until Lathrop offered to let him work on a subject more closely related to the Civil War. Gallagher chose to write on Confederate General Stephen Dodson Ramseur "because he left a wonderful set of papers that are in the Southern Historical Collection. The background reading for Ramseur I'd essentially been doing my whole life, so I was able to read through the letters and write my dissertation in about a year and a half." That became his first book.

When he graduated with his doctorate, Gallagher says, "there were no jobs. I don't mean it was a bad job market—it was a nonexistent job market in U.S. history." Fortunately, there was a position available as an archivist at the Lyndon Baines Johnson Library in Austin, Texas, and he worked there for ten years. At the end of that time, Forgie was on leave from UT, and Gallagher replaced him for one semester to teach the Civil War class. "That was my initial experience as a teacher," he recalls. While teaching that class, he was hired by Penn State, where he started teaching in the autumn of 1986. He taught there for twelve happy years before answering an ad for a chair in Civil War history at the University of Virginia. "It was a chair that tons of people applied for because it's such a great school and one of the best Civil War jobs that had been advertised in years. That's why I applied." Even though he had not been looking to go somewhere else, "this just seemed like an opportunity that I would have to at least take a chance with." He landed the job, and says, "I'm very happy here."

Gallagher is noted for putting together packages of essays on various campaigns and on different aspects of the Civil War. These books grew out of a series of conferences that he began running at Penn State. In talking with some of the participants, it became clear that books of essays would be a natural outgrowth of the conference presentations. "At first, these studies had a pretty traditional military focus," he says. He knew that among many academics there was a strong bias against military history and "to continue to have old-fashioned military history struck me as a little bit narrow." So he began to use those volumes of essays "as a way to cast military history in a little broader context." Besides essays on fairly traditional military history—questions of tactics, strategy, and leadership—he included studies on "the ways in which campaigns resonated behind the lines—their political impact, how they shaped or influenced political decisions and civilian morale, the development of emancipation, and so forth." In all, thirty to thirty-five scholars have contributed to the nine volumes published so far.

Gallagher saw this project as "a way to make military history embrace a greater range of elements of the Civil War, because I think too often there's this huge divide in the literature on the conflict." He believes most academics are satisfied to write and teach about the war "with the military history almost completely left out." But that's not desirable, he says, because "it was a gigantic war and you just can't understand it by leaving the war out." On the other hand, many nonacademics are often interested in only the military aspects. "It just seems to me that neither one of those approaches gets you where you need to go. Those two spheres intersect in so many ways that I think it's important to think more broadly about the Civil War."

Gallagher credits Lathrop and some of his undergraduate professors, "who took the time to work my prose over, showing me no quarter whatsoever," with teaching him how to edit. They taught him to write clearly. "Life's too short to read bad writing," he says. "Why not read something that's actually fun to read?" He believes you don't have to sacrifice complexity; "I think you can make complex arguments and deal with complex ideas in straightforward, vigorous prose that anyone can understand."

Editing isn't easy, Gallagher says. When there is heavy editing required, "there's nothing harder, because it's easier to just write it yourself than to try to salvage something that is hard to understand." The editing, he says, "usually comes in trying to make arguments clearer." He isn't concerned that the essays included in a volume agree with each other—"in fact, I like it when they don't. That's very instructive, because there isn't *an* answer to anything in history. It's very complicated and can be murky and maddening."

Besides the essays he has edited, Gallagher has written many himself—"I love to write essays," he says. He finds that he can do a lot with that format and believes that "a lot of books would actually make good essays." He says you can "make most of your points in an essay, sort of shake things up." So far, he has published two books of his own collected essays.

But essays are not his only published works. In addition to his book *Stephen Dodson Ramseur: Lee's Gallant General,* in which he was able to "get at the junior high command of Lee's army," he has written two other books. *The Confederate War* is his "reaction to what I perceived as directions in the literature that seemed to overlook very obvious things to me: the notion that the Confederates lost the war because of internal dissent, they didn't really try as hard as they could have, and that military history shouldn't be front and center." He has been happy with its reception. "It made some people angry, but many other people liked it," he says. "It's worked out just the way we hoped—which is to promote debate and further scholarship." His most recent book is *Causes Won, Lost, and Forgotten: How Hollywood and Art Shape What We Know About the Civil War.*

In choosing subjects to write about, Gallagher admits that he "likes to go against the conventional grain in some ways, and especially against the conventional academic grain." If the extant literature seems at odds with, to him, fairly obvious evidence, "I like to write about that." What he writes often has a historiographical dimension to it, coupled with his own argument that is based on his reading of the sources. "So it's not just historiography, it's a combination of playing off the current literature in a fairly specific way, and then drawing on my own research to put my ideas out against the ones that I'm holding up for debate."

This has led him to being labeled by some as a revisionist, or even a postrevisionist, but he says, "much of the revising I attempt to do often hearkens back to earlier ideas, although not in exactly the same way." He has written about the idea that Robert E. Lee "was a misguided general who didn't understand modern war and so forth," arguments propounded by Alan Nolan and Thomas Connelly in opposition to Douglas Southall Freeman and other writers who had only praise for Lee. Gallagher believes Lee was a good soldier, although his view differs from that of Freeman. He has been called a postrevisionist in that case because Nolan and Connelly are considered the revisionists. "People who haven't read my work as carefully as they might, think I'm just going back and praising Lee blindly, which isn't the case." He does think Lee was a modern soldier; "I think he understood better than his modern critics what was going on."

Gallagher goes where the sources take him. There is such a "fabulous richness of sources on the Civil War that you can argue *anything* and find things to support it." But he believes one must play fair with the evidence. If in ten pieces of evidence, eight of them say A and two of them say B, it isn't "cricket to argue the two sources and ignore the other eight" just because you want to argue B. "I think you need to go where the evidence leads you." Too often, he believes, "books are thesis-driven and go against the evidence to argue that point."

Gallagher works at home, at a stand-up desk because he has a "problematical back—I haven't sat down and worked in twenty years." If his legs get tired, he'll shift position or walk around or take a break and sit for a brief spell.

Early on in his career Gallagher took research notes on half-sheets of paper. "But it's been a long time since I did that," he says. "I now just take notes on computer files; I have everything on the computer." As he enters quotations, he immediately proofreads it, then proofs it again. "Every note that I take I proof twice, right at the time." When he visits a repository, he photocopies everything he can so that he can check his accuracy in quoting against the copy of the original. By copying items, he saves time and money; he can go through the material faster and spend fewer days in motel rooms and eating out.

Because he has a large personal library, the only research he does outside is in archival material. He has always diligently collected primary accounts. "I have hundreds and hundreds of them," he says, "including individual journal issues that would have sets of letters or reminiscences or something in them." If it has been published in some form, there's a good chance that Gallagher has it in his library.

Before he begins to write, Gallagher likes to have the vast majority of his research finished. "I always have to go back and add a few things, check a few more things, track down a few more things, but for the most part almost all of the research is finished before I start to write."

When writing, he prints out the notes he plans to use for that day's section. "I might have twenty single-spaced pages of quotations," Gallagher says. "Then I go through those pages and make organizational notes out in the margin in red ink." As he works on a particular topic, such as desertion, those red-ink notes in the margin pop right out, helping him locate the quotations he wants to use.

Gallagher has "always written in rooms where I'm just absolutely surrounded by books. I love to work with real books," he says. His *Official Records* are "still the big black-bound volumes, and I sometimes will have them spread all over my working room so I can just go from one to another." Books are essential to him. "There's just something about holding the book that's very important for me. I don't ever want to live in a world where you just go to the computer. There are few things in my life that have been as satisfying as just wandering the stacks of a really wonderful library." And there are advantages to "wandering the stacks." "You always find things that you're not thinking you're going to find, things that just happen to be shelved in the same section with the things you're looking for."

Besides being surrounded by his beloved books, Gallagher likes to write to music. His tastes are eclectic. "I switch among progressive country music, rock, and opera, Puccini mainly; those are the things that seem to work the best for me."

Gallagher edits as he goes along. "If I write five pages on Monday, the first thing I do on Tuesday is read those five pages and make changes in them and then go from there." By the time he has finished his first draft, "it's not a rough draft at all." At the end, he usually has to do just a light edit before sending it out to friends for their feedback.

Gallagher writes when he can, finding it "hard to carve out a particular time each day." Sometimes he'll get up early in the morning and write for five hours or so, but he's also written a good bit late at night. He found nights especially good when he was an administrator, "because then the phone wasn't ringing, I knew somebody wasn't going to pop into my office, and that was time I really could count on." When he was younger, he would sometimes write until eleven or twelve o'clock at night. "I can't do that anymore," he says, because he "found out that I can't *will* myself to be as productive as I used to be. I'm not sure I should be; there's actually more to life than writing, and that's a good thing for me. If I thought it was important to be as productive as I was earlier in my career, I'd be very bitter because I can't do it."

Gallagher believes teaching and writing complement each other: "I use things from my research to revise my lectures all the time." And he finds that he learns from his graduate students. "I've been lucky," he says, "to have some very good ones. I have learned a lot from them and some of them have become quite influential themselves in Civil War history."

When he has a year off from teaching, Gallagher finds that he misses being in the classroom. "There's something in me, I like getting positive feedback and so I like lecturing to classes." He teaches a variety of classes, from small undergraduate courses to large lecture courses, preferring the latter. "It's very rewarding to have people seem pleased with what you're yapping at them about."

Keeping up with the literature in the field is overwhelming. "I really can't keep up with the Civil War literature any more, there's so much of it," he says. Besides reading new publications, he reads many manuscripts for a series he edits for University of North Carolina Press called *Civil War America*. There are already eighty-one titles in the series, and for every manuscript that is published, there have been two or three he read that were not published. His outside reading includes *The Washington Post* and *The Economist*. After that, there's not much time left for discretionary reading. "I force myself to read some mystery novels, and a few other things outside my field. But I'm not nearly as well-read as I should be," he says.

Gallagher admits to procrastination when it comes to writing. "I have periods where all of a sudden I become a whirling dervish at everything else—the lawn, the dishes, I get out the vacuum, I clean shelves, I clean out closets, I take longer walks—I do everything except write, all the while knowing exactly what I'm doing. It's not as if I'm fooling myself." He will sometimes put off the writing until he absolutely cannot procrastinate anymore, "and then I become very productive," he says. "I've always been pretty good at meeting deadlines." And he enjoys the end product. "I get great satisfaction from finishing a piece of writing that seems to get my point across the way I want to get it across. I really do enjoy that. In that sense the writing is very rewarding for me."

When he runs into conflicting material, Gallagher first tries to resolve it by "looking at enough material so that I can get a sense of which part of it might actually be right." If that doesn't work, he believes the historian needs to "play it straight with readers—say some of the evidence says this, and some of the evidence says this, and taking into account other factors, I would lean toward this interpretation, but I may be wrong."

The most exciting adventure Gallagher has had in his career was finding the manuscript of Confederate artillerist Edward Porter Alexander's *Fighting for the Confederacy.* "No one knew it existed," he says. "That was an absolute joy." And he came so close to not figuring out what he had found. With just a few hours left of a week of researching at the Southern Historical Collection at the University of North Carolina at Chapel Hill, he found a letter Alexander had written to his wife from Nicaragua that enclosed his chapters on Gettysburg. In the letter, he described to his wife how long the full manuscript was and how many maps there were. "I went back through the papers and found that and then checked his other letters to find the other ones, and in the end there's this perfect manuscript, 1,200 pages long." It had essentially disappeared under the cataloging system used by the librarian. "That's the only project I've ever worked on that I honestly and truly was sorry to finish," he says. "Porter Alexander was such great company, so smart, and that account is so great."

Gallagher finds writing more difficult than researching. "There is no such thing as 'research block' as far as I'm aware," he says. "I can always get up in the morning and go to the Library of Congress or the National Archives or go systematically through books and take notes." However, he believes "there are greater rewards in writing than there are in the research. Though it's fun to find things, it's more fun for me to put together an argument or an account in a way that satisfies me."

A good historian, Gallagher believes, comes up "with questions that matter," either by asking a new question or going back to an old topic and coming at it from a different direction. In doing that, "it's absolutely critical that you play it straight with the evidence, even if it just *kills* you to have to abandon some notion you had about something."

Historians need to be careful about letting ideology drive their conclusions. "I'm not naïve enough to think that we can just check our political beliefs at the door and none of that will come out in our writing," Gallagher says. "I think there is some of that in everyone's writing." But if it becomes polemical, he believes, "the people who indulge in it shouldn't call it history, because it's not history."

His unique contribution to history, Gallagher believes, is "broadening the way we approach military history, trying to get people to think of the Civil War as a really big tent rather than different groups thinking of it as smaller tents of specific kinds." His *Civil War America* series has books on a wide range of subjects within the field of Civil War history, including military biographies, political biographies, books on the home front, on women, and on soldier life. "This underscores just how vibrant and broad a field it is. I have worked toward that in many ways over the years, and I think that I've had some success." Considering the books he has written himself, *The Confederate War,* Gallagher believes, is the most important one, but *Fighting for the Confederacy* will be the most cited.

In addition to his classroom teaching, Gallagher recorded a series of forty-eight lectures on the Civil War for The Teaching Company. "I have been stunned by how well that course has done," he says. "I think it's one of the best things I've ever done because it has reached a lot of people." He frequently receives e-mails about the course, and "every time I give a talk somewhere, two or three people will come up and tell me that they have enjoyed it." He finds that those who started with little knowledge of the Civil War, as well as those who are well-versed in it, have all enjoyed it and learned something from it.

The only other career he can imagine for himself would be an antiquarian bookseller. "That's the *only* other thing that would have appealed to me at all." He laments the loss of so many booksellers, put out of business by the Internet. "What a joy it used to be to go into a bookstore and just go up and down the shelves and discover things." On the Internet, you find there "are nine copies and you just decide which one you're going to buy. It's nice in one way," he admits, "but there's something about the old pursuit and joy of discovery that is gone now."

In choosing history, Gallagher positioned himself to indulge his bibliophilic passion. He owns thousands of books and finds it "comforting for me to be in a room that has bookcases everywhere. It is a security blanket, I won't pretend otherwise." At one time, he says, "I had a bunch of really wonderful antiquarian, desirable, scarce Civil War books," but circumstances forced him to lose "the heart of the book collection" on two occasions. If something has been published, the chances are pretty good that it is in, or has passed through, Gallagher's personal library.

As much as he loves books, Gallagher has a realistic perspective about the durability of his own publications. He recalls reading a passage in Bruce Catton's *Glory Road* recently. He believes Catton is "the *best* of the great Civil War narrative writers," but fears that people have gotten away from reading him. "I certainly don't labor under the illusion that anything we do is going to be there forever." He believes the only thing he has done that will still be used in fifty or sixty years is the Porter Alexander book. "That will be there forever," he says, "because it's Porter Alexander, because it's by a participant."

Gallagher did choose historian over antiquarian bookseller, and he loves what he does. "I've never been confused about how lucky I am to be doing this," he says. "Almost nobody gets to have a job like this, where you teach and write about what you love and nobody tells you what to do and you have the summers off. You don't get rich doing it, but you look forward to going to work most days, which a lot of people can't say."

William C. (Jack) Davis

Jack of All Trades

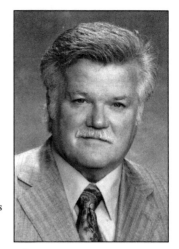

"To me, research is like having a party; writing is like the clean-up afterwards."

"If there's no story, there's no history."

"I've carried on in the tradition of...keeping history alive by making it sufficiently interesting for people to read."

"I've been extraordinarily lucky all my life. I got to do what I wanted to do."

———————◆◆◆———————

At a young age, from the time he was eight or nine years old, William C. (Jack) Davis, like many other historians, became hooked on the past. Part of that interest in history he credits to television shows such as Disney's *Davy Crockett* series and part to his history-conscious grandparents. He spent time with them as he grew up, and during the summer "they would put me in the car and drive me all over the country and stop at historic sites."

He is not certain which came first—"I don't know if that spurred my interest, or if they found my interest and that's why they did it." However it happened, the interest was spurred.

Davis's grandfather's hobby was genealogy, and he owned many family photographs and memorabilia. "A nine- or ten-year-old kid," Davis says, "thinks anything old is kind of cool. I used to pore over the old autograph books and journals with the old photos." He became interested enough in genealogy himself to discover some of his forebears. "Finding out that I had an ancestor who was involved in something like coming over to Jamestown in 1608, or being a soldier in the Civil War, gave me a desire to know what their experiences had been like, so that got me into their life stories."

Davis was born in Independence, Missouri, and grew up in Kansas City. By sixth grade, his interest in the Civil War kicked in. He believes that reading his grandfather's copy of Bruce Catton's *This Hallowed Ground* got him started. He recalls being particularly fascinated by the maps. "I remember taking tracing paper and tracing out the maps—God knows why!" He also discovered that his family had the cartridge case that his great-great-grandfather had carried as a Yankee cavalryman during the Civil War. "Somehow, I think those things in juxtaposition, plus the coming of the Civil War Centennial, got me interested in the Civil War." He was just the right age: "I was a thirteen- or fourteen-year-old boy, and the Civil War was all blood and thunder!"

During high school, he decided he would like to teach high school history, but when he got to college in northern California, he began to think instead about teaching at the college level. Sonoma State College was only two years old when he started there and had 600 students. (Today, renamed Sonoma State University, it has eight to ten thousand students.) Davis remembers it gratefully—"I got a pretty damn good education there."

He particularly remembers one of his teachers, Theodore Grivas. "There was one lecture, it was on a Tuesday or a Thursday in 1966, when instead of doing his usual thing, he talked about the research for the one book he published. It was just fascinating to hear him talk about research, going to the Library of Congress and National Archives, and getting your hands dirty on the good honest dust of scholarship. That sounded like what I'd like to do."

For some time, Davis had had an interest in John C. Breckinridge. In reading the account of the battle at New Market, Virginia, in May 1864, Davis wondered "what would make Breckinridge, the Confederate commander, a former United States vice president, become the ultimate traitor." After the inspirational lecture from Grivas, Davis decided to see if he could get something written and published. He wrote an article on Breckinridge and sent it off to the *Civil War Times Illustrated.* "And, of all things," he says, "they accepted the article and I got paid $50!"

Davis continued to write articles for them throughout his college years, and finally decided to write a biography of Breckinridge. He started it during his senior year at Sonoma, and for his master's degree he wrote another three or four chapters. The history department, he recalls, was "extraordinarily lenient in letting me do what I wanted," and he wrote papers on Breckinridge in "everything except courses on the Ottoman Empire." It would be several years, though, before the biography appeared.

After receiving his master's degree at Sonoma, Davis was accepted at the University of Chicago to study for a doctorate, but he never got there. In the summer of 1969, bound for Chicago with his master's in hand, he was offered a summer job at *Civil War Times Illustrated.* "That summer job lasted twenty-one years!" he says. When later offered a full-time position as editor, Davis took stock of what he wanted to do, and decided that "I could never discipline myself to learn something that I really wouldn't use"—like mastering foreign languages, a requirement to earn a doctorate. Also, the job market in history was not promising.

Even though he passed up the opportunity at that time, "I still expected that one day I would go back and get the doctorate, but I never did. I did get an honorary degree. I think I got it for giving an after-dinner speech." His many publications became "more than sufficient that if I had wanted to get a job in academia I probably could have," he says, "and I'd rather have them than the doctorate degree." And it hasn't kept him from academia—he is now a full professor of history at Virginia Tech.

In 1974, *Breckinridge: Statesman, Soldier, Symbol* was published, followed in quick succession by *The Battle of New Market* (1975), *Duel Between the First Ironclads* (1975), and *Battle at Bull Run* (1977). There have been many more since.

While writing books, Davis continued to work at *Civil War Times Illustrated*. He started as an editorial assistant and eventually became vice president of editorial and president of the marketing division. Robert Fowler, owner of the *Civil War Times Illustrated*, always gave Davis the go-ahead on any ideas he had. This led to some big successes, including one that Davis came up with during a sleepless night in 1971. "As I lay awake," he recalls, "I came up with a marketing plan that would allow us to market [the reprinted 128 volumes of the *Official Records*] successfully in eight-volume installments."

In 1990, Davis moved to England where he "did some consulting on marketing—American book sales for a couple of English publishers." He retired from that, moved back to the United States, and remained "retired" from 1991 until 2000, "just writing and doing some consulting and TV work" out of his home in Pennsylvania. Part of his consulting work was for Stackpole Books, which solicited him to build up its list of history books, particularly in Civil War, U.S., and British history.

Davis has also worked for the History Book Club as their reviewer of Civil War books since 1974. The club sends him manuscripts or galley proofs that publishers have submitted to them. He writes a brief report evaluating the work—"its documentation, writing style, what's been done on this subject recently, how likely it is to be an important or controversial contribution to the literature." He will usually include a recommendation to offer it or reject it, and if chosen, whether it should be a main or an alternate selection. "Usually," he says, "if I reject a book, they will drop it out of hand, but my recommendation doesn't guarantee that it will be accepted."

When deciding what to write about, Davis now opts only for what he finds interesting. In the past, however, "I wrote anything that would pay." He says he will never write a military book again— "I'm sick and tired of writing about battles, the same ones over and over again. Essentially, I'm not a military historian. I tell a good story, but I don't think I have anything profound to say about the military art. To me as a reader, it all starts sounding very much the same—you just sort of interchange the numbers of the regiments, the enfilade and right flank and left flank, and it just sort of all runs together for me." But he does not discount the importance of the field: "I'm not saying it's not an important aspect of history and that it's not interesting; it's just not interesting to me. Military history has come a long way in recent years and there are top-notch people now who are doing a whole lot more than just this regiment went here and that regiment went there."

Over the years, Davis has been remarkably productive, writing one or two books every year since 1990. He has virtually all of his research done before he begins to write. Research for him is "so much fun that I frequently end up acquiring a lot of material that I can't use."

To Davis, researching is akin to being an astronaut today, "as close to pioneering as you can come these days, that feeling that maybe you're the first person to see something or to put some things together." There are few surprises in archives, where many people have been through the documents. On occasion, though, a researcher will discover something that has not been used before because the previous researchers "weren't looking for *it*, they were looking for something else."

But Davis prefers to look for new information. "I've always had a lot of luck and have had a lot of fun tracking down sources that are in private hands by tracing descendants and that sort of thing. Finding a new source, and the anticipation of what could be beyond the next page, that's always exciting." To find descendants, he goes through the telephone directory where his subject came from to find addresses of people with the same last name, and then—"taking a chance"—sends out letters. For the New Market book, he managed to track down a descendant of every Confederate regimental and brigade commander. "Not all of them had things," he says, "but some had one, two, half a dozen items."

He also likes to use sources that many historians don't use, for example, state and county courthouse records. "It's incredible what you can pull out of the county courthouses," he says, "and a lot of historians don't go to those." Then there are business and industrial archives. "New Orleans has this incredible collection of New Orleans Notarial Archives that hardly anybody knows about; millions of documents going back to the 1700s, and they're all originals—business transactions, slave sales, slave manumissions, registered contracts with the builders of some of those plantation houses in Louisiana, and in those material archives you can find the contract that sets out the number of nails and the kind of wood to be used."

Even public sources aren't fully used, Davis says. There are regional facilities of the National Archives that many researchers are unaware of. In Fort Worth, Texas, there is a facility that has "tremendous stuff on the early Old Southwest. Nobody knows about it. All the court cases are there, and everybody's in court litigating something in those early days."

In the past, Davis took notes by hand which led to problems "because my handwriting is so bad that sometimes I can't read it." Now he takes all of his notes on a laptop. For a long time, he printed them out onto three-by-five cards, but recently he began sorting them into files on the computer and writing from there. Notes are usually arranged chronologically, and in browsing through them "sometimes a story emerges that I hadn't spotted before."

After the fun part comes the writing. "I sort of liken it to a party," Davis says. "To me, research is like having a party; writing is like the clean-up afterwards."

He usually writes at home on a computer, but his first several books were written on a manual typewriter, and old habits die hard. "Even today when I'm working on a computer, I bang on the keys like it's an old manual. To me, that's the sound of creation, that bang, bang, bang, of the typewriter."

To illustrate the point of old habits dying hard, Davis tells of a friend who began writing in the 1960s, before word processors were available to the average person. Now that they are, his friend still "will sharpen a bunch of Dixon-Ticonderoga No. 2 pencils to a pinpoint and line them up sort of anally by length on the table next to him, and then turn around to the PC and start writing on it." The sharpening of pencils is "still his signal to start writing."

Davis generally has relied on the clock for his signal to start—and stop—working. If he has decided to start writing at 10 A.M., he wouldn't begin at 9:55, but precisely at 10, and stops "pretty precisely on a predetermined point of time." He writes to a "pretty rigid schedule." For years, he wrote from 10 A.M. until 7 P.M., with a two-hour lunch break, seven days a week. He produced the same amount of text each hour. "Usually when I started a book," he says, "I could pretty much predict the day I would finish it because I knew how long I thought it would have to be." A day's work would be fourteen pages—about four thousand words. When the preset time to end his day comes, even if he is in the middle of a sentence, he turns the machine off and walks away from it.

But, Davis is not so strict about his writing days. "I've gotten sufficiently comfortable with writing that now I actually enjoy putting the story together. Now it seems that I don't need the rigid discipline I enforced on myself earlier, so I can be more relaxed about my schedule."

Davis admits to some odd writing habits. The men in his family overheat easily, and when he writes, "I generate a lot of heat." When he wrote the Breckinridge book, he recalls, "I'd start writing clothed, then after a while I'd be opening the window to let cool air in, and then I'd start stripping down, so I wrote a good bit of it in my undershorts." He goes through a lot of liquids while he's writing and keeps a small refrigerator nearby stocked with soda. "As a result," he says, "I usually write pretty close to a bathroom since I'll be churning a lot of that liquid through."

Davis doesn't answer the phone—"the enemy of creation"—or the door while he's working. The only time he disregards his set stopping time is when he's on the last chapter of a book. "Frequently, I wind up staying with it and writing twice as much as I did the day before. The momentum kicks in toward the end, and that's sort of a final sprint."

Procrastination doesn't present a problem for Davis. "When I work, I work intensely, but when I relax, I relax intensely, too. I could just sit in a chair and stare out the window for hours and be very content." Although he admits that the Protestant work ethic "hit me pretty hard," he feels no guilt about a day of utter relaxation.

At Virginia Tech, Davis is not on the regular faculty, but serves as the director for the Center for Civil War Studies. His time is pretty much his own, and most of the work he does involves marketing projects for the Center. He teaches occasionally, usually a graduate course. The university allows him to teach anything within his field, although he recently taught a class in the history of the development of theater in Tudor and Stuart times, focusing not on literary criticism, but rather on "where theaters themselves came from, their dynamics, the playwright's life and work routine."

Graduate courses are preferable to Davis. "They at least know they're expected to have done everything, and they're expected to take control of the course," a plus for Davis, who doesn't want to do two-hour-and-fifty-minute lectures. The university enrollment is large—twenty-eight thousand students—so undergraduates can "get through four years without ever raising their hand or speaking once in class because they may be in a classroom with 70 to 200 others." Graduate students understand that they must participate.

To be a good historian, Davis believes, one must be curious and have an interest in storytelling, "because those are the last two syllables in the word history. If there's no story, there's no history." A historian also needs to be disciplined and imaginative. "I think to be a good historian, you can't be complacent and be satisfied just with what you can find in a Google search or the published bibliographies of people who work in the same area. You have to take that as a departure and then show some imagination."

History, Davis says, is revisionism. "New information leads to changes in how you can look at things or what we think we know about them." As an example, he uses General Joseph E. Johnston— "the more we learn about [him], the more we learn what a bag of wind he was; I think his narrative of his military operations is the greatest novel of the Civil War." Johnston's reputation "has been steadily revised downward."

Associations with other historians have been important to Davis over the years. He had contact with so many of the great Civil War historians—Bell Wiley, T. Harry Williams, Clement Eaton, "Big Daddy" Rankin, and Charlie Roland—when he worked as the editor at *Civil War Times Illustrated*. He fondly remembers Wiley, in particular, taking him under his wing. "He'd introduce me around, he'd let me hang out with him at the conventions—I got to meet a lot of people." He found that interacting with people like that "invaluable for the sense of admiration I would come away with when I was young and think, man, I want to be just like them." Those experiences motivated him to work hard. "The awful thing," he laments, "is now I'm one of the old guys!"

Davis says he would like to think "I've carried on in the tradition of people like Catton and others, keeping history alive by making it sufficiently interesting for people to read." If a book goes unread, he says, "then you really haven't written a book." He also believes he has "opened up some new directions in research sources. I've been the first, or one of the first, to use sources that were previously not taken advantage of, but now get used more and more." Overall, though, he thinks "it's the fullness of research and readable writing that I probably would be known for."

These days Davis finds his interest straying from the Civil War to the Old Southwest. "I love Louisiana," he says, "and the story of that early frontier—Louisiana, Alabama, Mississippi Valley frontier—I find very interesting." He finds it "nice to have something new, to learn a new literature." As far as the Civil War is concerned, he probably won't write another book on the subject "unless I stumble across something else really interesting." And today, he says, "there are so many people working in the field that I'm content to leave it to them and find something else to do."

When he was in fifth grade, Davis remembers, his ambition was to be an architect, and he actually designed the house he lives in now. It might have been fun to do something like that, he says, "but

I can't imagine I'd have made a living doing it, or have had nearly the kind of travel and the associations and the friendships that I've had here and abroad as a result of being a historian."

"I've been extraordinarily lucky all my life," Davis says. "I got to do what I wanted to do, and I always got to look forward to opening the mail."

James I. (Bud) Robertson, Jr.

Civil War Ambassador

"I warn them that if they've got a queasy stomach, don't come because I will do my best to make you sick—and I do."

"I always watch the students. When they start crying, I know I've been a success that year."

"If you put me in front of a keyboard, I can peck words like a rooster in heat, using every adjective and adverb in the dictionary."

"If you don't understand the emotion of the Civil War, you'll never understand the war."

"If we don't learn from history, we've got no where else to go. If we don't remember how we got here, we'll never have much chance on where we're going."

"I INHERITED MY INTEREST IN HISTORY," SAYS JAMES I. (BUD) Robertson. "I'm from Southside Virginia; my great-grandfather and my great-uncle were both Confederate soldiers in the Fifty-seventh Virginia," and in Pickett's Brigade when it was "shot all to pieces at Gettysburg." Both of them survived the battle. "When you consider that four out of five men in Pickett's Brigade were casualties, there is no reason that I should even exist—the odds are against it."

Robertson's grandmother lived to be ninety-one, and he remembers when he was "a little boy sitting in her lap and listening to her tell me what her father had done in the war." Robertson's father, too, was strongly drawn to the Civil War. Robertson grew up in Danville, a railroad terminus, supply depot, hospital center, and the last capital of the Confederacy for the final seven days of the war. "So I just grew up in Civil War history."

When he first entered college, he thought he would go into medicine. That did not last long. In his freshman year he discovered "that chemistry and I had no chemistry," so he switched to history, and "I have never regretted it."

Robertson did his undergraduate work at Randolph Macon College near Richmond and went to Emory in Atlanta for his master's degree so he could study under Bell I. Wiley. At the end of his master's year, Emory offered him a teaching fellowship. Figuring that by the time he earned his doctorate he would also have three years of teaching experience to his credit, he accepted.

Wiley was not the only major influence in Robertson's career. He numbers among others many giants of Civil War history. He says he had the good fortune to come down the road when the masters were there—David Donald, Richard Harwell, William Hesseltine, Avery Craven, Bruce Catton, and Allan Nevins. The Civil War Centennial in the 1960s gave him the opportunity to meet all of them and to become close friends with some. "I got post-postgraduate instruction from each of them," he says. From Wiley, he learned the need to write well; Nevins taught him the thoroughness of research— "vacuum cleaner research, always pursue every little nugget that you can find"; Catton, whom he believes was his real inspiration, taught him the joy that comes from writing well. "To learn to write like he did, to get into the emotion and the human drama of it, is something I've always tried to do."

To be a good historian, Robertson says, you need to be a good writer. "The Ivory Towers," he laments, "are not producing people who can tell a good story," leaving the field open to "the pop guys, nonacademicians, who come forward and do a tremendous job."

He believes the historian needs to be dedicated. "Once you start it, you've got to stay with it and get it done." The historian also needs to be an organized and careful researcher: "You can't bluff your way through it. Unless you can find the source material, you've got nothing. You can't make it up. Intellectual honesty is a very important factor."

With his doctorate newly in hand, Robertson began his career at the University of Iowa, where, in addition to teaching, he edited the *Civil War Journal,* "the only really scholarly publication on the Civil War at the time." He was there for two years before President John F. Kennedy appointed him Executive Director of the United States Civil War Centennial Commission. "Kennedy didn't have a clue who I was," he says. He received the appointment, in a roundabout way, through Congressman Fred Schwengel, the representative from the district where the University of Iowa is located. Schwengel was a Lincoln scholar and vice chairman of the Centennial Commission.

Kennedy became upset with the plans for the commemoration that the original Commission came up with—"it wanted to do more celebrating than commemoration." The president purged the Commission and brought in as chairman Allan Nevins, a close friend retired from Columbia University and a scholar-in-residence at the Huntington Library. Nevins wanted someone else to take daily charge of the Centennial, a young scholar and an intellectual. Schwengel said to him, "I know exactly who you want." At first, Robertson turned down the offer, but Richard Harwell pointed out to him that the position would enable him to "make more contacts and become better known than I ever would by bouncing around from one campus to another." After meeting with Nevins, he accepted the job.

Robertson spent the next four years—1961 to 1965—in Washington, D.C., and at the end of that time he had "had a stomach full of Washington and I wanted to get as far away as possible." So he and his wife Libba moved to the University of Montana. They had "a great two years out there, but two years was enough." Virginia Tech was looking for a Civil War historian, "so I came and interviewed, took the job, and we came here in 1967." He is still there.

At Virginia Tech, Robertson is famous for his legendary Civil War course. At one time the class had 577 students, the biggest in the world, the maximum number the largest lecture hall on campus would hold.

Now he is teaching the children of students he had when he first arrived in 1967. "On a football weekend, I'll go into class," he says, "and there will be the students, and a lot of them will be with Momma and Daddy, one or both of whom had been former students in class." On those occasions, he delights in playing stump the parents, asking difficult questions that only the parents are allowed to answer and who usually cannot. "The students just get a big kick out of it." What Robertson finds particularly heartwarming is that the course is an elective. "Every single one of those students is there because he or she wants to be."

There are some notorious aspects to the course. He spends two days on Civil War medicine, "and I warn them that if they've got a queasy stomach, don't come because I will do my best to make you sick—and I do." He believes that most Civil War history leaves out the emotion, and he tries to bring that in by getting "down and dirty with maggots and pus and suffering and pain." The last lecture is a tribute to the veterans, where he shows slides of them growing old and at their reunions. In the middle of those slides he begins playing a recording of *Auld Lang Syne.* "You look at these old men teetering and tottering, with watery eyes. I always watch the students. When they start crying, I know I've been a success that year."

Robertson is a skilled speaker, but he can't explain why that is. "If I speak well, that's just the way it is," he says. Someone once told him that he writes like he speaks, "which I took as a great compliment." He is involved with the media, and one of nine alumni distinguished professors at the university. "Basically we are ambassadors and are supposed to be on the road speaking to groups all the time," he says. He also does a lot of television work, and a weekly broadcast for WVTF, a public radio station. "I think the older you get, the more you speak, the more you polish up."

Robertson grew up as a Methodist, but was drawn to the Episcopal Church "because I loved its conservatism, its formality, the beauty of the prayer book." But in 1980 the prayer book was rewritten, and church authorities "removed everything that had drawn me to the church." Over a million Episcopalians withdrew from the church and formed the Anglican Church—the Church of England—and received the blessing of the Archbishop of Canterbury. In the Anglican Church, Robertson studied for three years and became an ordained deacon. He can do everything except bless the elements for communion.

In another part of his busy life, Robertson spent twenty-eight years as a college football referee; the last sixteen were "big time—an Atlantic Coast Conference football official, with nine major bowl games." He retired from that several years ago—"at my age, there are parts of me that ache that I didn't know were capable of it"—but still misses it some "because I stayed in shape." In other respects, though, he is happy to be finished with it—"from Labor Day weekend to Thanksgiving weekend, you're gone. In the fall, I got nothing done."

Robertson's writing career began when he was in graduate school and the University of Indiana asked him to edit some classics for them—Sarah Dawson's diary, General James Longstreet's memoirs ("the only time I've ever been positive toward the general"), and the memoirs of Walter Taylor. The first book he wrote himself was *The Stonewall Brigade,* his doctoral dissertation, published in 1963; it has been in print ever since. Working as Executive Director during the Centennial slowed him down some, although he did do some editing, and then he began writing again when he returned to academia. "I was really a latecomer in the writing field," he says. "I won't say I wasted a lot of time, but it just wasn't a real productive time because I was busy with other things."

In 1987, Robertson published *General A. P. Hill: The Story of a Confederate Warrior.* He wrote the book, he says, because he "had this fascination with him," particularly with the mystery of what ailed him. Several theories had emerged over the years—asthma, tuberculosis, manic-depression, and so on. Robertson knew that to do a proper job, he needed to nail down the enigma of Hill's poor health. When he visited the National Archives to research, he discovered that they have the records from West Point for the period of time he was looking at, including the hospital log. Thumbing through it, he found what he needed. "Hill was admitted to the hospital suffering from gonorrhea."

Now he needed to see if Hill's symptoms matched up with the diagnosis. He called on Richard Duma, better known as "Dr. V.D.," who headed the department of communicable diseases at the Medical College of Virginia and was a graduate of Tech. Over lunch, Robertson presented the information he had, and Duma filled in the gaps. In two percent of the cases, the gonorrhea bacteria lays dormant for eighteen years and then becomes active again. Eighteen years from Hill's visit to the West Point hospital came in 1863. "And BANG! there it was," Robertson says. "On the eve of Gettysburg, Hill became ill again. He followed the pattern." When the bacteria reactivates, it attacks the kidneys, the victim goes into nephritis or Bright's disease, becomes anemic, and dies. "A. P. Hill followed that grid." Hill, however, did not die of it; he died by gunshot in April 1865.

Robertson relates a story of going to see Hill's granddaughter— 104 years old, blind, and hard-of-hearing. "When I met her she was hooting and hollering, saying 'God bless you!'" She was delighted that he had proven that her grandfather was not crazy, but "simply an all-American boy who just went out for a good time and paid a price for it."

Ten years later Robertson published *Stonewall Jackson: The Man, the Soldier, the Legend*. Jackson biographies were getting worse, topped by one that came out about 1987 written by a novelist that had a picture on the dust jacket that was not Jackson. "That was the living end!" he says. Shortly after that, he presented a paper at a symposium at the Stonewall Jackson House in Lexington, as did several other historians. Sitting in a motel room one evening, one of them said that somebody should do a decent and thorough biography of Jackson. "Suddenly all eyes turned to me!" he recalls. "I thought about it and then just took off."

But first he had to warn his wife of his decision. Before he began working on the project, knowing that he is a workaholic, he sat down with Libba and "over a bottle of wine I told her she was going to be neglected, I'd be forgetful, I'd ignore her, but I was going to do a big book and it was going to take a lot of time. She said, 'Go, go, go!' That's why I dedicated the book to her. I couldn't have done it without her love and understanding."

Robertson says there are different motivations for the books he writes. "With Jackson, there was just so much junk out there and we just seemed to be getting farther and farther away from the truth; A. P. Hill was just something that needed to be done." *Soldiers Blue and Gray* was his tribute to Bell Wiley, updating Wiley's *Johnny Reb* and *Billy Yank* studies published in the early 1950s.

Unusual for an academic historian, Robertson has also published books for young readers. He believes education in the United States "is in crisis and nobody seems to pay much attention to it." It bothers him that children are not getting proper instruction in the basic educational system, so he wrote a general history of the Civil War for schoolchildren. After his Jackson biography, Antheneum, the young readers' division of Simon and Schuster, asked him to do another book for youngsters, so he wrote *Standing Like a Stonewall*. It became the biggest seller they ever had, so he followed it up with a biography of Robert E. Lee for teenagers.

Robertson calls himself a "people's historian." So many historians, he says, write to impress one another. They produce "intellectual tomes dripping with footnotes," and if they sell a thousand books, all of which probably go to campus libraries, "they become brilliant scholars." He recalls Nevins once saying that there are two kinds of historians—those who write for their own cult and those who write for the public. Robertson takes great pride in being the latter.

Robertson always has writing on his mind. He carries three-by-five-inch cards all the time, "because I'm always thinking of something I've got to write. Maybe a good sentence or good thought will come to mind and I quickly jot it down."

Unlike most writers today, Robertson does a first draft in pencil on a legal pad. "If you put me in front of a keyboard," he says, "I can peck words like a rooster in heat, using every adjective and adverb in the dictionary." But if he sits down with a pencil and paper, he says, he's going to get to the point as quickly as he can "and be done with it." He likes short sentences: "I think that sentences can be too long, but it's not possible for a sentence to be too short."

Robertson likes to get an early start to his writing day, ready to work by 7 or 7:30 A.M. By about 4 P.M. he finds he's burned out. At the end of a good day, he will have written fifteen to sixteen legal-size pages in longhand. One requirement he has for writing is quiet. He owns a cottage at the New River, "a beautiful mountain river" several miles from his home, and does much of his writing there.

When he is finished with a day's writing, he puts it away for at least three weeks before looking at it again: "You back away and let it season a little bit." When the manuscript is completed to his satisfaction, he supplies the connecting links, so "the end of this chapter fits in with the beginning of the next one." For a long book, he never sits down and reads a manuscript from beginning to end; the shorter children's books he will read entirely. Anyway, he says, even though the author has done a perfect job, when it gets to the editors "they go scratching around and chew on it a little bit. That's why they're paid; they've got to make changes."

Although Robertson is not bothered with procrastination, he finds he does spend far too much time on the first sentence. "If I procrastinate at all," he says, "it's insisting that I get the first sentence down first without getting off into the main text. That first sentence is so important."

Robertson tries to have at least 90 percent of the research finished before he begins to write. When he begins researching a project, he writes to all the depositories in the country, describing his subject and asking what they have that might be of interest to him. He takes notes on five-by-eight cards that he organizes according to the subject matter he's working on. If it's a biography, the notes are arranged chronologically; if it's topical, such as *Soldiers Blue and Gray,* they are sorted topically. The research notes are then organized in five-by-eight file cabinets.

When he runs into conflicting material, Robertson asks himself several questions: "Who was this guy? When was he writing? Did he have an axe to grind? Did he realize that what he was saying might later become public?" He applies those criteria to almost any letter he reads, as well as to printed works. When he published the Stonewall Jackson biography, he was criticized for dismissing Henry Kyd Douglas. He did so, he says, because "I think the guy abused the truth from beginning to end." He admits that's a personal opinion, "but one has to make a judgment and treat the things accordingly."

The most emotional discovery Robertson ever made while researching was Jackson's little book of maxims. The book was long-thought to be lost, and in a sense it was because it was in a collection of papers that had been miscategorized in the archives at Tulane University. In the early 1900s, a graduate of the school had collected an enormous amount of Jackson material and given it to Tulane. It had been listed under the donor's name, Charles Davis. It wasn't until the university began to computerize its manuscript holdings, about the time that Robertson began his research, that it was discovered to be part of the Jackson papers. When he lifted the lid from the first of four boxes of papers, "there sitting on top was Jackson's little book of maxims. I cried; I couldn't help it."

Robertson finds research much more enjoyable than writing. "That's putting the jigsaw puzzle together," he says. The writing part is hard, but he considers it to be the more important part of the process. He tells his students that the most difficult thing they need to do is "get that little thing out of your brain to your fingertips."

When reading for pleasure, Robertson does not read Civil War history. He reads fiction, and particularly enjoys Larry McMurtry's writing style. "He just has a wonderful way with words and expressions."

Of teaching, Robertson believes that "if you don't understand the emotion of the Civil War, you'll never understand the war." He says that it's easy for us to sit back long after the event and criticize the people for what happened. "But they were driven by emotion," he says, "emotion out of control." He deals often with the health of individuals, believing that has much to do with how a person acts in a given situation. He believes too many academic historians have lost the sense of the human element in history. "History poorly taught is the dullest subject in the world," he says. "It ought to be the most exciting! It's about human beings."

He believes political correctness is "one of the basic things wrong with education now." He finds textbooks are "skewed, they're slanted, and it's a terrible situation." Those kowtowing to political correctness are "antihero, they want everybody on the same level." This attitude tells us why giants like Lincoln, Grant, and Lee are "being blasted out of the water. I find this outrageous."

Revisionism, Robertson says, is inevitable in history. Each generation interprets the past in the light of its own experiences. But he doesn't believe in "revising history simply to tell it a different way."

Asked about his unique contribution to the field of Civil War history, Robertson says, "I try to make it come alive; I try to make it human, to get readers to feel the emotions as well as the action that's taking place." He believes that we have to remember that we are dealing with human beings, with all their virtues and faults. "If we don't learn from history," he says, "we've got no where else to go. If we don't remember how we got here, we'll never have much chance on where we're going."

There is one other career that Robertson would have been happy to pursue—a railroad engineer. "I'm a railroad nut!" he confesses. "I can sit by a bank along a railroad track all day watching trains and be as content as a child." Growing up in Danville, a busy railroad center, family friends who were yard engineers let him work inside the steam engines shoveling coal from the time he was eight or nine until he was fifteen. Not long ago he had the opportunity to climb into the cab of the locomotive of a coal train and ride it for about a hundred miles into West Virginia. "Lord, I thought I'd died and gone to heaven!"

James M. McPherson

The Go-To Historian

"Why did this war happen, what were the issues that led to it, what did it resolve, what were its consequences for the future of the country? These big questions have always been, if not at the forefront of everything I did, certainly in the background."

"If you're going to write a book that will take years, you have to have the commitment and the stamina to stay with it. It's hard work."

"I try to write just what I think is right. In the end you just have to write it as you see it."

"Writing history can be a fairly lonely thing; lonely in the sense that you're doing it by yourself and you're solely responsible for the success of failure of it."

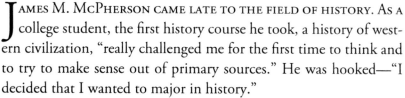

James M. McPherson came late to the field of history. As a college student, the first history course he took, a history of western civilization, "really challenged me for the first time to think and to try to make sense out of primary sources." He was hooked—"I decided that I wanted to major in history."

McPherson attended Gustavus Adolphus College in his hometown, St. Peter, Minnesota. The college was a small liberal arts institution; most of the faculty were not publishing scholars, and he thought his career would model theirs. However, when he was a junior, his advisors encouraged him to think about graduate school. By then he was firmly convinced that he did indeed want to teach at the college level, but had not given much thought to writing. In his senior year, after doing a couple of major research papers, "I grew more and more convinced that research and writing was something quite rewarding." He describes his undergraduate years as "a gradual process of awakening to what I might do as a historian."

From Gustavus Adolphus, McPherson matriculated to Johns Hopkins, which did not have a master's program. So he went directly to the doctorate. The university's research-oriented graduate program and the example of his mentor—the preeminent historian of the South, C. Vann Woodward—"really moved me in the direction of research and writing as well as teaching."

At this point, McPherson knew his interests lay in U.S. history, but he had not narrowed that down to a particular area. Working under Woodward, who taught Southern and nineteenth-century history, McPherson became drawn to that period. Initially, his interest focused on either side of the Civil War—the antislavery movement before the war and Reconstruction after. He believes he was drawn to that in part by contemporary events. He was at Johns Hopkins from 1958 to 1962, "the years of the Civil Rights movement, sit-ins, conflict between the federal government and Southern political leaders who were vowing massive resistance to national law. Federal troops were being sent into the South, and I became fascinated by the parallels between the 1860s and the 1960s."

The dissertation he wrote became his first book, *Struggle for Equality,* in which he looked at the abolitionists after emancipation to see what happened to them. He came to the conclusion that "they continued to see themselves as a cutting edge activist movement."

"It was only gradually that I zeroed in on the war itself," says McPherson. Much of the work he has done for more than a quarter-century after he zeroed in grew out of proposals from publishers or editors of series. *Ordeal by Fire,* a history of the Civil War and Reconstruction, was a suggestion of the editor of the college division of

Knopf. When Woodward was the general editor of the Oxford History of the United States series, he suggested a project to McPherson that eventually became *Battle Cry of Freedom,* now widely considered the best single-volume history of the Civil War.

"The experience of writing those two books," he says, "generated a lot of other ideas or projects or questions that were kind of spin-offs. I grew increasingly fascinated with Lincoln, and over a period of several years did a number of essays or lectures on him; that became my book of essays called *Abraham Lincoln and the Second American Revolution."* At the same time, McPherson found himself increasingly curious about what motivated Civil War soldiers; that study became *For Cause and Comrades.*

The general theme of his work over the years "has been the centrality of the Civil War to all of American experience, and how and why that is the case": "Why did this war happen, what were the issues that led to it, what issues did it resolve, what were its consequences for the future of the country? These big questions have always been, if not at the forefront of everything I did, certainly in the background." McPherson believes this is relevant to our times because "this would be a much different country today if those things had not happened or if they had come out differently."

McPherson finds that he is especially captivated with the letters and diaries of Civil War soldiers. He began reading them in 1987, and at the end of ten years he had published two books, *What They Fought For* and *For Cause and Comrades.* "It was a wonderful experience to get into the minds of these people and learn to understand them and appreciate them and admire them." He found himself "reluctant to stop doing that research. The temptation to keep doing research and never write is a pretty powerful one for a historian," he says. "Sooner or later you have to just tell yourself, look, you've got to stop; you'll never write this book if you don't just sit down and start writing it."

McPherson's wife Patricia works closely with him. She has been a research assistant on some of his projects, and they co-edited a book together. While researching *For Cause and Comrades,* they discovered a set of naval letters that they deemed worthy of publication. That resulted in *Lamson of the Gettysburg: The Civil War Letters of Lieutenant Roswell H. Lamson, U.S. Navy.*

At the time of this interview, McPherson had two projects underway. One, now published, is a study of Lincoln as commander-in-chief, how he envisioned and defined that role. It began with the suggestion of a publisher to update T. Harry Williams's *Lincoln and His Generals,* but McPherson saw it as a more comprehensive project. It's not only Lincoln and his generals, but also "a much broader conception of commander-in-chief in time of war." His second project is for a sesquicentennial series on the history of the Civil War, edited by Gary Gallagher for the University of North Carolina Press. McPherson's volume, one of twelve projected, will be on the naval war.

McPherson spent his career at Princeton University. At the time he was completing his doctoral dissertation in 1961–1962, the academic hiring process was "radically different from what it is now; it was really an old-boy network." The chairman of the history department at Princeton simply called Woodward, asking him to recommend a young man for an instructorship at the school, and Woodward suggested McPherson. He had a pro forma interview with several members of the history department "in a very relaxed atmosphere in a hotel room" during a meeting of the American Historical Association. "They offered me the job and I came," he says. "That's the way people got jobs in those days."

He has been satisfied with his employment. The university has "a very liberal policy of leaves, about one year out of every five." He also received outside support for his research and writing, mainly from the Huntington Library, where he spent three different years as a resident fellow. He has also been awarded grants from the Guggenheim Foundation, the National Endowment for the Humanities, and the Behavioral Sciences Center in Stanford. "I was lucky," he says, "in that for about every book I was doing, I would be able to have a year off and spend most of my time doing research or writing or both."

Big projects like *Ordeal by Fire* and *Battle Cry of Freedom* took McPherson five or six years to complete, with one full academic year off for each cycle. The rest of the time he taught full-time. But teaching at places like Princeton, he says, has "a lot of built-in off time where one has the opportunity and time to do research and writing." Still, "it would have been impossible to do either of those books in the time frame that I did without having a full year off in each case."

When he is home, McPherson writes in his study. He needs a fairly quiet atmosphere—"there can't be a whole lot of disturbance going on." He sometimes listens to classical music as he writes, "but if it's something that requires a lot of complicated thinking, I will turn the music off."

He does his best writing in the morning, McPherson says, but "sometimes I feel like I'm on a roll and I'll work right on through the day." Otherwise, he tends to use the afternoon for additional research or fact-checking. If he's writing a talk or an essay or an article or book review, he might work three or four hours on it and then move on to other things he needs to do.

When he has completed a chunk of writing, McPherson goes over it making the necessary changes—stylistic, substantive, and filling in information he may not have known when he wrote the original draft. On the second and third drafts he usually is just trying to improve "the flow of the writing."

To get a good start on the next day's writing, McPherson likes to stop when he knows where he wants to go for the next paragraph or two, perhaps making some shorthand notes to remind himself where he plans to go next.

He always writes his first draft in longhand. "I just find it easier somehow to transfer thoughts to paper that way than any other." For a long time, he did the second and subsequent drafts on the typewriter. "Now," he says, "I will do the final draft on a computer, but I still haven't made the complete transition to computer." He still has "a couple of beloved old electric typewriters that have sentimental value, and every once in a while I have to get them repaired, but for now they seem like comfortable old friends."

McPherson writes from "old-fashioned note cards," which he spreads out on a table while he writes. As he works, he keeps his footnotes current and complete, putting them on a separate sheet of paper as he goes along so they don't get mixed up. "I've had colleagues who have the most awful time; they spend as long a time after they've written something getting the footnotes in shape as they did to write it in the first place." His method ensures that he will not have to do that. The notes are taken by hand in places where the noise of a typewriter or computer would be distracting to others, but he will type them out if he is working at home.

When writing, McPherson deals with the notes in different ways, depending on the project. For his two big books, *Ordeal by Fire* and *Battle Cry of Freedom,* he worked on one chapter at a time. After deciding what he would cover in a chapter he would read the relevant sources, taking abbreviated notes with page references, and then line up all of the notes and the books he planned to use for that chapter. "I'd have books all over the floor and on the table," he says. "It was kind of a mess; my wife could never figure out how I could ever find anything, but I somehow did." After each chapter, or part of a chapter, he would begin the process all over again. "For that kind of book, there would be this constant cycle of research and write a draft and then move on to the next chapter or section of a chapter." By the time he finished an 850-page book, he estimated he had gone through the cycle two or three dozen times.

For shorter works, McPherson does all of the research first, ending up with many hundreds of note cards. At that point he goes through them to establish a framework—how many chapters he needs and what to include in each one. He tries to finish at least 95 percent of the research before he begins writing, augmenting it to fill in holes here and there.

McPherson owns an extensive personal library, but he also lives less than two miles from one of the better university libraries in the country, "so there are a lot of books that I might want to own, but I don't really need to." Too, he says, "there is only a certain amount of room in my house."

He admits to some procrastination. "The hardest thing about writing," he says, "is starting. There are all kinds of things that you can think you need to do before you start." When he gets started, though, "it's a lot easier to keep going." Although he has never had serious problems with writer's block, "I always worry about it; I dread the possibility of it happening."

"Research is both easier and usually more enjoyable than the writing," McPherson says. But he also likes writing—"especially when I've finished it. Looking back, I can say, 'Gee, I managed to accomplish this.' That's a great feeling." Still, he finds writing harder than the research. He believes each is equally important, however. "They are interdependent on each other—you can't write well unless you've done all the necessary research to do it." Inadequate research shows in the final product. "Good writing is dependent on good research."

McPherson credits Woodward with his ability to weave together both serious study and narrative story. "There's always a central idea in his writing and a powerful analysis or interpretation," McPherson says, "but he was able to clothe that in such attractive narrative writing that there was always a story in what he was writing." McPherson believes history is basically a story, "but it can't be just a story without some kind of a point to it." On the other hand, "if people are going to read it, it has to be interesting, it has to engage their attention and pique their interest."

When confronted with conflicting material, McPherson sometimes feels he deals with it "almost by intuition—there is a kind of sense that some of this evidence just seems truer than the other." He tries to find two or more sources that agree on a particular point, but sometimes that is not possible, and that's where his intuition kicks in. He admits that bias may also enter into it, "because every historian has a point of view on what he thinks is the right interpretation of something. It's human nature to select the evidence that supports the interpretation you think is right." But foremost, the historian must be honest: "If he finds the weight of the evidence conflicts with his interpretation, he needs to be flexible enough to change that or admit that." If there is no way of knowing the truth, it is the historian's responsibility to present the opposing arguments and let the readers draw their own conclusions.

His research for the book on soldiers' motivation gave McPherson his most revealing breakthrough. When he began the study, the standard interpretation was that most soldiers didn't think much about why they were fighting, that their basic idea was "to get the job done and to survive." But what he found in reading their letters and diaries was that a surprising number of them "really did have a deep-rooted conviction about what this war was about and what they were fighting for."

McPherson is often thought of as the preeminent, best-known Civil War historian—the go-to scholar. He is involved with many extracurricular projects that eat away at his research and writing time. At the time of this interview, he served on the historians' advisory committee for the new visitors' center at Gettysburg and for the new Civil War museum at the Tredegar Iron Works in Richmond. He is frequently asked to be a "talking head" on television documentaries—one of the more recent was for Central China Television. McPherson says he has had many conversations with a colleague about "why don't we say no to 90 percent of these things instead of only 60 percent of these things." But he admits, "it's hard to say no," even though he sometimes feels his time is fragmented into too many different directions.

Although he makes an effort to keep up with the periodical literature in the field, "the journals accumulate" until such time as he realizes that for something he's doing he needs to check them out. He is better at keeping up with important new books. For one thing, he is frequently sent books by publishers requesting that he write a blurb, a foreword, or a review. Colleagues send him manuscripts they are working on seeking his advice. At the time of this interview, he served as a juror for the Lincoln Prize, so everything that appeared on the Civil War came to him. "In one way or another," he says, "I tend to keep up better on books than I do with journals."

For leisure-time reading, he likes light fiction, especially detective and mystery novels. Here again, Patricia is a partner. She reads a lot more light fiction than he does, "and she tells me which ones she thinks I'll like." On occasion he reads historical fiction—"some of it's good, some of it's not." McPherson rarely watches television, "except at crisis news times."

To be a good historian, McPherson believes the first requirement is that "you have to have a kind of love affair with the material itself. You have to be passionately engaged with it." But the historian must also "have a kind of balance in the way you approach any subject— you have to be evenhanded." The historian also needs a lot of energy and stamina, both physically and mentally. "If you're going to write a book that will take years," he says, "you have to have the commitment and the stamina to stay with it. It's hard work."

McPherson has received some flak from readers who thought he had been politically incorrect on some issues. He recalls that his treatment of the Know-Nothings in the politics of the 1850s and the controversy over temperance and Catholicism and nativism provoked letters from both sides. A Northern Ireland Protestant thought he had bent over too much to present the Catholic as well as the Protestant view on the nativist movement, whereas a U.S. Catholic said he was too hard on the Catholics. McPherson believes it just comes with the territory. "If you write something that offends some ethnic or racial or religious interest group, you're going to hear from them about it." For his part, "I try to write just what I think is right. In the end you just have to write it as you see it."

On occasion McPherson has undertaken projects with other historians, usually with friends and colleagues who he knew pretty well and who agreed on what they wanted to accomplish. But over the years most of his work has been solo. "I think for the most part writing history can be a fairly lonely thing; lonely in the sense that you're doing it by yourself and you're solely responsible for the success or failure of it."

McPherson taught at Princeton for forty-two years, mostly nineteenth- and early twentieth-century history. From the 1970s on, he focused increasingly on the Civil War and Reconstruction period. He served as director of graduate studies a number of times, and mentored twenty-six of his own doctoral students. He believes teaching enhanced his writing career. "There is a very close reciprocal relationship between teaching on one hand and research and writing on the other." He believes working at making things clear to students helps one write more clearly. "When I envision an audience for my writing, it's often similar to a Princeton undergraduate who has an interest in the subject but not a specialized knowledge in it."

Students have often sparked new ideas or insights, particularly with their senior theses, "a major piece of research for these students." Some of the more interesting ones he has read have been written by pre-med students. "I can remember over the years four or five really good senior theses on Civil War medicine that were eye-opening to me, especially one on Confederate surgeons." That one came from a student, now a doctor, who did research in Confederate medical journals that McPherson had not known existed. The student's father, a physician himself, had access to obscure Confederate journals that he shared with her. "She came up with a wonderful thesis with new information."

Of all the work he has done, McPherson believes *Battle Cry of Freedom* is his most influential book. Not only did it have a far greater readership than anything else he has published, and win a Pulitzer Prize, but also "judging from the feedback I've gotten over the years, it's had a far greater impact than anything else I've done."

McPherson sees his unique contribution to the field of history has been putting the Civil War into a broader context and showing how crucial it was to understanding the society we live in today. The Civil War was not just a military and political conflict—it had all kinds of ramifications for U.S. culture and society. "I think my major contribution has been to show how it impacted all of these different areas of American life, not just the 1860s, but it reshaped the direction of American history."

"People have asked if I ever regretted the commitment I made to become an academic historian and a historian who reached beyond the academy," McPherson says. He hasn't. "I can't think of any better career. I've never had any regrets about the path I chose."

Carol Reardon

Military Maven

"It got to the point where if somebody was shooting, I was probably teaching it."

"I like developing the ability to take my subject and connect it with the work of other scholars who don't consider themselves military historians or Civil War historians."

"You have to be willing to admit that you have played out a question and there are no more answers; you don't take a giant leap of faith and call it fact."

CAROL REARDON CREDITS HER FATHER IN LARGE PART FOR HER becoming a military historian. He "had a lot to do with it," she says. It was in her genes.

Her father was in the army reserves so she saw him in uniform a couple of times a week, and he was active in the local VFW post. Indeed, the VFW became a family activity, "which meant that I spent a lot of time there." There were special activities for the boys and girls, and she and her brother were there often enough to have frequent contact with veterans of World War I, World War II, the Korean War, and Vietnam. "I grew up around a lot of it, and to that extent it was sort of a natural extension of my life. It wasn't all that difficult for me to reach the conclusion that that's what I really enjoyed." She "just found it incredibly interesting from early on."

Her father's particular interest is twentieth-century military history, but Reardon says she "just happened to get caught up in the Civil War Centennial so that sort of shaped where I was headed." She clearly remembers her first visit to a Civil War battlefield. Her neighbors in Pittsburgh, Pennsylvania, were Civil War buffs, and in May 1963, they invited her to take a day trip with them to Gettysburg.

The early budding interest in the Civil War, however, was just a hobby for many years. As an undergraduate at Allegheny College she majored in biology—positioning herself, she says, "for getting a job afterwards that would pay pretty well and be rewarding." Allegheny offered an excellent biology program, and the ecology movement was in its early phase. "I like anything that takes me outdoors," Reardon admits, "so I went the biology path and got a degree in biology." But three months into her graduate school studies in ecology at Rutgers University, "I woke up one morning and I said, 'No, this is not what I want to be doing.'" She doesn't recall anything that triggered that epiphany—she wasn't unhappy, and school was going well—"I just literally woke up one morning and said this is not what I want to be doing."

She returned to Allegheny College to run the biology lab for two years while she read history to prepare for her true calling.

Reardon's great inspiration was Jay Luvaas. At that time he was a professor at Allegheny before moving on to the Army War College. While an undergraduate she often joined other students on Luvaas's annual spring trip to a Civil War battlefield. "My good friends were all history majors, but they didn't know anything about the Civil War," she recalls. "I was a biology major, but I knew a lot about the Civil War and that made me very useful."

Luvaas was a prankster, and his pranks had a history basis to them. "He used to send people down trench lines that disappeared into swamps and things like that, knowing full well how nasty it was going to be." Reardon acted "as a sort of ringer, somebody who could figure out what he was trying to do before he actually did it." It took a while for Luvaas to catch on, but by Reardon's senior year "we had a declared war going on."

Reardon credits Luvaas as the person "who ultimately made a difference." When she returned to Allegheny, Luvaas organized a reading program for her and assigned her the equivalent of a graduate-level research paper. It wasn't for credit, she says, but "partly to test my commitment and partly to make sure I had the skills I needed." She proved that she had both the commitment and the skills, and Luvaas helped her choose among graduate programs.

Reardon picked the University of South Carolina for her master's study and then matriculated to the University of Kentucky for her doctorate. She chose Kentucky because Luvaas had warned her not to become a "one-war wonder—there was more to military history than that one war." At Kentucky she studied the Civil War under Charles Roland and the Vietnam War with George Herring, along with other specialists on the faculty. She says that move "was one of the best decisions I ever made in my life." And she kept a promise to Luvaas when she recently published a book on Vietnam, *Launch the Intruders: A Naval Attack Squadron in the Vietnam War, 1972,* something that had nothing to do with the Civil War.

Reardon graduated with her doctoral degree in 1987 and went to work at Kentucky as associate editor of the Henry Clay Papers. She had already done some documentary editing at South Carolina on the John C. Calhoun Papers project and was a natural for the job.

In 1989, Reardon landed her first teaching position. For two years, she taught at the University of Georgia—U.S. history surveys, a military history course, a Vietnam course, and a Civil War course. "Basically," she says, "it got to the point where if somebody was shooting, I was probably teaching it."

In the fall of 1991, Reardon moved to Penn State, where she has remained. When she first arrived, Gary Gallagher was already there teaching military history. He preferred teaching only Civil War, so Reardon did the other military history courses, including naval history.

Reardon's first book, *Soldiers and Scholars,* an outgrowth of her doctoral dissertation, looked at the education of military officers from 1865 to 1920. It centered on the Civil War, but since "Civil

War" is not in the title, "most of the Civil War community and the buffs didn't pick up on it." Because of that, Reardon calls the book her "stealth Civil War book." She hasn't repeated that mistake. "I've learned a lot about marketing since then. If I had it to do over again, I would put Civil War in the title."

Another book of hers, *Pickett's Charge in History and Memory,* had a longer gestation period. It started as Reardon's master's thesis. As a graduate student, she was challenged to take a standard interpretation of a historical event or personality and see how that interpretation evolved over time. She chose Pickett's Charge, finished the master's degree, and put the paper aside when she moved on to Kentucky and other interests.

The summer after her first year at Penn State, Gallagher hosted a Civil War conference at the Penn State Mont Alto campus devoted to the third day of the Battle of Gettysburg. He asked her if she knew anything about the events of that day, and she told him of her master's thesis on Pickett's Charge. "Okay," he said, "you've got the gig." Originally, she thought she would just give the presentation in its current form. However, since she had written it twelve years earlier, "historians had embraced the whole concept of historical memory." As she looked at the thesis she realized, "first of all that, man, it was bad! But secondly, I did have the nugget of something very good there." She delved into the literature on memory studies, and how our interpretation of the past changes because of shifting priorities and values in subsequent years. "I began tracing the image of Pickett's Charge and how it evolved, and all of a sudden I realized I had something pretty neat."

When she chooses a subject, Reardon searches for new questions. She doesn't enter the research process with the intent to revise an old interpretation, but rather to "find a fresh way to ask important questions; using a fresh set of lenses to look at an old question." A topic she now itches to ask new questions about is Pennsylvania in the Civil War. She believes that so much of Civil War history focuses on the South, that "there is still a lot of room for open-field running for researchers in the Civil War in the North."

Reardon much prefers research to writing. "There is still that sense of adventure, that there's something out there that you're going to find that's really going to provide an *aha!* moment. By the time you're writing, you already know what the *aha!* moment is, so it's not nearly as much fun." Still, though not as much fun, she sees the writing as equally important. "I don't see them as two separate parts; they are inseparable," Reardon says. "The best writing in the world won't make up for sloppy research, and if you can't tell your story, if you can't make use of the source material you found, that doesn't help, either."

Reardon fits research and writing around her teaching schedule. In the fall she teaches two courses—her "standard" U.S. military history course, and at the time of the interview she also taught the 100-level Civil War course. In the spring she usually teaches a course on the Vietnam War. On the graduate level, she teaches a reading course on topics in military history or on military thinkers and theorists, "which can cross generations and cultures." At Penn State, there is "an embarrassment of riches on the faculty when it comes to Civil War historians, so I have to share and teach courses on other topics."

Research is primarily done during the summer, "at least the research that requires travel." The writing, she says, "happens whenever there's time to make it happen." She's always writing something, "even if it's a shorter piece, regardless of the time of the year."

When she researches, Reardon prefers to take notes on her laptop, using longhand only when the archive demands it. If she is reading a book she owns, she highlights what she wants to use. When working on something complicated, she says, "I'll even color-code it in a couple of different colors to help me find what I need when I'm in the writing phase."

Reardon likes to have 75 to 80 percent of the research completed before she begins writing. "I like to know what the terrain of my final piece is going to look like before I really get started," she says. "But I'm always open to finding something new, and oftentimes the writing will reveal a hole in the research."

When she is organizing notes for writing, Reardon prints out what she has on the laptop and adds them to copies she has made out of journals and documents from archives, and so on. She then breaks down the material into chapters. "I have an outline in my head of what will go into each chapter and I just make piles which are basically chapter piles." If there is something that she will use in more than one chapter, she'll make extra copies so that everything she needs for each chapter is in the appropriate pile. Everything is always on full sheets of paper, "just so no half sheets or scraps fall out of that pile."

And she literally means a pile. "I'm not ultra-organized," she says, "but I've never lost anything that I absolutely needed to have, either." As she works through the pile, she marks the paper, indicating that she has used it. "I always know at any point that I can go through that pile and say, 'Okay, I've used this, I haven't used that.' I'm pretty methodical about that. It looks more chaotic than it actually is. It's a system that works for me." All of those notes eventually end up in "one file dedicated to that project alone, but sometimes not for a while, since smaller projects often spin off from the major one."

Reardon does not follow a regular writing schedule. "I can't get into that kind of a rut—it really bugs me," she says. She generally writes in her office at school—"at home I can get distracted too easily." When asked what distracts her, since she lives alone, she responds, "Oh, it's amazing what can be distracting! The laundry has to be done, I have to go out shopping, pay bills, water the plants—it's real easy, trust me. And during football season, it's even worse; I can always find distraction there." She admits to being a fanatic Pittsburgh Steelers fan—"I grew up with them."

She writes "easily" in the late morning and early afternoon. "I'm definitely not a morning person," she says, "so I'm not writing at eight o'clock in the morning. Between 10 A.M. and 3 P.M. I'm pretty good at it." Late afternoon is not optimal writing time for her either, so she schedules her teaching for that part of the day. She also finds she can't write well in the early evening, but after the eleven o'clock news, she says, "I can write like crazy. I can do some of my best writing between 11:30 P.M. and 2 A.M."

Reardon writes on a computer, but other than that she has no special requirements—other than Mountain Dew® in large quantities and, in "extreme emergencies," nacho cheese Doritos®. "Once I'm ready, I start," she says. She often listens to music, oldies from the '60s and '70s, "and if it happens to be the Rolling Stones, that's perfectly okay." She prefers music with a beat. "I probably could not write to classical music because it would likely put me to sleep. The music I listen to sometimes gives me enough of an adrenaline rush that it just keeps me going."

Reardon's writing does not always move forward smoothly, with one thought following the next. Sometimes she has been working on a problem in her head, and when she turns on the computer at the beginning of a writing session, "I want to get it down before I forget what I decided what to do with it. So I'll just start wherever that inspiration takes me and finish it off." It's important to her to get her ideas down first, and "then wait until I have a substantial body of material to go through before I start moving it around and shaping it."

"I don't consider my writing ready to be set in type until the day it goes out the door," Reardon says. She does a lot of rewriting, and appreciates the ability to just highlight, click, and move things around on the computer. "It lets me focus on getting my ideas down while they're hot," she says, "and then moving them where they need to be later."

When a piece of writing is completed, Reardon goes back to do three things. First, she works on smoothing transitions between sentences and paragraphs. Second, she works on being sure that she has paragraphed in a way that makes sense. Finally, she checks her verbs, replacing passive verbs with active ones. "Then I'm happy," she says.

Although she has never run across any Civil War source material that she shied away from using, she did find that working on the Vietnam book was a different situation. "A number of my sources are still alive and a number of people I wrote about are still alive. There were a few cases where, out of respect, I chose not to use some specific information." The information she chose not to use did not compromise the validity of the historical narrative she chronicled; "it was information of a personal nature that I backed away from."

When there is conflicting material, Reardon believes it is the job of historians to figure out why the sources saw things so differently, "and then come up with our best assessment of which of the various versions is correct." But those decisions should not be judgmental—"somebody who we decide might not have told the most convincing story might not be wrong; he might believe that this is in fact what he saw." If a historian runs across conflicting evidence, which despite her best efforts cannot be resolved, "then simply admit it and go on."

When that conflicting evidence is related to Civil War military history, Reardon often finds that disagreements can be resolved by visiting the battlefield and studying the ground. For an example, she points to the Tennesseans and Alabamians serving under Pettigrew during Pickett's Charge who, in the 1880s, criticized General James Kemper for not giving them credit for their part in the attack. But when the track of Kemper's men is followed on the battlefield, it becomes clear that Kemper most likely did not see any troops other than Pickett's Virginians during the entire charge because of the lay of the land. "Standing on the ground," Reardon says, "helps to resolve inconsistencies, confirm observations, and cast doubt on boasts in written diaries, letters, and memoirs."

Reardon believes her biggest breakthroughs come when she conceptualizes a book. When she wrote the Vietnam book, nobody had ever done what she was trying to do, and she had *aha!* moments "all over the place." *Launch the Intruders* follows an entire naval aviation squadron through its 1972 combat cruise. "Although there are plenty of individual memoirs from the cockpit of an aircraft, and big-picture analyses of the air war in Vietnam, nobody else had ever approached the subject as a full-blown unit history before." When she wrote *Soldiers and Scholars* she related military history to the history of education, the history of professionalism, and the history of the Progressive Era. "I like developing the ability to take my subject and connect it with the work of other scholars who don't consider themselves military historians or Civil War historians," Reardon says. "When I can do that, that's always fun."

Reardon finds she has a heavy reading schedule. Being a military historian rather than just a Civil War historian, she has "an immense amount of things to read. I have to cover a lot of territory, so I always have a lot of things on the bookshelf to read." At the time of the interview, Reardon was president of the Society for Military History, and "trying to keep abreast of what my members are writing. That means I may be looking at a World War II book now and tomorrow it's Vietnam and the day after that it's Gettysburg." She skims a lot and reads selectively, "but it's an ongoing process—there's always something on the bookshelf." Periodicals tend to get short shrift unless there are articles on something she is currently working on, although she does read *The Journal of Military History* faithfully.

A good historian, Reardon says, must have a curious mind—"somebody who enjoys asking questions as well as answering them." It is important for historians to be honest, to have a healthy ego "that fuels confidence," but who also knows "when to rein it in." The historian must be willing to revisit an issue when the evidence indicates that a conclusion already reached may be inaccurate. "You have to be willing to admit that you have played out a question and there are no more answers; you don't take a giant leap of faith and call it fact."

The historian must also have great personal discipline. "I'm not driven by tenure or promotion or that sort of thing," Reardon says. "I'm driven more by my demand to meet the challenge I put out there for myself. You have to have a good bit of confidence in your own abilities."

It is essential for the historian to be able to tell a story. She believes James McPherson was correct when he wrote that Civil War historians need to satisfy different audiences—professional peers, who demand that the methodology be correct, and audiences well beyond academia. "If you don't tell a good story in the process of analyzing great events, they aren't going to care and they aren't going to read your work," says Reardon. "And that would be a shame, especially if those ideas and the thought process behind them are really good."

Reardon makes her writing come alive by going back to the soldiers' words. "I like to have people in my stories," she says, "so if I'm writing about Pickett's Charge or I'm writing about a naval aviation squadron in the air, I'm going to have Private Jones or Lieutenant Smith telling me something about what's going on. That way you have a sense of how it feels, not just what happens."

As a female military historian, Reardon believes the embracing of diversity has been her friend. When appointing committees, oftentimes someone would suggest they needed some diversity, "and for a while it seemed like diversity was *me* because there weren't a whole lot of other women in the field. So I got to do a number of things in my career earlier than I might have if I were a guy." Now, she says, there are plenty of women at meetings of the Society for Military History and she doesn't see it as an issue any more.

She says, "I'm a female military historian; plenty of my colleagues don't consider me politically correct for that alone!" Her greatest beef, however, is with those who focus on the causes and consequences of war, but "dismiss the importance of the military experience; there actually is a war in the Civil War era," she reminds us. As renown military theorist Karl von Clausewitz noted, war is a political act, and political and social historians need to understand what the military experience is like to understand what makes a soldier willing to fight.

Reardon frequently interacts with other historians, in both the Southern Historical Society and the Society for Military History. She particularly relishes the latter, "probably because so many of us consider ourselves intellectual outsiders in our own departments." She has gotten "great ideas" and "some great leads for research sources— all the kinds of things you want to have happen when you deal with colleagues who take your work seriously, who want to cooperate in furthering knowledge, and who don't hoard important sources."

She is particularly proud of the "presidential panels" she instituted at the Society for Military History annual meeting, inviting scholars from other historical specialties and even disciplines outside history to share their work on topics of common interest. Thus, recent meetings have featured panels from organizations as diverse as the Peace History Society, the Hemingway Society, and the American Schools of Oriental Research.

She always believes her favorite book is the next one. Her three major books "are so unlike one another that the experience for each was different." Her first book, which broke new ground in military intellectual history, led to all sorts of unexpected experiences. She was invited to become a member of the Board of Visitors of Marine Corps University at Quantico, and she became involved in professional military education, leading staff rides to Civil War battlefields. From these rides, she says, she learns as much from her students about today's military as they learn from her about Civil War history.

Reardon believes she has made several unique contributions to the field of history. With her first book, *Soldiers and Scholars,* she helped open the whole concept of intellectual military history, looking at how U.S. soldiers have used history to develop doctrine, analyze campaigns and command issues, and hand them down from one generation of soldiers to the next. The Pickett's Charge book helped popularize the utility of the memory concept, and the book has been picked up for use in a number of methodology courses and historiography courses, "to demonstrate to students of history what various concepts mean." And she was the first to do an in-depth study of a squadron-level unit in the Vietnam War.

She has never regretted leaving biology and ecology for history. She recently looked at her family tree and discovered that in Gaelic the name Reardon means "son of the royal poet." She also discovered that for many generations the Reardons have been soldiers and scholars, something she did not know when she chose the title for her first book. "So," she says, "I sort of figure I'm doing what I'm supposed to be doing."

· PART 4 ·

THE WIDER WORLD

MANY OF OUR HISTORIANS ARE MULTIDIMENSIONAL; SOME NOTED FOR their work in the Civil War era have also shone in other fields of history. This section showcases them.

Daniel E. Sutherland's interests are wide ranging. Besides several Civil War studies, he has written about nineteenth-century domestic servants in the United States and has undertaken a biography of the famed American painter, James McNeill Whistler.

Perry D. Jamieson straddles two worlds. By day, he looks at contemporary events as a historian of the U.S. Air Force; in his free time he studies the Civil War era. Because of the different requirements of each, Jamieson has had to develop two entirely different mind-sets, methods of research, and styles of writing.

Another of the historians also lives in two different worlds even more diverse than Jamieson's. Following family tradition, Robert T. Maberry, Jr., became a dentist. History, however, was always his passion, and after establishing an extremely successful dental practice he pursued that passion. Maberry professes a love of history in general. "It didn't matter the subject," he declares; "all history is interesting.... There are wonderful things to be discovered everywhere in the past." His interview describes how he has been able to combine his two radically different worlds.

Ari Hoogenboom started his career in history studying Civil Service reform, which led to a biography on Rutherford B. Hayes and a book on the Interstate Commerce Commission. Outside of his work on the Civil Service, Hoogenboom worked off and on for forty years on a biography of

Gustavus Vasa Fox, Lincoln's assistant secretary of the navy, a pivotal figure in Civil War history.

Eugene Genovese and Elizabeth Fox-Genovese represent our only married couple doing history. Much of their work has been independent of one another, but they have also collaborated in fields of mutual interest. Their deep respect for one another is clear from their interviews. Sadly, Fox-Genovese passed away in early 2007.

Genovese has spent his professional career studying slavery and the world of the slaveholders. Over the years, his thinking and approaches to the subject have continued to evolve. In response to critics who attack him for changing his mind, Genovese says, "I hope so."

Fox-Genovese's entire life was steeped in history. Born into a family of historians, from an early age she was surrounded by stories of the past. Her early focus was on French history, but gradually her attention turned to U.S. Southern history and women's history. Shared interests, and working styles that meshed, enabled the couple to collaborate on several projects. She believed that historians need to make every effort to correctly under-stand and describe the past. "It's essential," she says, "to understand what we have in common with previous civilizations.... We could do with a lot more serious reflection on the fall of Rome these days."

When two of his undergraduate history professors took opposing views on the philosophy underlying the Constitution, Forrest McDonald was hooked. He switched his major from English to history and has been at it ever since, becoming the Constitution's premier historian. "The only legitimate reason for doing history," McDonald believes, "is because you love it." His many and varied publications are proof that he practices what he preaches.

Although David Herbert Donald was a two-time winner of the Pu-litzer Prize, he believed his most important contribution to the field of history was the many students he trained, "who will be for the next genera-tion the leaders and pioneers in their field." He was proud of their accom-plishments and thought that might be "the best legacy that I could leave." Sadly, Professor Donald has also passed on since his interview. The legacy he leaves is large, rich, and all-encompassing.

Daniel E. Sutherland

ALL-COURT PLAYER

"I think that's the proper way to go about something, without any preconceived notions of what you want to find or what you think you're going to find, but just start reading and see what you discover."

"The very act of writing, of pushing the pencil across the page, I find far more energizing than sitting and typing keys at either a typewriter or a computer screen."

On political correctness: "I run screaming away from it and I'm almost to the point where I'll do anything purposely to get those people agitated. I just shudder to think of the ways in which history is being distorted and misused."

———◆———

"I THINK I GREW UP LEARNING TO LIKE HISTORY," SAYS DANIEL E. Sutherland. Although he grew up in Detroit, his grandparents on both sides had been born in the South. "There was always talk in my family about the Old South and about the Civil War and about history generally."

He credits an elementary school teacher, named McBrien, who further stirred in him an appreciation for the drama and excitement of history and the great stories of the past. McBrien had a particular interest in the Civil War, Sutherland says, "which reinforced the stories about the war that I was getting at home."

In college, however, Sutherland's interest lay in sports, particularly football. He had played football throughout high school and attended Wayne State University on a football scholarship. After graduation in 1968, he spent two years in the navy at an office job in Pensacola, Florida. Men in his office often discussed history and politics, and "I knew just enough more than they did to seem like the resident intellectual where history was concerned." They encouraged him to get a graduate degree in history, but when he left the navy he first looked for a job with the Detroit public schools as either a coach or a social studies teacher. He found that no coaching jobs were open at the time.

With money from the Veterans Administration, Sutherland decided to go to graduate school, "at first part-time, to take some graduate courses in history, and wait for something to open up." His heart was set on coaching, and he was also "rather afraid to become a history major because I thought the formality of college courses would drain all the excitement out of it." Although he had minored in history, and then added it as a second major in undergraduate school, he still did not believe the formal study of it matched the excitement of coaching football. But that attitude soon changed.

"Lo and behold," he recalls, "my first day in graduate school, my first course, I walked into Grady McWhiney's Civil War class. Talk about serendipity! McWhiney had just come to Wayne State, and this was his first course." Sutherland soon became McWhiney's research assistant, and the professor talked to him about "taking the history game more seriously and recommended me for a fellowship the following year." It was only then, in his second year of graduate school, that "I started to devote myself to a career in history—teaching history at the university level and writing history as a profession."

To Sutherland, the reason to be a historian is "simply to investigate and test either the truth of something or simply to find out more about an event or a person that relatively little is known about." He has faithfully followed that rule in his choice of subjects to study and write about. As McWhiney's research assistant, he "read through the dozens, perhaps scores, of published antebellum travel accounts looking for references to the status of and attitudes towards officers in the old army, before the Civil War." That was the subject McWhiney was working on at the time. As he read those accounts for material McWhiney needed, he found that frequently the writers commented on domestic servants in the United States. His interest piqued, he chose travelers' views of U.S. domestic servants as his master's thesis. For his doctoral dissertation, he continued with the same theme, going beyond the travelers' accounts and incorporating "all sorts of other published and unpublished sources." That became his first book, *Americans and Their Servants: Domestic Servants in the United States, 1800–1920.*

His next book, *The Confederate Carpetbaggers,* originated in his reading of Fletcher Green's book, *The Role of the Yankee in the Old South.* "I said, well, gee, isn't that interesting! Why don't I do the reverse of that, and I'll look at the role of Southerners in the antebellum North." As he compiled a list of names, he found many more than he expected who had gone North after the war. He began looking for information about them. At the time, he says, he was not thinking of "any kind of historiographical construct or proposing any questions." But as he acquired material, the questions evolved. "I think that's the proper way to go about something," he says, "without any preconceived notions of what you want to find or what you think you're going to find, but just start reading and see what you discover."

In 1995, Sutherland published his first book on the Civil War itself, *Seasons of War: The Ordeal of a Confederate Community, 1861– 1865.* He wanted to write something on the war in a way that had not been done before and originally thought about writing an imaginary diary of a Southern civilian witnessing the war and commenting on it day by day. As he discussed this idea with other historians, "people whose opinion I respected," they told him he would "get a lot of flak, a lot of criticism, for writing essentially a novel." It was suggested that he use the same premise, viewing the war from the microcosm, but write a "documented actual historical account of the war."

So the search was on for a suitable venue. "I needed a place where something was going on throughout the entire war. It had to be a place that was actually witnessing some of the more important events of the war years." After careful consideration of a number of places, he chose Culpeper County in Virginia. Not only was it an active arena during the war, but there was also a wealth of archival material: "letters and diaries and published accounts in newspapers, as well as reminiscences, and so on, of people either from Culpeper, the citizens, or soldiers who had passed through Culpeper during the course of the war." Sutherland wrote it in the present tense, still clinging to his initial idea of a diary, "and writing it as though I was some omnipotent figure who was hovering over Culpeper and observing everything that was going on during the course of the war."

Another book, *Fredericksburg and Chancellorsville: The Dare Mark Campaign,* was a contract book, one that the University of Nebraska Press asked him to write for their Great Campaigns series. In an unusual move, the press lumped the two battles together, although they had previously been considered separate campaigns. Sutherland thought he would have to contrive a way to forge them into one. However, "the more I looked at it, the more I thought there were far more parallels and connections between those two battles than earlier historians had considered. I found it fairly easy to construct Fredericksburg and Chancellorsville as a single and legitimate and logical campaign, from both the Union and Confederate perspectives."

He had to do a lot of archival work for the book, "because the secondary work available wasn't making the connection that I wanted to make." Using the letters and diaries of politicians and soldiers, he found the connection. "But no one," he says, "had pieced it together before I tried to do it." Some people still don't see his argument as a valid melding of the two. "The more I looked at it, the Chancellorsville campaign was a natural continuation of what had happened at Fredericksburg, but I still have a hard time selling that to some people."

As his career has progressed, Sutherland has found he has more time for research and writing as his teaching load has diminished. The research phase of any subject is lengthy—probably about two-thirds of the time it takes from the beginning of research to publication of the completed work.

Sutherland takes all of his notes in longhand on eight-by-eleven-inch sheets of paper, one letter or one thought per sheet. When organizing the notes for the writing phase, he sorts them into folders according to his planned chapters. At the time of this interview, he was working on a book about guerrillas in the Civil War. "Essentially," he says, "I'm writing a narrative of the Civil War, the entire war, but writing it from the perspective of the guerrilla war." The only way to organize it, he found, was to arrange it by states, and then to break down each state into three subdivisions: general comments about the guerrilla war in that particular state, then Confederate perspectives on it, and finally Union perspectives on it.

Sutherland tries to complete all of the research before he begins writing. Because of his penchant for taking notes in longhand, rather than on a computer, the first draft of his work requires that he write either in his office or his home, "wherever I have a stash of notes." Working at a summer cottage or someplace away from home "would mean taking with me truckloads of notes and books and other things."

Other than that, his writing requirements are minimal—a pad of paper and five pencils. He always writes his first draft in longhand, which he credits in part to McWhiney and Forrest McDonald. Both of them taught at Wayne State when Sutherland was in graduate school, and at that time, both wrote their first drafts in longhand. They taught Sutherland to write one paragraph per page. That works on two levels. First, it focuses attention on just one paragraph, with a particular topic and a particular theme, giving it cohesiveness. Second, it makes it easier to rearrange the paragraphs into the most satisfactory form when the first draft is completed.

Sutherland admits that rearranging is easier on a computer, but he has other reasons for writing that first draft in longhand. "I never became very much of a typist," he says. "The very act of writing, of pushing the pencil across the page, I find far more energizing than sitting and typing keys at either a typewriter or a computer screen."

When the first draft is finished, Sutherland is ready to put it into the computer, changing things as he goes along, creating in the process a second draft. From then on, the rewriting is all done on the computer and he can work on it anywhere, no longer tied to his office or home.

And those five pencils? They force him into a pause mode. "When I've used those five pencils down to the nub then I have to get up and resharpen them. That's my way of taking a forced break from time to time, and of stretching and breathing deeply before I go back to work."

Sutherland writes best from early morning—6:30 or 7 A.M.—until 2:30 or 3 in the afternoon. He doesn't try to keep a regular schedule but does try to set a minimum number of at least two or three days each week to write. On each writing day he organizes his thoughts by making an outline of what he hopes to write, "but it's a rare day when I really finish what I thought I was going to accomplish."

Before beginning a writing session, he reviews the previous two or three pages to get back to what he was doing the time before. Although he doesn't follow this as closely as he would like to, he remembers a bit of advice from McDonald. "He always said that he quit writing before he was ready to. He'd be right in the middle of describing some really exciting scene or something that he was excited to be writing about, and he found that if he quit right at the peak of his excitement and interest that it would be a lot easier the next day to get back into the story."

Late afternoon and evening is Sutherland's time for research, general reading, or playing sports. This interview was conducted in the winter, and he admits, "the greatest release right now is to go play hockey in the evening and just knock people over." Sports continue to be important to him. "I was an athlete long before I was a historian. I've been athletically inclined since I was nine years old. I must simply be busy playing something—I don't intend to give that up," he says.

When asked about procrastination, Sutherland admits that he has a rather unusual problem with it—he gets excited about the next subject before he finishes the one he's currently working on. While working on the guerrilla book, he became fascinated with the painter James McNeill Whistler. At the time of this interview, he had been dividing his time for the past five of six years between the two subjects. "I could have finished this guerrilla book two or three years ago and been done with it," he says, "but I just keep being drawn back to Whistler." At long last, in 2009, the University of North Carolina Press published *A Savage Conflict: The Decisive Role of Guerrillas in the American Civil War.*

Sutherland spent 2005–2006 as a visiting fellow at the University of Cambridge in England, studying art history and beginning his work on Whistler. "The benefit for the guerrilla book," he says, "is that it forced me to focus and finish most of that manuscript before going to Cambridge. I had a deadline." While he was in England he could rewrite and tinker with the guerrillas "while spending most of my time on Whistler."

Working on Whistler brought Sutherland his most exciting breakthrough as a researcher. The painter had attended West Point, and while working in the National Archives, Sutherland looked at the post's medical records. Whistler was sickly, complaining throughout his life of poor health, and Sutherland thought that perhaps his poor health contributed to his flunking out of the academy. "What I came across was something that no biographer ever mentioned before," Sutherland says, "and so far as I know I was the first person in 150 years to have this bit of information in my grasp." Early in his second year at West Point Whistler visited the cadet hospital on several occasions because he had contracted gonorrhea. "I still remember sitting there and having this sensation. I was almost trembling. I said, 'Dan, nobody in the universe knows this but you.'"

If an event seems controversial or far-fetched, Sutherland has a rule of never using that information from just one source. He always looks for at least two sources that agree. If there is only one source, he believes the historian must be honest with the reader, explaining either in the text or a note that it is the best available evidence or account.

Sutherland's view of the relative enjoyment of research and writing has changed over the years. Early on, he most enjoyed the research, finding the writing more difficult. But at some point, he can't remember just when, the research became more of a chore and he began to look forward to the writing phase—"That, now, is more fun." Sutherland works at getting the language just right, using the precise word for what he wants to convey to the reader. He evokes Mark Twain, who said that "the difference between the right word and almost the right word is the difference between lightning and the lightning bug."

When asked if political correctness influences his work, Sutherland admits that it does. "I run screaming away from it and I'm almost to the point where I'll do anything purposely to get those people agitated," he says. "I just shudder to think of the ways in which history is being distorted and misused."

Revisionism, he says, is what historians are all about—correcting the record, rooting out misinterpretation, correcting erroneous conclusions. However, that has to come out of honest research, not out of a desire to purposely set out to revise or change our view of the past because the historian "almost willfully wants to reread the evidence in a certain way."

Associations with other historians have been important to Sutherland throughout his career. For one thing, they offer venues for presenting papers to an informed audience that can generate useful feedback in the early stages of a piece of work. The other aspect, he says, is the informal network of friends he has accumulated from such meetings. Social interactions, like having a beer in a bar, open opportunities to float ideas and get suggestions from friends, which can have a useful impact on one's work.

Sometimes, Sutherland admits, he finds having students a burden, thinking about all he could accomplish if he didn't have to spend time reading their work. But he says, "I think back that somebody had to do this work for me, somebody had to correct my early writings and my early seminar papers. People like Grady and Forrest did that for me, and so it's just payback time now on my part."

Sutherland believes his book on guerrillas may be the best book he has written. He believes that if it is not the most important element in the Civil War, it is "certainly the most influential overlooked element in telling the story of the war, and that if you don't understand what was happening in the guerrilla war, then you really can't explain the larger war."

He hopes that people looking at his work will find that it is "well-researched, that I wasn't looking for evidence to tell a particular story in a particular way, that I told the story from the evidence that I had, and that given my resources at the particular time I did a pretty thorough job of accumulating and considering that body of evidence." And he would like to be known as a good storyteller. "I do understand that in the end that has to be the ultimate measure of my work—what the story turns out to be."

If not a historian, Sutherland admits he would have relished being a rock star or a football star in either college or in the pros. He also, at a very early age, thought he would like to be professional soldier, like his idol, George Armstrong Custer. He recalls at age seven or eight copying Custer's letter of application to West Point and thinking to himself that he would use that letter when he applied to the academy.

"But," he says, "I grew out of that and wound up a historian. Once I became a semi-mature adult and began to think seriously about career paths, I can't imagine doing anything but this as my life's work."

Perry D. Jamieson

One Man, Two Worlds

Forrest McDonald told Jamieson that the best historians "probably appear to be schizophrenic. They have to be tremendously introverted,...have the ability to go into an archives or library and sit by themselves, work alone, hour after hour, day after day, sometimes week after week, doing research...." Jamieson agrees..."and extroverted enough and enthused enough to convey the excitement of history to other people."

"Just by definition if you're a military historian working on current things you're seeing a lot of material that quite properly, to protect our national security, just can't be discussed."

"I've never had the idea that my academic friends really have it made.... They have a lot of demands on their time, and the better researchers they are and the better record they have in publishing, the more demands there are on them to do other things."

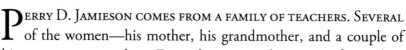

Perry D. Jamieson comes from a family of teachers. Several of the women—his mother, his grandmother, and a couple of his aunts—were teachers. From them comes his passion for reading and for history.

So when he matriculated to Michigan State University in the 1960s, Jamieson majored in English and minored in history. Looking back, he believes "things really worked out well for me. English is a skill that is fundamental to all historians; we do all that research, but then we want to write it up clearly so other people can read it and understand it."

It wasn't until he entered the working world, teaching English in a public high school in 1969, that he realized he had his major and his minor backward, that he "really wanted to be a historian." He had met Stephanie, a nursing student, at Michigan State, and in 1971 they married. "She was good enough to be willing to support me while I went to school," Jamieson says. And he already knew that he wanted to study the Civil War.

He remembers clearly when that interest took hold. A sixth-grade teacher assigned several boys to pick a war to study and report on it to the class. Jamieson's research consisted of going to the *World Book Encyclopedia*. "I can still remember what some of the illustrations in there looked like. It all made a tremendous impression on my young mind."

While working on his master's degree at Wayne State University in the early 1970s, Jamieson met Grady McWhiney. "I was enormously impressed with him," he says, "and he was very gracious and very helpful to me even though I wasn't his student; I was just taking classes from him." He also studied under Forrest McDonald at Wayne State. "I learned an enormous amount from them as historians and scholars." Jamieson admits that he didn't fully appreciate the time and interest he received from McWhiney and McDonald until after he completed his doctoral degree. In talking with colleagues at the University of Texas at El Paso, and with other young postdoctoral students at conferences, he discovered that he had had an atypical graduate-student experience—that no one else had even approached the preparation and help that he received from his two professors.

"I didn't realize or appreciate fully—I knew these were wonderful men, and I appreciated them in the 1970s—but I didn't appreciate them *fully* until after I graduated and started comparing notes with other people." One of the things he appreciated the most was the emphasis they put on writing, "which seemed pretty obvious to me; you ought to know how to do that as a professional historian."

But he found that few had had the same kind of systematic and professional scholarly training that he had received.

Jamieson's first book, *Attack and Die: Civil War Military Tactics and Southern Heritage,* was a joint project with McWhiney. McWhiney suggested that Jamieson look at Civil War tactics for his doctoral dissertation. When it was completed, McWhiney added a first and a final chapter on the Celtic heritage of Southerners and how that played out as the Confederates fought the Union armies. The book created a sensation, primarily because of the Celtic thesis that McWhiney brought to it. The fact that it created so much controversy doesn't bother Jamieson—"No one ever got very upset about what *I* wrote"—and the controversy has kept the book in print since its publication.

Jamieson had another professor, Phil Mason, who also served him well. Mason taught courses in archival management, very unusual at the time. Oral history played a key role in his courses, a skill that Jamieson found "very, very valuable" as his career took an unexpected turn into public history.

McDonald told Jamieson that the best historians "probably appear to be schizophrenic. They have to be tremendously introverted, they have to have the ability to go into an archives or a library and sit by themselves, work alone hour after hour, day after day, sometimes week after week, doing research, and then they have to be extroverted enough to convey in speech to students who may not always be terribly interested at 8 o'clock in the morning in what it is they've found." Jamieson agrees that "you do have to have this odd mix. You have to be able to do this research on your own and yet at the same time you have to be personable enough and extroverted enough and enthused enough to convey the excitement of history to other people."

Jamieson may appear to be even more schizophrenic than most historians because he has had essentially two simultaneous careers. By day, he works as an Air Force historian. Here, he has little choice in what he writes about; most of the subjects are assigned to him. The Air Force, the military branch most dependent on high technology, is generally interested in its immediate past and the Air Force of to-day. They have little knowledge or interest in their own more distant past; the two World Wars, Korea, even Vietnam, are ancient history to them.

On his own time, Jamieson does have a choice of work. Then he chooses the nineteenth-century army, from the mid-to-late 1800s. After the publication of *Attack and Die* in 1982, Jamieson began work on *Crossing the Deadly Ground: United States Army Tactics, 1865–1899*. Because of his work with the Air Force, this book took much longer and was published in 1994. His next study, *Death in September: The Antietam Campaign,* published in 1995, he admits was "a labor of love. I love that battlefield—it doesn't have the tourism and clutter of Gettysburg, it's very pastoral." At the time of this interview, Jamieson was working on a book on the last campaigns of the Civil War for the University of Nebraska Press's series of campaign studies.

Jamieson has different research habits for his two careers. In his day job, he works with Air Force documents, primarily e-mail or electronic documents, and with oral history, frequently interviewing people and recording the session, then working from notes or a transcript. For the Civil War research, he heads for the primary sources before looking at the secondary works.

At the beginning of his career, Jamieson took notes by hand on a legal pad. He did little photocopying and still likes to do it the old-fashioned way, although these days it's usually on a laptop. "I think you get better intellectual control over what you're working with and a better understanding of it if you copy it out word-for-word into notes of your own rather than just standing in front of a machine and photocopying hundreds of pages."

When writing nineteenth-century history, Jamieson thinks through the topic overall and then breaks it down into chapters. He also decides who he thinks his audience will be. His plans are always flexible. "Even when you think you've finished your research, your understanding of the material changes," he says, "and then the way you want to organize it changes." Again, though, he contrasts his

Air Force work with his non-Air Force writing. "In my Air Force writing, because of deadlines, I can't continue to make changes in organization any more than I can continue to do research beyond a certain point."

For his Civil War writing, Jamieson says there is often a certain formula. If it's a campaign, there's usually an introduction that includes what happened earlier in the war. He introduces the commanders on each side, their forces (i.e., numbers, arms, morale, logistics), and so on. Then he looks for a balance in the length of the chapters. For this writing, he tries not to tie himself to a regular schedule. "I like to spend as much time as I can on it without a goal of working on it three hours tonight or ten hours tomorrow on a day off."

Writing for the Air Force—where there is always a deadline—is a different story. He needs to quickly review the information he has compiled or listen to the interviews and then decide how many major topics he can deal with in the time allotted. Here he tends to plan by the week, not the day. "There are too many unforeseen things that can come up in any one day for me to be sure I'm going to get X amount done. If I have requests to help people with other things, then I'm disappointed if I didn't make the goal of X. So I find that if I do it by the week, I can usually meet a goal."

Jamieson finds that he writes best in the morning—early morning. Since 1980, he says, he has been getting up at 4 A.M. If he's doing Civil War work, that's when he begins writing. For the Air Force work, he tries to start writing by 8 A.M., but if other things come along, "I just have to accept that as part of the rules of the road, and I may have to work on it in the afternoon." His day job entails working out of two different offices, giving him "a kind of unusual and complicated and sometimes unpredictable schedule."

His early mornings take a toll by the end of the week. "I find early in the week I do my best work in the morning, and I'm still doing pretty well in the afternoons. As the week goes on—I hate to say it, but it's an aging thing—I don't do as well on Thursdays and Fridays. Getting up at 4 o'clock every morning, by the end of the week I don't have a lot of enthusiasm." Bed time changes over the week, too. Monday night he "can enjoy myself into the evening, but by Thursday and Friday night at 8 o'clock, 8:30, I've conked out."

Jamieson likes to be alone when he writes, in a quiet atmosphere. In both of his worlds, he does his writing on the computer. When he first began, he wrote on legal pads or typed on a typewriter. He is struck by how easily he transferred to the computer what McWhiney and McDonald taught him thirty years ago—to write one paragraph per page on a legal pad so the material could be readily moved around and revised. "Now I do exactly the same thing, only now I use computer software to move things and change copy. None of us would ever have imagined it when I was in graduate school." But Jamieson finds that the ease of revising makes it difficult to stop tinkering with the text unless he sets a deadline for himself.

Before he begins a day's writing, Jamieson reviews his previous work. For his Air Force projects, he goes back one day, but his other work is often put on hold for long periods of time. When that happens, "I may have to go back a whole chapter or skim a whole manuscript to see what I was thinking and where I was going."

Balancing the time spent researching and writing differs between his two worlds. For his Air Force work, Jamieson knows approximately how long it will take him to complete an assignment. After blocking out the time, he knows how much time he can devote to the research. On his personal projects, "the problem I have is that I find research a lot more fun than writing, or at least than getting started writing." Early in his career, Jamieson preferred to have the research "pretty well corralled" before he started writing, but with the ease of revising on the computer, "it isn't the great problem that it used to be, where you'd have to retype hundreds of pages of manuscript to add something new."

Jamieson handles conflicting material in different ways. When writing nineteenth-century history, he believes experience helps in sorting things out. "The older we get, the more experienced we become," he says, "not only as historians but as human beings. We begin to develop a certain understanding of how human beings interact and how they rationalize things, how they think. It comes down to experience, and using common sense." At times, he says, it really can't be untangled, and then the historian just has to admit that.

As an Air Force historian, however, he is often writing about people who are still alive, and perhaps still on active duty, "so it's just beyond what I can do to be very critical of their decisions." He has to present the record as it is: "Here is what the documents say, here is what the officers and others who were there at the time tell me happened, and how the decision was made." Future historians, he says, who perhaps have more evidence, or who aren't working under the constraints that he has, may take a different view.

And there is another challenge for a public historian. "I've always believed we really can't do a good job for the Air Force or the taxpayers unless we're honest, but on the other hand we're working for the Air Force and if the Air Force is in a dispute with the Army about how a particular weapon is best used, we tend to see the Air Force side of it—those are the documents we have and those are the people we're talking to."

Jamieson explains the difference between his Air Force public history and academic history. Academic historians are wary of addressing contemporary events and issues. "We don't really have a context for it yet; it's too recent, it's hard to sort some of these things out and really analyze them professionally until a certain amount of time passes, until the issues cool off." For his Air Force history, he does have access to records and material and people who are making history at the time, or very shortly after the history is made, but some of it can't be published immediately because of its sensitive nature.

When asked if he has ever found material that for one reason or another he couldn't use, Jamieson says, "that's a fat pitch for an Air Force historian." He has a high-level security clearance and sees a lot of highly classified documents and briefings. "Just by definition if you're a military historian working on current things you're seeing a lot of material that quite properly, to protect our national security, just can't be discussed."

Another difficulty Jamieson faces in his work with the Air Force is the language that the military uses, full of acronyms and jargon. "It's not their fault," he says, "it's their language, the way they talk to one another, and they assume everyone knows these acronyms and these expressions and this slang, and it's hard to get them to see, working as they have to on projects that are due tomorrow morning, that we're writing for an audience twenty-five or thirty years ahead and no one's going to know what this acronym means or what this program was, so we have to do a lot of translating." Acronyms, he says, "junk up a text and make it harder to read and understand." He tries to translate these to take the mystery out, to remove the bureaucratic expressions or politics that the general reader would not understand.

His most thrilling moments, Jamieson says, have been in his Air Force work "because of the clearances we have and our access to Air Force officers and Air Force generals." Right after the Gulf War (Desert Storm), the historians interviewed General Charles Horner who ran the air campaign for General Norman Schwarzkopf, and many of the pilots. "That was very exciting," Jamieson says, "to have access to these officers before other historians did, or before the general public could talk to these people or see the documents."

On September 11, 2001, the morning of the terrorist attacks on the World Trade Center and the Pentagon, Jamieson attended a staff meeting of Air Force General John P. Jumper in the basement of the Pentagon. "I've had opportunities like that where I've been at the scene of a historic event, or soon after." He admits that these experiences "are not the same as discovering a nineteenth-century manuscript that nobody else has seen, but in a way you have the same kind of feelings, saying, boy, I've talked to this person before other historians have."

Jamieson has no problems with political correctness in his work. He doesn't find the military services defensive about either gender or race, "nor should they be." He believes the percentage of female Air Force officers, especially in the mid and fairly senior grades, "is probably higher than in the corporate world." The same case can be made for ethnicity—"in the ranks of the airmen and officers, if you look statistically at how well blacks or Latins are represented, it would be the same thing—they have probably fared much better than they have in the corporate world."

Jamieson has found associations with other historians helpful. He enjoys his Air Force work where he is in the company of so many historians who are interested not just in Air Force history, but in U.S. military history generally. Ideas and writings are passed around "to friendly critics and colleagues." He attends Southern Historical Association meetings, primarily for the social contacts he has there. He also finds it professionally helpful because the participants are all historians, "we all use the same skills, and it's interesting to see the new ideas in the profession and what the younger historians are working on, and what's going on in the larger profession."

Jamieson spends time reading on U.S. military history in all periods, from the colonial to the present. For fun and relaxation, he reads mysteries—Nero Wolfe and the Amos Walker books, which are set in Detroit—"I'm still a Detroiter at heart." He believes the pleasure he finds in mysteries is related to historical research—"puzzling things out."

Jamieson believes *Attack and Die* is probably his most important work because it has remained in print for so long. *Death in September* he believes has been influential in helping visitors to the Antietam battlefield better understand what happened there. It is also used as a textbook at West Point.

His unique contribution to the field of history, Jamieson believes, is his double career. Although his day job is as a public historian, he has "kept one foot in the academic history world as well." Outside of his Air Force career, he has operated like an academic historian—"the topics I've worked on, presentations I've given to general and academic audiences." He believes there "are probably not a lot of historians over the last twenty years who have had the good fortune to have a two-track career."

Jamieson also contrasts his Air Force work with the job academic historians do. He works at least forty hours a week with the service, "and I don't always have a lot of energy left over." But he says, "I've never had the idea that my academic friends really have it made, that all they have to do is read those same old lectures that they wrote many years ago and the rest of their time is theirs, because the really good historians don't do that. They have a lot of demands on their time, and the better researchers they are and the better record they have in publishing, the more demands there are on them to do other things."

Jamieson believes there is one other job he could have stayed with and still done history—being a mail carrier, a summer and winter-holidays job he had as an undergraduate student. "I found carrying mail on a walking route keeps you in shape, and once you become very familiar with the route you can have your brain free to brainstorm about things, like how to break a book into chapters. It would have taken me a lot longer, but I can see how I could have stayed with the post office, made a good steady income, gotten a government retirement, gone to night school, and gotten an advanced degree eventually in history. I could have been a full-time postal worker and part-time historian." Fortunately, for the field of history, he chose instead to be a full-time historian.

Since this interview, Jamieson has retired from his position as an Air Force historian and is focusing exclusively on his Civil War work.

Robert T. Maberry, Jr.

A Passion for History

"There are wonderful things to be discovered everywhere in the past."

"I'm a person who likes to live vicariously in the past; that's what is fun about history."

"To read primary sources is in some ways to live people's lives, to know what they felt and to almost be present in the past."

"Once I discovered the pleasure and pain of writing, I had found what I had been seeking all along."

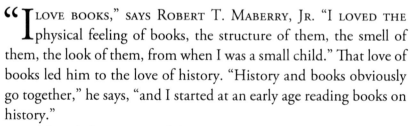

"I LOVE BOOKS," SAYS ROBERT T. MABERRY, JR. "I LOVED THE physical feeling of books, the structure of them, the smell of them, the look of them, from when I was a small child." That love of books led him to the love of history. "History and books obviously go together," he says, "and I started at an early age reading books on history."

Although his parents did not read to him, there were always books in the house. His father, Maberry says, is a "sort of a Renaissance man," reading books on poetry theory, science, history, theology, "and all sorts of different subjects." Consequently, his father had hundreds of books, and even before he learned to read, Maberry says, "I just pretty much pulled one down and looked at it—just looked at the books themselves."

When he could read, Maberry devoured history books written for young people. He recalls the Random House series of *Landmark Books* that he read in their entirety. From those he progressed to historical adventure stories, such as C. S. Forester's Hornblower books.

Maberry remembers good history teachers in school, in particular Julia Catherine Garrett. Garrett earned her doctorate at the University of California–Los Angeles and then "devoted her life to teaching at Arlington Heights High School in west Fort Worth, Texas—a very inspiring teacher."

Despite his early fascination with history, Maberry became a dentist. It was "sort of a family tradition." His father, his father-in-law, and his grandfather-in-law were all dentists. "It was the easy path," he concedes. He did, however, experience a "crisis" in college when he announced that he was not going to be a dentist after all, but a history professor. "That panicked my father," Mayberry recalls, who visited him at the University of Texas (UT) in Austin, bringing along a friend who was a history professor. Between the two of them, they convinced the young Maberry to go to dental school after all, arguing that he could always go back to school and become a historian. "I actually bought that argument and they just knowingly smiled, I'm sure, behind my back, thinking, 'Well, he'll forget this.'" But he didn't. "I always kept the history dream in the back of my mind and that, in fact, is what kept me going."

In his undergraduate studies, Maberry majored in history, with the same number of hours, twenty-four, in classics, "just another form of history with language and literature thrown in." He studied classics under William Arrowsmith and Douglas Parker.

After UT, Maberry attended the University of Texas Dental Branch in Houston, graduating in 1975, and establishing a flourishing practice over the years. Still, he was "always looking for some sort of intellectual outlet." He kept reading on his own and learned the rudiments of classical Greek and spent time translating Homer and medieval French poetry. He was "looking desperately for an outlet, for something that would save me from the humdrum existence of a middle-class professional."

Then in 1982, Maberry approached another of his father's friends, Ben Proctor, a history professor at Texas Christian University (TCU) in Fort Worth, about the possibility of taking courses, "just for something to do." Instead, Proctor encouraged him to work toward a degree, to somehow work it into his schedule. "I jumped on that," Maberry says, "and thanks to him I enrolled in graduate school."

To his delight, he discovered that TCU was an excellent place to work on a degree in history and still maintain his dental practice. "The department was accommodating," he says, "they were used to having some nontraditional students." Although he really wanted to be a classicist, "there was absolutely no way, with the dearth of classics programs in the immediate area, that one could do graduate work in the field."

But that made no difference to Maberry. "It didn't matter the subject; all history is interesting. I could be a historian in any field and be happy. Something would be interesting about it; the mechanics, or the fundamentals, are all the same pretty much—reconstructing and analyzing life in the past. It doesn't matter if it's the history of Poland or the history of the Trobriand Islands—there are wonderful things to be discovered everywhere in the past."

Because his goal was history—any history—Maberry decided to go with the "best graduate professor available to me at that particular time." That turned out to be Grady McWhiney, who specialized in Civil War and Southern history. "He had a wonderful reputation and turned out to be a wonderful man as well as a *great* teacher," Maberry says. "He took me on without ever questioning my motives. He understood my passion, he didn't wonder why the hell I was there. While most of the department dismissed me as being a dilettante, he took me at face value and treated me just like any other student."

Finally, Maberry found himself where he wanted to be, and it was even better than he had imagined. "The most wonderful thing that happened to me in graduate school was that I discovered the glories of the primary source. I'm a person who likes to live vicariously in the past; that's what is fun about history. I always identify with my subject; I love learning everything I can about people in the past and how they lived. To read primary sources is in some ways to live people's lives, to know what they felt and to almost be present in the past."

Using primary sources for his master's studies in the Civil War, Maberry became interested in the Confederate Army of Tennessee: "This army seemed to embody the ethos and the hard-luck fate of the Old South." As he surveyed the primary sources, he realized it was an enormous subject, and he would have to set limits on what he could accomplish with his dissertation. He eventually narrowed it down to the history of Texans in the Confederate Northwest in the first year of the war, soldiers who later served in the Army of Tennessee. His dissertation primarily told the story of Texans fighting in the Indian Territory of Oklahoma as allies of slaveholding Indians aligned with the Confederacy against Unionist Indians. "The story I now focused on was fascinating," he says. "There was a lot to be told about that first year of conflict, and not just about the events themselves, but about what the combatants were like, their lives, their economies, their social systems, a whole way of life now lost." It turned out to be much more than Maberry had originally thought. "I never planned to write social as well as military history; things just kind of evolved."

McWhiney had a profound effect on Maberry. "I didn't have to be inspired by anyone to be interested in history," he says, "but Grady made it possible for me to actually become a historian. It would never have happened otherwise. He improved my writing, he taught me how to organize, he taught me how to do research, he taught me *what* to research. If you were fortunate enough to study under Grady McWhiney, you had all the tools you needed to become a competent historian." And through McWhiney he discovered the real joys of history. "The really glorious revelation was how wonderful research and writing are. Writing especially. Once I discovered the pleasure and pain of writing, I had found what I had been seeking all along."

The knowledge acquired while writing his dissertation led to Maberry's next project, a study of the flags of Texas. The state of Texas maintains an extensive collection of historical flags, most of them from the Civil War. Haphazard handling over the decades left a large number of them with lost records and identities.

John Nau, chair of the Texas Historical Commission, and Mike Andrews, a former congressman from Houston, resolved to salvage the deteriorating flag collection and set out to raise money for an extensive conservation effort. Because conservation is costly, they needed to separate the flags that were most important, and to that end, identify those that had lost their identities. They needed a historian with knowledge of Texas history. "While I really had no broad knowledge of Texas history at the time," Maberry says, "I did have the tools to acquire it, and I did know about Texas in the Civil War era."

Meanwhile, Maberry had been working with the United Daughters of the Confederacy (UDC), a heritage group of Texas women, to help document their collection of artifacts and was planning to write a small book on their Civil War flags. In 1998, Mike Parrish, a Baylor history professor, notified Nau and Andrews about Maberry's activities with the UDC, and they asked him to help with their project. "I said yes, little knowing what I'd be getting into."

"In all modesty," Maberry says, "I was the right person for this project. I loved the idea of saving and documenting the flags. I knew the primary sources well, and I have a pretty good memory for obscure things. I can recall tiny details from historical documents I may have consulted years before." So he went back to various primary sources to identify flags and reconstruct "histories long forgotten." One of the flags, he discovered, had been with Hood's Texas Brigade, and "this knowledge increased its value exponentially." Several of the flags he identified from descriptions in primary sources.

"Texas flags was a wonderful topic for a historian to get hold of," Maberry says. "It was a subject people were interested in, there was a practical need for its study, and the sources for finding out about the old flags existed. So it was just a wonderful stew."

A completely unexpected outcome of his study on the flags was the opportunity to curate an exhibit at the Museum of Fine Arts in Houston. The innovative director of the Museum, Peter Marzio, suggested the exhibit and asked Maberry to be the curator. The exhibit would range beyond the state collection and could include any historic Texas flag. Maberry found himself traveling around the state and the country searching for historic flags and selecting those he found most interesting. "It was a dream job," he says, "to be curator at a major museum. To put together a major exhibition was really starting at the top!"

Part of his job as curator was to write an exhibition catalog. He planned to have a photograph and a short history of each flag. But as he researched, he found many untapped sources for the history of the flags. "There was material no professional historian had ever consulted, let alone written about," Maberry says. "It was wide-open territory, and there were all sorts of surprising things I found that even self-proclaimed flag experts didn't know."

Maberry became interested in more than just the flags. He immersed himself in learning what "the flags represented and what the people who made and flew flags were like and why a flag was so important to them." And most of all, he wanted "to present a narrative composed of good stories. That's something Grady always taught us; you can be a great historian, but if you don't tell a good story, no one's going to have the benefit of your expert research and all of your hard work." In the end, he says, "The flags became a vehicle that I used to relate some higher truths in Texas history."

He had help along the way. Vexillology, the formal study of flags, began in 1959, and the field still has a lot of amateur scholars—"I was constantly struggling to keep them focused on using proper research techniques." The struggle played out on the Internet. Shortly after his project began, Maberry received an e-mail from someone involved with an Internet group interested in Confederate flags, the "Flag Fanatics." When he discovered them, he says, it "was the beginning of an astounding research collaboration," with members of the group sharing their research through e-mails. One of those he encountered online is Vicki Betts, librarian at the University of Texas in Tyler. Betts had extracted hundreds of articles about flags from nineteenth-century newspapers, and she made that information available to the Flag Fanatics. "I got material for almost two chapters out of her work," Maberry says.

Without the Internet, he says, the project would have been much more difficult—"it could never have happened, not like it did." He worked under severe time constraints, with just fifteen months to produce a book and to plan the exhibition. He had a running start because of the research he had already done in the state archives for the UDC, "but with the expanded scope, there was much more to do." To have the book ready for the opening of the exhibit, he needed to write a chapter each month and have the entire manuscript ready five months before the exhibit opened.

To meet the deadlines, Maberry says, "took discipline. I had to keep rigidly to a schedule." The organizational skills he learned from McWhiney proved essential. He took all of his notes on the computer in files by chapter and topics. He never tried to have all of his research completed before he began writing because "things evolve; I find out new things as my writing proceeds. I don't know how you could ever do all your research beforehand."

When beginning to write, he printed out the references for each chapter, sorted them by subject, and lined them up "paragraph by paragraph just the way Grady taught us to do." As he laid them out, they "would suggest an inner sense to me; I would understand the reality of it once I had all the information assembled. It would all just meld." This melding created an outline, which Maberry says is important to him. "I love working from an outline; that's the way I like to organize my thoughts—outline a whole chapter, line up the notes, and then do the writing."

Four nights during each week, after the day at his dental practice, he spent two or three hours editing, organizing, or rewriting. Most of the writing he did on his three-day weekends, working up to eight hours each day. He found that it took him a week to organize a chapter, a week to write the first draft, and two weeks to rewrite and revise.

"Fortunately," Maberry says, "my family tolerated my obsession. They knew I was engaged in an important project and were very supportive." He needs absolute silence when he writes, and if someone came into his study, "I couldn't even acknowledge their presence, lest I lose my train of thought." If his concentration was broken, he says, "it might take me thirty minutes to get back up to speed."

Maberry says writing *Texas Flags* was "the most intense experience of my whole life. It was almost mystical. I can see why ancient writers often referred to experiencing divine inspiration. The act of writing was like something took me over on some of those eight-hour days when I never got out of my chair. I began at 8 A.M. and all of a sudden it was four o'clock in the afternoon. I hadn't had lunch, I didn't know what had gone on around me. I was just there—time had contracted, and I'd have ten pages done. The experience was like being in another state of reality, it was that intense. I used to marvel at the end of the day, with a happy and terrible exhaustion, thinking, 'My God, what have I just been through?' Beginning a session was something I dreaded, knowing that this was going to be so engrossing, but once I got started, I lost myself in the process."

He still had his day job, but he says, "I'm able to compartmentalize my life." Dentistry never really challenged him, "it was always fairly effortless." But he maintained his professionalism, tending up to twenty-five patients each day. "I never neglected my practice or my patients. I was very successful in those years."

Maberry writes in his upstairs study equipped with a desk, a computer, and a side table where he lays out his notes. There are also two long tables and a set of shelves that hold the books and references he is currently consulting. Other bookcases "all around" hold ancillary references. "Everything is within arm's reach—all the notes I need, all the books I need; I can spread out over maybe ten feet of space."

The computer? It's "absolutely essential for me." Without it, he says, he would be writing everything out in longhand, "and you can't do revisions very well on legal pads." He does a lot of revising and says this is why he needs to write more books: "That comes with practice, by just doing it."

Maberry credits Forrest McDonald with helping him with his writing style. McDonald advised him to use "interesting expressions and precise vocabulary," using words that are "mellifluous but meaningful." Use passive voice only if there is a strong reason to do so. Split an infinitive if you need to. "I think developing a style is extremely important," Maberry says. He strives to "get a rhythm in my writing, something that has an oral quality to it." Everything he writes, he reads aloud to hear how it sounds. "That's what writing really is, what it originally was, to be read out loud. In the ancient world, there was no such thing as silent reading." Whenever he is conflicted about how to express something, "how it sounds when read aloud is the deciding factor."

Maberry believes subjects to research and write about "grow best out of the soil of your previous knowledge and your previous studies." The next project he is contemplating grew out of his research on the battle flag of San Jacinto, "a work of fine art" painted by James H. Beard of Cincinnati, Ohio. The book would be about Beard, an artist who has never been studied or written about.

But he finds it difficult to get motivated for the project. "*Texas Flags* was such a successful book that it's hard to get excited about the next one." Too, he has found that "one characteristic pattern of my life is that once I've accomplished something, I'm ready to try something else. I'm always interested in new things, often completely different things. So even though the Beard book needs to be done, the compulsion that motivated me before is not there. I may never be able to do the book. But that wouldn't be the end of the world."

But, he says, "my life of study goes on." Now that the flags project is finished, he has returned to his classical and literary studies, which he had neglected in favor of the flags.

Despite his heavy schedule, Maberry always finds time to read for pleasure, usually having eight or ten books going at once. He says in the past he "read a lot of bestsellers and historical novels, science fiction, and things like that." Then he read some Dickens "and discovered that it was simply better than that other stuff. It's full of humanity and insight. Reading Dickens is like being in a time machine, it's like walking the streets of Victorian London. There's no question—why read tripe when there is so much better stuff out there?" He now reads Dante, Cervantes, Evelyn Waugh, Somerset Maugham, and T. S. Eliot. He has recently become fascinated by "the religious conversions of the literary intelligentsia in the twentieth century: Thomas Merton who became a Trappist brother, C. S. Lewis, Dorothy Sayers, Evelyn Waugh, T. S. Eliot—all these people underwent orthodox religious conversions, and these were some of the most brilliant, sophisticated people in all of society."

Maberry's associations are with other historians, not with dentists. He says he went through a period when he had no one with like interests to talk with. "I would read an exciting book and there would be nobody to discuss it with. There was little reason for me to do research because I had nothing I could do with my discoveries. Just being with like-minded people, with similar interests," he says, "makes all the difference in the world."

Maberry believes passion is a must for a historian; indeed, "the number one thing for any great endeavor." Integrity is also a must—don't plagiarize, and don't "hide available truths to make a point." He remembers McWhiney admonishing his students that if they found a key fact that contradicted their thesis, they could not leave it out. He always said, Maberry recalls, "We are historians, not lawyers."

Like many of his fellow historians, Maberry is appalled by the academic system today. There is no merit system in academics, he says, only credentials—where you earned your degree. "It's such a silly, nasty system in the way it's set up. In most places political orthodoxy—read 'political correctness'—is more important than truth. People with diverse beliefs would not stand a chance of being hired at the most prestigious schools."

Political correctness plays too large a part in the world of academia, Maberry says. "I believe that the universities no longer maintain the intellectual leadership of the country. There are certain subjects and points of view that are taboo. You have to think in a certain way to be successful in many universities. It scares me to death."

He believes revisionism is a meaningless term. As the historian follows the facts where they lead, "any new interpretation of history is revision—'re-vision.'"

Maberry sees *Texas Flags* as his unique contribution to the field of history—"maybe my only contribution," he says. "I'm really very selfish intellectually. It's nice to be able to make a contribution, but basically it was for me. I did it for love." He finds that studying history "allows me to exist on a different plane of reality." Research and writing is for his own pleasure. When the book was written, "it was not that exciting any more. It's something that's done, it's been accomplished and...ho hum...next project."

Maberry says that in the past he believed that if he had it to do over again he would skip dentistry and just be a historian. "But now I'm not so sure," he says. "As I approach the end of my dental career, I realize it has been a rewarding occupation." On occasion he contemplates what would have happened had he made history his career. He knows he would probably not be as well off financially. But he wonders about the books he might have written, the skills he might have honed: "I would have written more and evolved more as a writer."

But he would be one of the first to say it is never too late.

In 2009, Maberry sold his dental practice in Fort Worth and accepted an invitation to join the history faculty at McMurry University in Abilene. But even there, he straddles his unlikely worlds: he is still a dentist one day a week—every Friday.

Ari Hoogenboom

HISTORICAL HANDYMAN

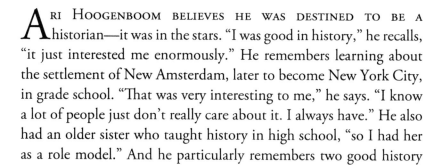

"The lifeblood of history is in the story, the narrative, how it happened."

"I don't think there's anything mysterious about it. It's work! Writing is like keeping in shape, you've got to stay active."

"The research is like being a Peeping Tom, a voyeur."

"I don't type very fast. I type about as fast as my brain works."

"We should not be judgmental or apply twenty-first century moral values, but it's hard to escape them."

ARI HOOGENBOOM BELIEVES HE WAS DESTINED TO BE A historian—it was in the stars. "I was good in history," he recalls, "it just interested me enormously." He remembers learning about the settlement of New Amsterdam, later to become New York City, in grade school. "That was very interesting to me," he says. "I know a lot of people just don't really care about it. I always have." He also had an older sister who taught history in high school, "so I had her as a role model." And he particularly remembers two good history teachers that he had at John Adams High School in Queens.

Following his destiny, Hoogenboom chose to study history in undergraduate school at Atlantic Union College in South Lancaster,

Massachusetts—a Seventh-Day Adventist school. There he had three history teachers—Godfrey Anderson, Albert W. Werline, and Willis King—"who were patient with me, and did not hesitate to give me their time."

Initially, he planned to teach history in high school, but when he matriculated at Columbia University in New York City to work on his master's degree, "I got a little more ambitious about teaching college." There he first studied under Richard B. Morris, but when he began work on his doctoral degree, David Herbert Donald became his main professor. Donald "really made a great difference in my life," Hoogenboom says. "He spent a great deal of time with me and his other graduate students, far beyond what one would normally expect a university professor to do."

Donald gave much to his students, but in return, he expected much from them. "He was really tough, no question about that," Hoogenboom recalls. "Sometimes we wondered whether he kept a record as to whether this was the meeting where he gave us a kick or whether this was the meeting he gave us a pat on the back, so we wouldn't get too discouraged."

A good historian, Hoogenboom believes, needs to know how to tell a good story. "The lifeblood of history is in the story, the narrative, how it happened," he says. "Analysis should be a part of the unfolding of events, or the unfolding of a life, or the progression of a life, or the evolution of a life, or of a movement." That's what makes history an art—"to try to weave the analysis in, make it palatable, and not lose sight of the unfolding of events, because people are interested in the story." He believes historians should "stick to what people enjoy reading. People enjoy history, they buy a lot of history, but the history they buy tends to be the history that tells a story."

Hoogenboom confesses that his subjects usually choose him, not the other way around. In graduate school he began a biography of George William Curtis, a literary figure and the political editor of *Harper's Weekly,* who headed the Civil Service reform movement. Discovering that someone else had already written a dissertation on Curtis, Donald suggested that Hoogenboom focus instead on the history of the reform movement. That study, *Outlawing the Spoils: A History of the Civil Service Reform Movement, 1865–1883,* was published in 1961.

From that, Hoogenboom says, "a lot of things simply flowed." In 1976, he and his wife Olive coauthored *A History of the ICC: From Panacea to Palliative,* which focused on the Interstate Commerce Commission. The University Press of Kansas asked him to write a volume on Rutherford B. Hayes for their presidency series, "since Civil Service reform was an important issue during his administration." *The Presidency of Rutherford B. Hayes* was published in 1988, and in 1995 Hoogenboom followed that with a full biography, *Rutherford B. Hayes: Warrior and President.*

The one subject Hoogenboom chose entirely on his own took him nearly fifty years to complete—a biography of Gustavus Vasa Fox, Lincoln's assistant secretary of the navy. His interest in Fox, he says, started with his own father, a Dutch sailor, who jumped ship in New York in 1920. He married a Brooklyn woman, who by marrying a foreigner lost her citizenship, and along with her husband became a naturalized U.S. citizen. His father, who always had a boat, heightened Hoogenboom's interest in naval subjects. Interest in the Civil War was quickened by Grady McWhiney, a fellow Donald doctoral student. "I certainly got a lot of Civil War just hanging around him," Hoogenboom remembers.

Little had been written about Fox. "He was basically chief of naval operations in the Civil War," says Hoogenboom, "which means that in many ways he was more important than David Farragut or David Dixon Porter or John Dahlgren or any of the other admirals that have been written up." He was not in any battles, but he was deeply involved in shaping overall strategy and in supplying the navy with vessels. He was largely responsible for the controversial emphasis on ironclad monitors with their heavy ordnance.

After decades of being "waylaid by other projects," *Gustavus Vasa Fox of the Union Navy: A Biography* was published in 2008.

When he first started writing, Hoogenboom took notes by hand, but forty years ago he and Olive purchased a Contura Constat, which takes pictures of manuscripts. He soon began having printouts made from pertinent microfilm reels.

Directly on the copies and printouts, Hoogenboom draws a line beside information he wants to use and makes notations at the top of the page. On a separate sheet of paper he notes items that strike him as particularly good so he won't overlook them in the writing process. The material is then organized chronologically in file folders.

At this point, Hoogenboom does not have the material divided into chapters. "I'm not usually that well organized to start with," he says. To some extent, he believes that one can be too well organized and have it all so well-thought-out as to be "almost straitjacketed into a preconception that's not based on going through all the material. You really have to be aware that your outline is very tentative," he says. Otherwise, "you might find yourself culling things out that don't fit into your organization and you might be culling out things that you shouldn't be culling out." He finds that "a little bit of disorganization is useful because you will suddenly have some things in juxtaposition that apparently do have a connection that you become aware of, a connection that you would not have been aware of if you were so organized that these pieces were widely separated."

Having things organized chronologically when writing a biography allows the historian to "come across them in the same sequence that your subject saw them, so you might approximate your subject's state of mind at the time he was dealing with them," says Hoogenboom. "Sometimes you [and your subject] are dealing with a dozen things at the same time." The historian "can't do the dozen things all at the same time, but you have to do them within that chronological framework."

Hoogenboom likes to have a fair amount of the research completed before he begins to write, but he doesn't think "it's wise to postpone writing until you've nailed down every last possible source." Too often, he says, people, who have the idea that they must have everything in hand before writing, "simply don't get around to writing."

Hoogenboom now writes on a computer. In the early days he wrote in longhand, but because he had never learned to type, "my dear wife ended up typing a lot of those early manuscripts five, six, seven times, as they were revised and revised." In 1986, they bought their first computer, and at that point he resolved to learn to type. "I don't type very fast," he says, but "I type about as fast as my brain works." During summers, which he spends with his family on an island in Maine where he has no electricity, he runs the computer on a battery powered by a solar panel on the roof of their cottage.

When he is not in Maine, Hoogenboom works at home. He has a study and a "reasonably good" library where he "can generally look up stuff if I have to check a fact, get some data." He doesn't require absolute quiet—"I can concentrate pretty well, whatever is going on." He recalls in his younger days being able to work while remaining "somewhat aware of what my kids were doing outside, and every now and again I'd let out a roar out the window in the warmer weather telling my son or one of my daughters to shape up."

He tries to write mornings and afternoons. On occasion he can write at night, if he's "really keyed up on something," but usually finds that by the time he has finished doing the dishes after dinner ("which is my job around this place") he is "not much good for anything in the evening."

Now retired, Hoogenboom finds it difficult to keep to a regular writing schedule each day. He and Olive have young grandchildren with whom they spend one or two days a week. One of his daughters recently bought an apartment house in Queens that needs a lot of work, and he has been spending time there at least twice a week, "mainly scraping paint off of the woodwork." As he looked at his past week when writing *Fox,* he often said, "Yesterday I got in a great day on Fox, today I got in a great day scraping paint."

Usually, Hoogenboom reviews the previous day's output before beginning a writing session, "to see just where I am and to get myself in the mood." He does some revising, but he leaves a lot of that to family members. Olive "is a terrific editor," he says, and will always make suggestions, which he "almost invariably" accepts. His daughter Lynn works for *The New York Times* and is an "incredibly good editor, and she's kind enough to go over my stuff." Lynn was particularly helpful when he had to drastically cut his Hayes biography. "To me," he says, "it was like sawing off my right hand," but Lynn "went over it and suggested places where things could be discarded."

When he finds conflicting material, Hoogenboom believes in going with the contemporary source, someone acquainted with the subject or event. But he says, even in that situation, you have to guard against a bias the writer may have. It is well known that eyewitnesses "are notoriously unreliable, reminiscences are always suspect, and secondary sources are even more suspect." Hoogenboom believes it is vitally important to know your source.

In his earlier days, faced with a blank sheet of paper, Hoogenboom procrastinated by taking imaginary trips. "I have a lot of road maps in my desk," he says, "and I'd take out a road map and just start reading it—take a drive through South Dakota or something like that." These days he doesn't do that very often: "I think it's because I'm getting older and I know time is fleeting." He has never been bothered by writer's block, as a purely creative writer might be. Although there is creativity involved in writing history, he says, "we're pretty much bound by our source material, so we should not really have too much difficulty along that line."

Like many historians, Hoogenboom finds writing more difficult than researching. "I don't think there's anything mysterious about it. It's work! Writing is like keeping in shape, you've got to stay active." The fun part is researching. "The research is like being a Peeping Tom, a voyeur," he says. "You're getting into these letters, and you're reading about people's personal lives. You really get to know people very well." Donald, Hoogenboom recalls, "once said that he might have known more about Charles Sumner at one point than Charles Sumner knew himself." (Donald wrote two books about Sumner.)

His most thrilling breakthrough, Hoogenboom says, was discovering that Fox (despite his family connection with Montgomery Blair) thought that "black equality is the only way we can go," and believed strongly in black suffrage. Hoogenboom discovered this in the letters Fox wrote to his wife. She spent long periods of time with her mother in Portsmouth, New Hampshire, and the correspondence between husband and wife left a rich legacy for posterity.

Hoogenboom relished learning about Fox's view of freed slaves. Although he says he is not an ideologue, and he tries to be balanced, as a political liberal he appreciates Fox's position. "My conscience will force me to try to be fair," he says. "Although no one can be completely fair, it's worth trying. Ideology, even for somebody nonideological, is unavoidable, but, on the other hand, it should be avoided." He believes "we should not be judgmental or apply twenty-first century moral values, but it's hard to escape them."

Hoogenboom believes that in deliberately setting out to present a revisionist view of history, "there's a danger of picking only the kinds of sources, episodes, and information that will prove your point." The historian needs to be guided by the sources. "You can start out with an idea, but one has to be very, very willing to revise that idea, to overhaul, and to tinker with it." Ideally, this process may lead to a revision, and he says, "there's nothing wrong with a fresh view."

Hoogenboom today sees a strong emphasis on social history. He believes "it is good to know how people lived and it's certainly worthy of study." Although he thinks it is worthwhile to take note of so-called anonymous Americans, "anonymous Americans have not been as important in shaping the nation as have been, say, presidents of the United States and important political figures."

Hoogenboom learned a valuable lesson about historiography in a graduate school course. The students had to write a paper on how the life and times of a historian were reflected in his or her writings. He chose Charles Downer Hazen, a historian who, at the turn of the twentieth century, wrote on the French Revolution. "It was a good exercise," Hoogenboom says, "because Hazen tried to write good history, good accurate fare, and yet it was perfectly obvious that he was reflecting the period in which he was writing and reflecting his own values, as well as those of the French Revolution." The main point of the exercise, Hoogenboom believes, was to illustrate the necessity of avoiding "present-mindedness, but it also made us aware that it was very difficult to avoid it."

He remembers reading for the same course an article by Charles Beard, which "quite frankly embraced the idea of writing from a point of view and using history to illustrate that point of view." Hoogenboom believes that is a mistake. "I think what you end up doing is propagandizing for a particular point of view that will go out of favor. That's just the way life is, we move in cycles, it seems, and whatever we write will then be ignored and nobody is going to take it terribly seriously." He hopes that the work he has done "will be useful for future generations, and even if their values are different than ours, they'll still find merit in what we've done."

Over his career Hoogenboom found associations with other historians rewarding, and maintains membership in several organizations. Lately, he participates in meetings less than he did in the past. "I think what happens," he says, "being older, I don't know as many of the people, a lot of my old friends don't go anymore."

Hoogenboom believes his book on Civil Service reform may be one of his best. "My point of view, that Civil Service reformers were 'outs' trying to get the 'ins' out of office, I still think is valid; I think I had enough hard evidence to prove my point." He is also proud of his biography of Hayes and is pleased with his biography of Fox.

Most of Hoogenboom's reading is focused on the subject he is currently working on, but on occasion he reads just for pleasure. He read Anthony Trollope for a while, and has "read Jane Austen through." His wife sometimes recommends a book, which he will read, "but it's very unusual for me to get involved in reading a book." He reads *The New York Times* every morning, and at night he'll work on the crossword puzzle in bed, but admits, "I keep falling asleep." As for TV, he and Olive watch *Washington Week* for a half-hour each week, "and that's usually it."

If history had not been his destiny, Hoogenboom believes he might have been a carpenter, following in the footsteps of his father. On weekends and during the summer his father would get him construction jobs, work he enjoyed, until his father died in a construction accident when Hoogenboom was just twenty-three years old. But he still keeps his hand in, wielding a hammer or a shovel when called upon—or scraping that paint off those window frames.

Eugene Genovese

SLAVERY'S SCHOLAR

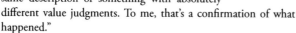

"When I wrote *Roll, Jordan, Roll,* one of the things that really delighted me was when I could find masters and black slaves giving pretty much the same description of something with absolutely different value judgments. To me, that's a confirmation of what happened."

"You have no idea how good your work is. Fifty years after you're dead people will make a judgment—if they remember who you are."

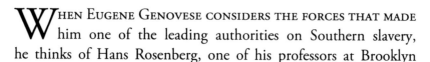

WHEN EUGENE GENOVESE CONSIDERS THE FORCES THAT MADE him one of the leading authorities on Southern slavery, he thinks of Hans Rosenberg, one of his professors at Brooklyn College.

In his younger years Genovese was an ardent Marxist and a member of the Communist Party. Rosenberg was a strongly anti-Marxist and anti-Communist professor, "steeped in the controversies around Marxism." In the college student body at the time were many like-minded with Genovese, party members and fellow travelers. Many of them took Rosenberg's courses despite his anti-Marxism because he was a first-rate teacher, "and he was tuned in to all the theoretical problems we were interested in." He "gave us a hard time and kept us on our mettle," Genovese remembers, and "war went on in his classroom every day."

One day Rosenberg invited Genovese to his home for a glass of sherry. This took Genovese by surprise. Such a thing was almost never done in that day—professors were teaching five days a week and busy writing books and generally inaccessible. "You just didn't go and bother them, let's put it that way," Genovese says.

"I remember sitting in his study," Genovese recalls, "and he said to me that these slaveholders were a social class that had risen to power in a more or less definable period of time, and went, as he put it, kaput in one year. He then said this is the closest thing to a historical laboratory that you could find, and I assume you are going to make them your life's work when you go on to graduate school, because now you will have an opportunity to test those crazy Marxist theories of yours seriously"—an opportunity "to see how a ruling class really works, as opposed to all the stereotypes."

"Well," Genovese confesses, "I was stuck. At first I thought he was crazy; the idea of spending my life on that." But Genovese soon discovered that "the *image* of the slaveholders was nothing like reality." Fascinated by this, they did indeed become his life's work. The foremost fruit of that work is *Roll, Jordan, Roll: The World the Slaves Made,* published in 1972, and it is perhaps the most insightful book about slavery ever written. In his continuing search for the reality of that world, he has further elaborated on the theme in works that have cemented his high standing and reputation in the field.

Genovese is no longer a Marxist, a Communist, or an atheist, and he has embraced Catholicism. In part this was because he had to "face the fact that our whole communist movement [which had collapsed] had never had a moral basis, that we had never had any place to ground our morals, and therefore to check ourselves." He believed it was too easy for socialism to generate totalitarianism.

But he has, through his career, been a worker. Early in their careers he and his friend and fellow historian Forrest McDonald, the authority on the U.S. Constitution, agreed that while preparing to be historians they could afford only four and a half hours of sleep each night because they each held full-time jobs to work their way through college. Both have since eased up and are sleeping more—"I figure I don't have to work more than six or seven hours a day any more," says Genovese. But their work ethics have carried both of them to the heights as historians, and they have fed off one another. McDonald is "a guy who knows what all the big questions are, who has no patience with trivia and cant, and it is a pleasure to disagree with him, to argue with him. He is somebody you learn from."

Genovese continues to probe for reality in the slave world. "Until the day I die," he says, "I'll never be satisfied that I really understand these people from the inside. I think that's probably true of any social class we study, any group of people we study, but I find them particularly complex and fascinating."

Genovese considers history both a science and an art—research being the science and writing the art. "Look," he says, "it claims to be a science. Let's start there. That's legitimate to the extent that we strive for maximum precision, and that's important to stress these days with all this postmodernist claptrap, which wants us to deny even the existence of historical facts. I think Aristotle was right when he made the analogy between history and poetry; what is critical and what separates useful historical digging from generally writing history is the impact of the historical imagination, and that's a matter of trying to piece things together and to see what degree of coherence you can bring to them."

Abetting his writing, Genovese is a polymath reader, a drive he shared with his late wife and fellow historian and collaborator, Elizabeth (Betsey) Fox-Genovese. "I came from a working class home," he says, "and until I was fourteen or so I read mostly comic books. I joined the Communist movement at fifteen, and that's when I started reading a lot of political stuff."

He discovered that he was "intellectually very curious." But he had some catching up to do. Comic books only take you so far. "When I went to Brooklyn College, which was overwhelmingly middle-class Jewish," he says, "I was drowning in the sense that I was surrounded by kids who had read, or at least knew that they were supposed to have read, an enormous amount that I had barely heard of. I really chafed under it; I knew I was every bit as smart as the smartest kid—I was not modest—but I didn't know anything. So I read voraciously, and not in a very disciplined way—I would go from one thing to another, taking the reading wherever it led me." Ever since, reading has been "what I do."

Every five or ten years or so, Genovese rereads Gibbon's *Decline and Fall of the Roman Empire*—"from cover to cover," he says. "I have read it many times, and I always find it a fresh work. Also, whenever I've gotten some awards for my writing and every time I'm getting to believe my press notices, I take Gibbon down and pick up any volume and read forty or fifty pages. It is a splendid way to remind yourself of how good you're *not*."

When he was turning twenty, Genovese was expelled from the Communist Party. "I was going through a very deep personal crisis," he explains. "I was making a mess out of every aspect of my life, and I was behaving in a very erratic way. The Party had to throw me out. I never held it against them; I was behaving very badly."

Genovese was an organizer in the party. "I was very good at it," he says, "and I had expected to go on to a career as a party organizer and a trade union organizer." When they threw him out, "my whole career was gone, my life was gone, what was I supposed to do with it?" But he soon found a niche. "If you are interested in that kind of politics [Marxism and Communism], history is a natural." At Brooklyn College he discovered he was pretty good at it, so history became his new career.

Reading as much as he does, one would assume that he reads fast. "No," he protests, "I read slowly. I've improved, but God's compensation is that I always wrote fast." And he has definite ideas on that subject as well.

He says about writing, "Let me begin by saying what an old teacher of mine used to say: 'There's no such thing as a dull subject, only dull authors.' I believe that. With the advent of social history, which I think is a great thing, you can get into the center of a society by studying the kind of buttons that people put on their jackets. The only problem is, you've got to be very smart to do it. What happened with the vulgar social history is that people were studying more and more buttons, as it were, without any sense of what the hell this was supposed to be."

That kind of history, he says, "the bottom-up stuff, always makes me sick because most of it was a romanticizing of working-class people by bourgeois brats who didn't know what they were talking about. I'm sorry—now I'm ranting. What I would say is, write on what you want, I don't care how small the subject, but you have to know that if it's really going to be important, you have to be able to put that into political context. Politics is what history is. All the things in history one needs to study manifests themselves in politics—the rise and fall of social classes, of states, of countries, of civilizations."

Throughout his career, Genovese has discovered that being a historian requires patience, a trait that he believes has never been his particular forte. "I do know one thing," he says, "you have to be cool enough to face the facts, and when you don't like them, when they're against you, you've got to find out how it is you can believe what you believe in the face of these facts. You can't walk away from them." He also believes a historian must be committed to its discipline. "I do believe you have to be engaged with material in a way that you don't let it rule and ruin you." History in his view requires disciplined passion. At its best, disciplined passion "sharpens historical understanding, it doesn't detract from it. But that's a very delicate balance and there's no formula for it."

As he does not read by any set formula, neither does Genovese research and write by any set formula. However, he does prefer writing in the mornings, starting as early as he can. How long he writes "depends on what else I have to do. Right now, for example, I've got a stack of books that I have to read in connection with the work Betsey and I are doing, so I'll probably be writing today until mid-afternoon, and then I'll read."

In his early days Genovese wrote in longhand and then typed out what he had written. But when Betsey made him cave in and get a computer, that became his preferred instrument. It is a progression through which many historians have passed in recent decades.

Not only has God compensated Genovese's slow reading with fast writing, but writing has also always been easy for him. "I'm unusual in that respect, I think. Writing has never been a problem. For most of the historians I know, writing is a real drag; they have to sweat it."

Writer's block? "No, never," he says. "Some people would say I've written too much; they may be right. But no, there's only one thing I've ever had writer's block about, if that's what it is: on a couple of occasions I've touched on autobiographical stuff, and I hate it. I really can't be comfortable doing it. I regret most of the little bit that I have done." With very few exceptions, he has never particularly liked the genre to begin with—"by and large I think people embarrass themselves."

He also does his research now with a computer. As many historians have done, Genovese started out taking notes by hand. "I've got a room full of notes dating back to when I started. But for some years now I've taken notes on the computer, especially if I'm going to quote, because that leaves out a step where you can make mistakes."

Like most historians, mistakes are the devil in the woodpile—hard to avoid. When he wrote *Roll, Jordan, Roll,* Genovese had become—"I think the euphemism is 'very controversial'—and I didn't want that book to be messed up, so I hired a crack graduate student to check all my footnotes, including for context." Since then, he has always followed that procedure for all of his books.

"For the book Betsey and I just came out with, *The Mind of the Master Class,* we had a couple of crack young men checking it and it's remarkable how many errors they came up with. It's very, very rare that it's anything of importance, but still, little things can be irritating, especially if your colleagues want to criticize you—if you have cited the wrong volume for a journal, for example. In quoting people you've got to be very, very careful and have everything rechecked. Once in a long while our assistants will say, 'I think your context is wrong.' Usually, they're right when that happens. You want a source to say something and he appears to be saying it, and you get sloppy, and the next thing you know you make him say something that's very different from what he actually said."

Genovese draws the line at using assistants to do his original research. "We have had absolutely first-rate students working for us," he says, "but I don't care how good they are, I would never trust anybody to do my research. Even the very best assistant can't read the stuff through your eyes. You can't trust it. It's not that they're not doing good work, but even Betsey and I trust each other only up to a point." On all the more important stuff, he says, "we have different sensibilities, different eyes."

Taking care in all phases of his research is absolutely essential to Genovese. He says, "I think I can honestly say I've made a great many more enemies in this business than most people, and some of them like to turn students loose checking the footnotes of people they hate. I'm pleased to say that I've never been embarrassed."

He has, however, received heavy criticism in his time. It hasn't particularly bothered him. "First of all," he says, "I was a Communist, and let me tell you something—one of the things I learned in my years in the party was that you couldn't do anything without be criticized, and I mean *criticized*. You develop a thick skin very early on."

Most of the time Genovese knows exactly where a note he takes is going to fit into his narrative. But at times he takes miscellaneous notes, not knowing precisely where he will be using them, yet he doesn't want to let go of them. He goes through these set-aside notes periodically to see if there is something he can now retrieve. He also has a discard file, which he also goes through and rereads on occasion, sometimes finding something and saying, "Oh, how did I miss this?"

Genovese no longer works at night, which he did when he was sleeping only four and a half hours in twenty-four hours. Generally, in the evening he unwinds in front of a television set watching baseball games. He's a San Francisco Giants fan; Betsey, a Yankee fan. He reckoned that if the two teams had ever played in a World Series against one another, "a beautiful marriage" would have been in jeopardy.

Besides pursuing their own individual projects, Genovese and Fox-Genovese worked on projects together for more than twenty-five years before she died in 2007. Generally they worked on the same project together at the same time, but for many years, not in the same room. For most of that quarter of a century, they worked as far from one another as the house permitted. He worked on the first floor and she on the third, he at the north end of the house, she on the south end. "We were in touch with each other all the time," he explains, "but if we had to work that closely we'd drive each other crazy."

During her last year, however, they abandoned separate studies at opposite ends of the house on separate floors "because Betsey was experiencing increasingly bad falls and waves of weakness." They agreed they needed to be close to one another. "To our pleasant surprise," Genovese says, "the diminution in privacy no longer seemed important. We enjoyed the proximity more than we ever imagined. Maybe we enjoyed it in consequence of our getting old. But I am not so sure. I wonder if we would not have enjoyed it many years earlier."

A primary task for a historian is often to accommodate conflicting evidence—people in the past looking at the same event and reporting it quite differently. "When I wrote *Roll, Jordan, Roll*," he says, "one of the things that really delighted me was when I could find masters and black slaves giving pretty much the same description of something with absolutely different value judgments. To me, that's a confirmation of what happened. Now the historian's problem is not what is objectively true between these two things, but how do you mesh the two points of view, what does it tell you about the mind-set and about the reality of the incident."

Witnesses, he says, "often describe things where you can recognize that they're talking about the same thing, but from a very different slant. As historians, our job is to say how they came to read it the way they did. What were their assumptions, what were their own experiences, and what does that tell us about trying to create an image of the objective reality of the matter?"

As might be suspected, Genovese shares the same view of political correctness most conscientious historians entertain—only more so. He considers political correctness as simply "a nice way of speaking about totalitarian hooliganism." And he is baffled by the word *revisionism* as applied to history in a pejorative way. "Every historian is revising," he insists. "Otherwise, why bother to write if you don't have something fresh to say, to put the matter in a somewhat different perspective. When I was in graduate school, revisionist history was the stuff that Richard Hofstadter and William Leuchtenburg and people like that were doing. I never understood what was supposed to be unusual about it."

Genovese has said of his career that he had hoped to reorient the study of Southern slave society. He now likes to think that he may have succeeded to some degree. "There are plenty of people who have credited me with it," he says, "but it's really for other people to evaluate. I always told my students that you have no idea how good your work is. Fifty years after you're dead people will make a judgment—if they remember who you are."

Pressed to choose what he thinks has been his most important work, Genovese believes that is also not for him to say. Certainly most would agree that *Roll, Jordan, Roll* is a seminal work. But there are also *The Slaveholder's Dilemma, The World the Slaveholders Made, The Political Economy of Slavery,* and *The Mind of the Master Class,* which are all important contributions in the search for the reality of slavery and the slave society.

"I think I have—or at least I hope I have—contributed to undermining the Manichaean view of the slaveholders," Genovese says. "If there was one thing I set out to do in a specific sense, it was that. The Manichaean view is still strong, stronger than it has been in a long time, but I also have the sense that there are people out there who are resisting and that this period we're going through will end."

"Reason will return—I hope."

Elizabeth Fox-Genovese

Versatile Historian

"There are as many good styles of teaching as there are personalities. What is required is that you be true to who you are and use those strengths and take the students seriously."

"I think what people don't get is that technological change... completely changes the ball game. It changes who we are, and the rules, and erases previous rules and patterns and experience."

"Historians with some integrity and some experience should be as open-minded as humanly possible, but we also are in a position to know some things."

"I BEGAN AS A HISTORIAN," ELIZABETH FOX-GENOVESE SAYS. "History was what came naturally to me." Indeed, it was firmly fixed in her genes. She recalls her grandmother on her father's side "as just a repository of her family's history, which stretched back beyond the couple of generations she remembered. It went into the history of the country, and the whole family goes back to the Massachusetts Bay Colony—in fact, to the first minister for the Bay Colony. I grew up on her stories."

Her father was an academic historian with a strong pull on his daughter. "My father was extraordinary, and when I was very young he would get up in the very early morning with me and we would have long conversations. He had the gift of talking to even very young children as if they were serious human beings."

Fox-Genovese and her family traveled extensively in Europe during her childhood, and she spent what would have been her freshman year in high school in France. Those experiences, she believes, developed in her "a tremendous feel for European history."

Following high school, Fox-Genovese decided to take a year off, which she spent as an extramural student at Cornell, where her father taught. "It was all right for me to take his course because it was a large class and all the grading was done by assistants, so he didn't ever have to grade me." She claims, "my father's survey course carried me through graduate school, and gave me a sense of structure, and a surprisingly detailed knowledge of several periods in European history."

The paper she wrote for the course centered on European history. She studied the additional acts to the constitution of the empire that Napoleon instituted during the years between his return from Elba and the Battle of Waterloo. "Looking back," she says, "it was a pretty sophisticated paper for someone who would have been a senior in high school."

Following her year "off," Fox-Genovese matriculated to Bryn Mawr, where she studied medieval civilization under David Herlihy. Her education, Fox-Genovese says, "was completely European." She was bilingual in French, and spent her junior year in France, taking courses at the Institute of Political Science. At the same time, she accompanied her father several times to Oxford where he was editing a historical atlas. There were two volumes, and Fox-Genovese worked on the U.S. volume—her formal introduction to U.S. history. "I got this far straight through high school and college, without ever taking any American history," she recalls; "knowing a fair amount, but having taken none."

When she completed her studies at Bryn Mawr, her parents persuaded her to apply to graduate school, although she had no expectation of a career. "No one expected us [young women] to earn a living," she says. Many in her class were engaged to be married when they graduated. But at the urging of her parents, Fox-Genovese chose to attend Harvard because that's where they had gone.

At Harvard she continued her studies, focusing again on France, and on the expansion of Europe, including America before it became the United States, and on early modern Spain and Portugal—"a vast sweeping field." Her best field, she says, "was medieval history," under Charles Taylor, who "trained the great medievalists of several generations. He was a great teacher; he was scholarship walking."

In her third year at Harvard, Fox-Genovese, assigned to teach a survey course, discovered she was very good at teaching. Her skill was made evident by her students' reaction to her. They "liked working with me and worked hard for me and I certainly worked hard for them. I loved it."

As with her addiction to history, she credits her teaching expertise to her forebears. "My father was a great teacher," she says, and both of her father's parents were "extraordinary" teachers. Her grandfather "could teach anybody basic math; that was his genius." Her grandmother, who never attended college, taught in a one-room schoolhouse and managed to teach a dyslexic boy to read when others had given up on him. "I came by it naturally," she believes, even as she developed her own style. "There are as many good styles of teaching as there are personalities. What is required is that you be true to who you are and use those strengths and take the students seriously."

But Fox-Genovese found it difficult to complete her studies because she didn't know quite what she wanted to do when she earned her degree. She took a year off from graduate school, and during that time decided that she would like to teach. To do so she needed to go back and finish her schooling. She changed her thesis subject from eighteenth-century European port cities to physiocracy, the eighteenth-century French system of political economics. She made the change because her original subject required her to research in France, something she didn't want to do at that time. Physiocracy, on the other hand, was intellectual history, which she could do from books. Harvard's Widener Library "had an absolutely extraordinary collection" from which she worked. But again, "I didn't want to finish it. I still didn't know what I wanted to be when I grew up."

Then she met Eugene Genovese, and everything changed. Brought together by a mutual friend, they hit it off immediately. "We talked all night long about history," she recalls of their first date. About 1 A.M., "he kissed me gently on the forehead" and headed back to his hotel room. "I shut the door on him," Fox-Genovese says, "and had a deep, still feeling, no romantic flutters, just absolute quiet, sort of the eye of a storm. Oh, my god, this is it! From then on, I didn't look back." Despite Genovese's marital past, "I knew I had found a man I could trust. That was all I cared about."

After they married, they moved to Rochester, New York, where Fox-Genovese at last completed her dissertation, writing "800 pages in six months," and received her doctoral degree. The thesis, *The Origins of Physiocracy: Economic Revolution and Social Order in Eighteenth-Century France,* was published in 1976.

Now she found herself drawn into U.S. history, her new husband's field. The University of Rochester hosted a conference on *Time on the Cross,* and Fox-Genovese presented a paper titled "Poor Richard at Work in the Cotton Fields," which became a chapter in *Fruits of Merchant Capital.* She wrote a long review essay of a book on Andrew Jackson and American Indian removal and taught courses on the expansion of the United States and on the Atlantic world in the age of revolution.

"Then," she says, "women's history broke upon the world, and it was quite obvious to everyone that since I was a girl, I was the person to teach it. I had stayed pretty far from women's history; I didn't want to be classified as that." She began her foray into the field with several articles: "something on women and property," two pieces on French women, "something on feminist theory, a long essay on Margaret Drabble, the British novelist." Women's history, she says, was the "vehicle" that moved her away from French history toward U.S. history.

Her writing attracted the attention of the State University of New York at Binghamton. They were establishing the first doctoral program in women's history in the country and invited her to be part of it. As an inducement to accept the position, they made her "a full professor and an American historian."

It was at Binghamton that Fox-Genovese began research for what eventually became *Within the Plantation Household*. Then in 1984, she and Genovese were accepted at the National Humanities Center at the Triangle University Center for Advanced Studies in North Carolina. There she was able to "get into the primary materials in greater depth, which was a pure delight." That's when, she says, the book "began to take shape in its final form." It was published in 1988 and has "done extremely well." It is assigned for college course work, but it also attracts general readers.

A couple of books on feminism followed. In 1991, she published *Feminism without Illusions,* "which was historical, but with a certain amount of political philosophy and theory." It is used in political science and some law classes more than in history. *Feminism Is Not the Story of My Life,* published in 1996, is historical, "but it was written for a more general audience and it's very contemporary history."

At the time of this interview, Fox-Genovese had a few projects in the works, and several more on the back burner. She and Genovese had just completed work on *The Mind of the Master Class,* and they had plans for a couple of complementary volumes. She was finishing a book on marriage with a "broad historical sweep and argument," and she edited the *Historical Journal,* which she and Genovese had founded. Besides all of her writing and editing projects, Fox-Genovese continued to teach.

She loves history and teaching it. She believes, "History is something you talk about, you think about, you want to know facts, you want to know who was who and the players, but you also want to get a feel for the dynamic and what the issues were, and it's been great teaching new kinds of courses just to feel so much at home in this thing."

The Mind of the Master Class is about the history and faith of Southern slaveholders. Fox-Genovese believes the book addresses many of the issues facing Americans today. It has a message about "what is most seriously wrong with the worst aspects of our contemporary culture." She fears that people today don't understand what technology has done to society. "I think what people don't get is that technological change, which has been so breathtaking in recent years, and accelerating, completely changes the ball game. It changes who we are, and the rules, and erases previous rules and patterns and experience—disallows them all. Then all you've done is reduce human beings to our technology. You've lost what's human about us. So I think the sense of history as the balance between that which occurs and that which changes is tremendously important to the moral and political health of our culture."

Fox-Genovese views history as "more than a game or a collection of facts, or a collection of theories, and it's certainly not something we just make up to reflect our own point of view." To be a good historian, one must maintain "standards of honesty and of craft. Obviously we are not going to recapture the past as it was at the time to those who lived it, but we sure can make every effort to get it right. I think it's very important to do so, because it's essential to understand what we have in common with previous civilizations, societies, people, as well as what differentiates us from them. We could do with a lot more serious reflection on the fall of Rome these days."

Fox-Genovese does the vast majority of her work on a computer, although she has "been known to write papers or comments or finish up something on an airplane or in a hotel room with a pencil and a pad of paper." She started writing longhand, fairly early transferred to a typewriter, and then the computer became her machine of choice. "I think for someone who writes well, the computer is a tremendous asset because it makes you much readier to change than you would be otherwise." She still resorts, however, to pencil and paper when faced with a difficult passage to write through.

She does a "fair amount" of editing. "I care a lot about language," she says, "and I am a pretty finicky editor. I almost always see something that I want to change." But she seldom edits on the computer—"I always work from a hard copy," admitting that she needs to see the material in that form.

When she researches, Fox-Genovese usually takes notes on a computer. If she must take a note by hand, "I won't feel safe until I get it into the computer." Her notes are on full sheets of paper, with the topic (one per page) at the top of the page. She learned how to take notes in her father's class. "If you had taken your notes intelligently enough, and you ordered them well," she says, "the paper literally wrote itself." Now, she says, she is somewhat sloppier with her notes. "I have a pretty good memory for what I think is important. I'll just make a note of where something is, or I'll just simply work it in immediately into something I'm writing." When reading, she makes little check marks or notes in the margin. "An awful lot of my books have marginalia in them," she admits.

When writing, Fox-Genovese rereads what she thinks are the more important things, but, she says, "by the time I write I will have assimilated them fairly well." She spends "a lot of time living with something before I write it, a lot of time thinking it through, letting it gel in the back of my mind, making just jotted notes of ideas about how things fit together." When she does sit down to write, she writes "fairly fast, sometimes very fast."

She writes when she has time, rather than to a strict schedule. The time of day does not seem to matter: "Once I'm geared up to write, once I know where I'm going, and often once I start to write I keep going pretty single-mindedly," she says. She is "likely to write ten or fifteen pages in a day, and maybe for several days in a row, to get something done." But then there are days when "my time is completely taken up doing other things."

When confronted with conflicting material, Fox-Genovese says she hopes she'll "have some knowledge of my own to balance it against." She is "more likely to dismiss points of view that frankly just strike me as silly, or where I have reason not to trust the author." Still, even if she doesn't fully trust the source, "I really try not to be bigoted and close-minded." In the end, she says, "it's all point of view and we just don't know and we'll never know, and everyone has his or her story, and virtually any account is as good as any other. There's no way of recapturing the past with any precision." In the end, it comes down to honesty. "I think there are standards of evidence, and I think there are things like deep knowledge as opposed to superficial knowledge. Historians with some integrity and some experience should be as open-minded as humanly possible, but we also are in a position to know some things."

When asked her preference between writing and researching, Fox-Genovese says writing comes pretty easy to her, and there is a good deal she wants to write about. But research is what her writing is grounded in. "I would prefer to be able to defend what I say and not simply write essays and opinion pieces. To have my work grounded in something serious makes research necessary."

Writer's block and procrastination are not problems for her, although she does admit that "I'm capable of letting less important things get in the way of more important things."

Fox-Genovese says one big breakthrough for her was when it became clear to her how strong the sexual division of labor was in the slave workforces on the plantations of the South. "The women were doing things that very fine historians, including my own husband [an authority on slavery], had totally missed. Many times what you could get from careful reading has been the most exciting for me, that which is right there in front of your eyes, but you hadn't been able to see it before."

Fox-Genovese believes *Within the Plantation Household* is perhaps her most important contribution to the field of history. It "brought black and white women together, and advanced an important argument about the nature of antebellum southern society. Just bringing the white women alive, and then to my surprise being able to bring the black women to life as well."

Reading is a compelling part of her life. She reads for teaching, not only what she is focusing on for that particular class, but also "around whatever it is that I'm working on at the moment." If she is working on a book about feminism, she might read political theory, sociological theory, on community and society and contractual relations. "Since I was trained in the European tradition, I'm used to reading pretty widely."

She also reads fiction. In the past she enjoyed reading Marcel Proust and George Eliot, "and the sweep of British literature." She teaches William Faulkner and loves his books. Of today's writers, she likes Gail Godwin, Margaret Atwood, and Toni Morrison. She used to read mystery stories, "but I don't have much time for that any more"—other than Dick Francis, who she enjoys because of "his love for animals, his respect for women, and the interest of his characters. He is grounded in literature and serious thought; he runs very deep, and he knows what evil is and he isn't afraid to name it."

Although she can't think of any one thing off hand, Fox-Genovese says that her students always have sparked new ideas or insights in her work. "I've trained so many and I've learned from all of them," she says. "Our work is close and the exchanges back and forth are continuous. So there's no one spark, but there's a kind of running conversation with my students, which is enriching and rewarding, and it's certain that I learn from them. One after another has opened up views of things that have expanded my sense of the world."

At one point in her life, Fox-Genovese had thought about becoming a psychoanalyst—"I think I would have been a pretty good one"—and studied at London's Tavistock, England's prime psychoanalytic institute. But by the time she had completed her doctoral dissertation, "it really confirmed that what I am is a teacher"—and a historian. She is eminently satisfied with the path she took. "I've had the life I wanted, and the marriage I wanted, and the students I wanted, and I can't imagine having had to sacrifice the freedom I've enjoyed."

"In a real sense," she says, "we're the last craftspeople left, practically, and it's being eroded. For those of us who are a bit older, it really has afforded us a surprising degree of freedom, given the nature of the modern world."

After a long and distinguished career in history, Fox-Genovese died in 2007 before this interview became part of the historical record. Her essays and articles, over 150 in a half-dozen fields, are being republished in four volumes, *The Selected Works of Elizabeth Fox-Genovese,* by the University of South Carolina Press, under the general editorship of David Moltke-Hansen, and a fifth volume, *An Elizabeth Fox-Genovese Reader* is also in the works. And Genovese, her beloved husband, wrote of their life together in *Miss Betsey: A Memoir of Marriage.*

Forrest McDonald

MASTER OF EPIPHANIES

"Hard writing makes easy reading."

"The only legitimate reason for doing history is because you love it, because it's fun."

When you're researching, you never know what you're going to find, and then "BANG! You understand something that nobody has ever understood before and that's why you do it—for those moments of epiphany and realization and understanding."

———◆◆———

FORREST MCDONALD CAME LATE TO THE FIELD OF HISTORY. HE already had his bachelor's degree from the University of Texas (UT) before history found him. "I grew up wanting to be a major league baseball player," he says. But when he went out for the baseball team in college, he discovered "I was good field, no hit, as they say." Curve balls have done in more than one would-be ball player.

His first year in college, McDonald remembers, "I messed around, went to an occasional class." At eighteen, he left school to enlist in the World War II navy. During his time in the service, he "decided that being a major league baseball player was not very realistic; what I wanted to do was write the great American novel, being 'realistic' this time." After his stint in the navy, McDonald returned to UT as an English major. "I actually did write a novel," he recalls, "which never got published—and it shouldn't have."

One of his U.S. history undergraduate courses, taught by Eugene Campbell Barker, covered the period from 1776 to 1828. But instead of covering the whole era, Barker delivered "a diatribe that went on all semester long against the writings of Charles A. Beard, particularly Beard's economic interpretation of the Constitution." Some semesters later, he took another history course, this one taught by H. Malcolm MacDonald, "a very hot-shot political scientist." In one of his lectures on the Constitution, the professor presented the Beard thesis favorably. McDonald was "mystified." After class he spoke to the professor about what he had learned from Barker regarding Beard. "He looked me straight in the eye," McDonald recalls, "and he said Eugene Campbell Barker is a senile old man."

McDonald was "stunned." It occurred to him that if "something so fundamental to American history as the formation of the Constitution can elicit such totally polar opposite points of view, this must be a field that is wide open." He switched his major to history, intending to write a rebuttal of the Beard thesis for his master's degree. To do the research, he hitchhiked from Austin, Texas, to Washington, D.C., in 1949, spent a day and a half in the National Archives, and then hitchhiked back to Austin. What he had found "cast considerable doubt on Beard," says McDonald. "Professor Barker was just thrilled by the whole thing." He doesn't say what Professor MacDonald thought about it.

As he began his doctoral studies, McDonald worked as a teaching assistant to Fulmer Mood. Mood convinced him that he needed a larger perspective on the subject, to study the issues that resulted in the final form of the Constitution. In 1951, McDonald received a research training fellowship grant from the Social Science Research Council in Washington, which put him two years "on the road." He spent twelve to eighteen hours a day in state archives and state historical societies up on down the East Coast, from Georgia to Maine, doing research in primary sources. He had decided he wanted to write "a grand opus tracing the history of the period from 1781 to 1789."

When the grant money ran out in 1953, McDonald had to get a job. Mood had connections in Wisconsin, and he introduced

McDonald to Clifford Lord, the director of the Wisconsin State Historical Society. Lord offered him a research project on the electric utility business. Although he knew nothing about it, McDonald discovered he had a couple of things working in his favor. "One was that though I didn't realize it, I have a natural gift for understanding financial matters, and understanding the electric utility business was in considerable measure learning the complex economics of the business." The other thing he had going for him was that he sat down and read *Popular Mechanics* from 1876 to 1920 to familiarize himself with the technology. "And so I was off and running," he says.

Meanwhile, he had not yet earned his doctorate. Mood pressed him to finish his thesis and suggested that he do so by "skimming off the top" of his notes. That, says McDonald, "was how the Beard book, *We the People: The Economic Origins of the Constitution,* happened to be written." He received his degree in 1955.

While writing the utility book, McDonald became intrigued with Samuel Insull, a utility pioneer who worked as Thomas Edison's private secretary in the 1880s. Insull went into the utility business, and he was the person who really worked out the economics of electric power. "He had a spectacular career," says McDonald, "climaxing in 1932 when he went bankrupt—the biggest business failure in the history of the world to that time." In 1962, McDonald published *Insull,* a book that received renewed interest in the early 2000s with the collapse of Enron and Health South, among others.

McDonald followed *We the People* with two additional studies of the Constitution: *E Pluribus Unum: The Formation of the American Republic,* published in 1979 and *Novus Ordo Seclorum: The Intellectual Origins of the Constitution,* which appeared in 1985. He also was drawn into writing on two presidents. The University of Kansas Press asked him to write a history of George Washington's presidency, which was published in 1974. Next came Thomas Jefferson. That happened when McDonald bought and began working a farm in Florida. "I got to wondering," he says, "if I was going to have to do Jefferson because I'm now laboring in the earth, so to speak, and Jefferson praised laboring in the earth." The volume on

Jefferson appeared in 1976, and in 1994 he published *The American Presidency: An Intellectual History.* He also wrote a biography of Alexander Hamilton, a project that grew out of his reviewing the twenty-six volumes of the Hamilton Papers as they were published. "One thing leads to another," he says. "You follow your subjects where they go and you follow your ideas where they go."

After a couple of years in Wisconsin as the director of the American History Research Center, a subsidiary of the state historical society, McDonald took a job at Brown University in Providence, Rhode Island. That began his teaching career, a path he followed until his retirement.

Before he writes, McDonald needs an outline of each chapter "in great, laborious detail, long detail." Then he sits down with a pad of eight-by-fourteen-inch yellow ruled sheets, and he writes by hand. "Writing by hand slows me down," he says, "and actually I've got a second and third draft by the time I've finished the first draft." His wife, Ellen Shapiro McDonald, types out the first draft on a typewriter, editing as she goes along. No computer; "We're very old-fashioned," McDonald says, and admits to still using a rotary telephone.

After three or four drafts, everything has been typed out. Then "I go back through it at least one more time, and she goes back through it at least one more time, and we edit and edit and edit." In his earlier books he always did seven or eight drafts; now he can do it in four or five, but he still does a lot of rewriting. "Hard writing makes easy reading," he says.

McDonald usually writes in the nude. He and Ellen live on a farm in "total isolation, nobody ever comes down here. For years the electric company couldn't find us so we had to read the meter for them." Besides, he says, "it's warm here most of the year so there's no point in wearing any clothes, so I sit on my front porch without any clothes on, with my notes and cards and books and stuff lying around, and the pad that I'm writing on."

When researching, McDonald takes notes by hand on "good quality paper with a ballpoint pen on full sheets." He does not order them by subject, but rather by source; for example, newspapers, tax records, parliamentary debates, and so forth. When plugging them into his writing, he first arrives at his generalizations and then looks for the documentary evidence. "If you make the generalization and you're going to make a statement of a particular fact, you know pretty well by then where you can find it," he says.

At one time McDonald kept to a fairly regular schedule, assigning himself a certain number of pages to write each day. Now that he is retired, he doesn't push as hard—"I'm not in a hurry any more," he says. Afternoons are the best time for him to write, so in the morning he plays tennis and works on his farm.

McDonald has little trouble with conflicting material. "I let the primary materials speak for themselves," he says. "They tell me what they tell me, and I don't care who has said what to the contrary." He does not keep up with the literature in the field—"I couldn't care less." If there is something he thinks needs to be examined, Ellen will visit the library to check it out for him. "But by and large I write without regard to what other people think." He believes the quality of historical writing has declined, and today's output is "simply not worth worrying about."

McDonald enjoys the research phase much more than the writing. "Research is just pure fun," he says. "It's true fun because I'm not doing it to find out anything, to support a point of view, I'm just going to the materials." He does not use the Internet for research. "I don't think I would like that very much," he says. "I've always done [research] in the physical primary sources, in the primary repositories."

McDonald credits Mood with helping him learn to write while he was working on the Beard book. "He was correcting like crazy and marking up every page." Mood told him it was important to all writers to have someone who can and will go over everything they produce. For most of his career, McDonald relied upon Tom Govan to criticize his writing. Govan was a historian who never wrote much, but he was "a wonderful critic."

When he was in Wisconsin, he turned to Livia Appel, a book editor who had her office down the hall from his. "I used to sit by the hour with Livia and she would work in microscopic detail, and we would have long, long discussions as to why this phraseology wouldn't do and that would do better, and this would be even better, and so on." That close contact for better than a year "taught me probably more in detail about writing than all the others put together."

McDonald also credits Ellen with improving his writing. "She's probably as good an editor of historical scholarship as there is around," he says. "On half of my books she could have been the coauthor, and I was willing to make her the coauthor, but she was modest and said no."

"The only legitimate reason for doing history," McDonald believes, "is because you love it, because it's fun." He remembers clearly an important moment that came early in his career. He had been on the road researching Beard's thesis for about six months when he found himself in Concord, New Hampshire, working through the microfilmed collections of early town records of the state. Suddenly, he had an epiphany that turned his whole interpretation of the 1780s upside down. "I had practically an intellectual orgasm," he says. "It was the most intense feeling of satisfaction I had ever had in my life—one of those moments that you do history for." When you're researching, he says, you never know what you're going to find, and then "BANG! You understand something that nobody has ever understood before and that's why you do it—for those moments of epiphany and realization and understanding."

McDonald has his research completed before he starts writing because that's where your epiphany comes from. "You've got to have had your epiphany about the whole thing before you can start," he says. "At least I do."

Besides working the farm and playing tennis, McDonald relaxes with crossword puzzles, doing six to eight each day. He reads suspense novels, and every day he and Ellen play games. They used to listen to opera, he says, "but now we've stopped because it bothers the cat." They play gin rummy, watch *Jeopardy*, and then while Ellen prepares dinner, he mixes the drinks and reads aloud.

Political correctness does not influence McDonald's work in any way. "I've been an outlander from the very beginning," he says. "I'm a conservative in a very liberal profession." He recently published a memoir, *Recovering the Past: A Historian's Memoir*, and one reviewer remarked, "Who else would include pictures of himself with Ronald Reagan, Richard Nixon, and George W. Bush?"

McDonald has had his moments as a revisionist. He points to the work he and Grady McWhiney did on the Celtic thesis, which "undermined the progressive school of historians—Charles A. Beard, Carl Becker, even Frederick Jackson Turner—undermined the hell out of Turner." Turner believed the American frontier encouraged people to become "brand new." But McDonald and McWhiney showed that that is not what happened. Immigrants brought with them their "folkways, mores, habits, customs, that kind of stuff." For many of those who came to the United States, there was rapid change occurring in the old country. The New World "gave you an opportunity to be with like-minded people in isolation from other people. You could avoid the forces of change, and that's what they did. That's the whole key to cultural conservatism as a force in America. The Celtic South could remain the Celtic South. They didn't have to stay in Scotland and Ireland and Wales and become Anglicized."

The two historians came to this understanding by different routes. McWhiney came to it through Wilbur Cash's *The Mind of the South*, and by reading foreign traveler's accounts. He noted that these writers talked about Southerners primarily raising animals, rather than the cotton and tobacco that gets so much attention in the secondary literature. McDonald, on the other hand, noticed when he lived in Spain for a year that various portions of the country were very different from one another. Looking at settlement patterns in the Americas, he realized that the immigrants tended to settle in different places, and that they seemed to take their old ways with them. Paraguay, for example, he says, "had a very violent history, and they were a very belligerent bunch of people. There are certain Spaniards who are that way, and I wondered if maybe it's because they were carrying their old ways with them."

At some point, McDonald and McWhiney put their heads together and realized they were studying the same phenomenon. "And then BANG! The thing was born that way. It was a mutual epiphany."

Although he does not belong to any historical associations, McDonald has enjoyable and fruitful relationships with other historians. He particularly appreciates people who understand "the philosophy of history and the ideas of history and what it's all about." In particular, he mentions Govan, who critiqued his work, and John Lukas, "just a whiz bang," a European historian who taught at a small college in Pennsylvania.

McDonald believes his unique contribution to the field of history is his "otherwise-mindedness, not accepting the revised standard version, and viewing things from a different perspective, in constitutional history, as well as in economic history, as well as in intellectual history, and various other things. It's always been from a different slant, from a different angle."

He finds it difficult to say which of his books has been the most important or influential. The book on Hamilton, he says, may be one of them, or the presidencies, but the one he likes the best is the Insull biography—"It was just so much fun to do."

When asked whether he regarded himself primarily as a researcher or a teacher, McDonald says, "I think the two are inseparable. Some people like to point out the whole notion of publish or perish, but it's been my experience that the people who are the best practicing historians in terms of research and writing are also the best teachers."

McDonald cannot imagine having done something else with his life. If he had not chosen history, his life would still have "been in some kind of scholarship, maybe in political science." He might have been in economics, though he had never had an economics course, "because it was just something I could understand." He had also toyed with the idea of being a lawyer, "but that would be a dead end, not very challenging."

Throughout his career, McDonald has enjoyed challenge, and in particular the challenge of history, of seeking new ways of looking at old problems and events. Even his old dream of playing baseball is at rest—"I'm satisfied about that," he says.

David Herbert Donald

The Mentor

"The students used to say, that I wrote more in red on their papers than they wrote in blue."

"You took those notes yourself, you filed them yourself, you pulled them out and you just read them, so if you don't remember what's in them it's probably not worth knowing."

"If you look over the country's colleges today, in many areas of nineteenth-century history, I'm very proud to say, the leaders are students who worked with me."

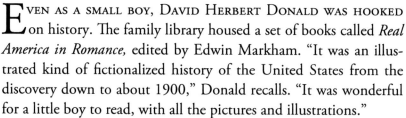

EVEN AS A SMALL BOY, DAVID HERBERT DONALD WAS HOOKED on history. The family library housed a set of books called *Real America in Romance,* edited by Edwin Markham. "It was an illustrated kind of fictionalized history of the United States from the discovery down to about 1900," Donald recalls. "It was wonderful for a little boy to read, with all the pictures and illustrations."

It was books and not teachers that stirred Donald's love of history. "I did not have very good history teachers in either grade school or high school," he says. He grew up in Goodman, Mississippi, a small town of about 650 people, equally white and black. White students from the outlying area were bussed in, and left at the end of the school day, and Donald had few companions in town; "I was sort of alone and didn't have much to do except read."

His family, he says, was "large and a little bit too chaotic" for anyone to take time to read to him, so he read on his own. He read widely, including things too advanced for his age. "I probably didn't understand them, but I enjoyed reading them and thinking about them." When he was about nine years old, there was a "great commotion" when Thomas Wolfe published his novel, *Look Homeward, Angel.* He overheard his mother discussing the book with a friend, talking about it being "a very naughty book, with terrible words in it." As soon as he could, Donald read the book. "That was the first time in my life I saw a cuss word in print," he confesses. "I don't think I understood the book, or read it all, but I loved the dirty words, anyway."

Donald's poor history instruction in public school continued in junior college. The history teacher typically was also the coach, whose primary responsibility was to the basketball and the football teams. He recalls one history teacher in junior college who worked directly from a "dull, dull textbook." He would read a sentence from the book, leaving out the last word. The students would then read from their textbooks to complete the sentence. "It was not," he laments, "an inspiring class!"

When he matriculated to Millsaps College in Jackson, Mississippi, that all changed. "My two years there were enormously stimulating," he says. "We had excellent people in history and in other fields as well." He particularly admired Vernon Wharton, one of the pioneers who revised the view of Reconstruction. To Donald, this was "enormously exciting. For the first time we were hearing about what really happened during Reconstruction, and it wasn't all just barbarism, but there were in fact notable accomplishments. This was quite revolutionary for us."

As graduation neared, Donald had no idea what he wanted to do. Others in his classes were talking about graduate school. Even though "I didn't know anything at all about graduate school, I thought I might as well apply, too." He sent applications to twelve schools, "not knowing one from the other, to tell the truth." When he asked Wharton for letters of introduction, the professor said he didn't have time—no secretary, teaching full-time, and a lot of students applying to graduate school. He told Donald to write the letters himself and he would sign them. "So I did, and he did." At the time, very few scholarships and fellowships were being given, but Donald's letter drew a note from the dean of the graduate school at the University of Illinois, which said, "admit this man with a fellowship. He has excellent letters of recommendation!"

"To get paid to go to school was remarkable!" Donald recalls. Besides, the University of Illinois was the school closest to his hometown to accept him. The Illinois Central Railroad ran right through Goodman and on to Champaign-Urbana, Illinois. "To a little boy from a small town, it seemed rather less frightening than trying to go across country." At Illinois he studied under James G. Randall, "the great Civil War historian, the greatest Lincoln scholar who ever lived." He also worked with Fred Albert Shannon, "a remarkable teacher, a rigorous teacher who put backbones into us, made us learn how to do footnotes and to look up citations and so on. Those years were great years for me."

Donald completed his master's in one year. Then he decided to matriculate to the University of North Carolina, where Wharton had received his doctorate. Donald planned to write about Mississippi and Reconstruction and thought that would be the best place to do it. "It was an interesting, stimulating year," Donald recalls, "but not an altogether successful one." World War II was raging, and the professor he particularly wanted to study with, Howard Beale, had been called away to relocate the Japanese from the West Coast. So even though he had "interesting and able teachers," they weren't encouraging the kind of research he wanted to do.

There were only four new students in U.S. history—"me [kept out of the service with poor vision], one girl, another boy who became a very good historian (he had lost a kidney playing football and was therefore not eligible to serve in the army), and a poor spastic fellow who also couldn't serve in the army." The four of them banded together and thought of themselves as "the halt, the lame, and the blind." All in all, "it was a somewhat impoverished kind of academic setting." At the end of the first quarter, Donald heard that the army had drafted Randall's research assistant and he was looking for a replacement. "Professor Randall very kindly welcomed me back," and Donald returned to Illinois.

There he did research for the first two volumes of Randall's four-volume *Lincoln the President*. Donald's job was to go through the manuscript and check every citation for accuracy, which meant looking up every book, manuscript, newspaper, and so on, that Randall had used. Learning sources in the process, he was able to compile a draft bibliography for Randall's work.

When he had finished that, he had a solid grounding in both Civil War and Lincoln studies and a different idea for a doctoral thesis. One day Randall mentioned to him that William H. Herndon, who had been Lincoln's law partner, had never had much written about him, and his papers had recently become available. Randall suggested that Donald look into it. He did, found it "exciting," and that became his thesis, which was published in 1948 as *Lincoln's Herndon*.

While working on it, Donald received a fellowship from the Social Science Research Council doctoral training program. These were awarded to a few advanced graduate students, giving them a year of research and travel. Donald used the money to go from one research library to another, from Boston to the Huntington Library in California. He met many historians along the way who "helped me find things and talked with me about what was new and interesting in their fields." The experience was invaluable. "I think perhaps that was the most stimulating single year of my life."

At the end of the year he returned to Urbana to work with Randall until he finished his thesis and received his degree in 1946. Soon afterward, Columbia University in New York City hired him to teach. "I enjoyed Columbia immensely," he says, "and found the students simply wonderful and so bright and so aggressively intelligent that I learned an immense amount." But after two years at the school, he says, "I wasn't sure that I wanted a life in such a high-pressured place as Columbia," so he moved to Smith College in Northampton,

Massachusetts. He found his time at Smith "interesting years, but not intellectually stimulating years, and I found myself longing for Columbia." At the end of two years he returned to New York.

At Columbia, Donald worked primarily with graduate students. At one of his first seminars he met Grady McWhiney and Ari Hoogenboom, among other "extraordinarily able people [who] stimulated me and maybe I helped them, too." That early seminar, he says, "was the model seminar that I have never altogether equaled since that time." He thought of them as members of his family, and when he married Aida DiPace a few years later, she, too, considered them family. "They were in and out of our apartment all hours, playing Ping-Pong until after midnight, and so on. It was an interesting, stimulating, sociable life, as well as an intellectual life."

Donald had "strong ideas about seminars, and what they ought to be and what they ought not to be." As a graduate student, he had not found his seminars stimulating—"there was very little interchange of ideas, there was very little criticism of each other or of anything else, and there was no particular plan of how our reading fit into the overall scheme of things."

Donald wanted to conduct a seminar that had a "theme and a central purpose." For that first group of graduate students, he decided that each person would take a thread of Charles Beard's economic interpretation of the Civil War and see how it played out. They worked on civil service reform, national politics, and monetary policy, among other topics. Irwin Unger, who worked on the monetary policy, won a Pulitzer Prize for his dissertation, *Greenback Era*.

The seminar achieved just what Donald had hoped. "We all had much in common," he recalls, "and they not only talked to me, but they talked to each other, they exchanged a lot of ideas, and I think the wonderful thing about it is that years and years and years later, they are all still in touch. They know each other, they know each other's families, they exchange manuscripts and ideas. That's my idea of how a seminar ought to work."

Donald made it a point to emphasize writing skills with his students. "I felt very strongly that one of the problems with American history in general is that it's written in such pedantic language that it can't attract a general following." Having read Francis Parkman and George Bancroft, "the great literary historians," Donald "saw no reason why present-day historians shouldn't get something of that kind of audience." Colleagues at Columbia, Henry Commager and Allan Nevins, had large popular audiences, and Donald thought, "Okay, my students ought to be able to do this, too." He taught them to revise, and revise, and revise. "The students used to say," he confesses, "that I wrote more in red on their papers than they wrote in blue."

Donald believes he learned his own writing skills from his avid reading of fiction. "I like to watch how great storytellers organize their materials to tell it so you are there in the middle of it, you can feel and you can see exactly what's going on. If you've grown up on Charles Dickens, for example, you're not likely to write arid prose." A technique he taught his students was to read aloud what they wrote. "If you can't read it aloud interestingly to yourself, there's something wrong; the sentences should come right off your tongue. When you think you have it down, have someone else listen to you read. If you see their eyes glazing over, you realize you're not making your point and you go back and write it over again, and over and over again."

After the publication of the Herndon book, Donald discussed with the publisher, Alfred Knopf, a project that would combine two of his interests—the Civil War and Reconstruction and U.S. intellectual history. Donald chose Charles Sumner as a figure that combined both subjects. "He was a man of enormous erudition," Donald says. "He was friendly with all the great New Englanders— Emerson, Thoreau, Hawthorne, Alcott, and so on—but at the same time he was a big political figure."

Originally intended to be one volume, the biography ended up as two volumes, published ten years apart. Between the two, Donald went to England as the Harmsworth Professor at Oxford. Knowing that he would not have the sources available to him to continue work on Sumner, he and Knopf decided to publish what he had already as *Charles Sumner and the Coming of the Civil War,* which appeared in 1960 and won a Pulitzer Prize. In 1970, he published the second volume, *Charles Sumner and the Rights of Man.* The two have since been published as one volume—"one huge volume!"—as originally intended.

When Donald returned to the United States, he moved to New Jersey to teach at Princeton for two years before moving to Johns Hopkins where he remained for eleven years.

In 1973, Donald made one final move, this time to Harvard University as the Charles Warren Professor of American History. He became director of a graduate program called History of American Civilization, a kind of American studies program. His students came from various departments—history, literature, philosophy, and so on—"a very interesting group of students," he says. Because he was working with people doing "various kinds of literary things, I had to acquaint myself with the new styles and fashions in literary criticism." This eventually led to another biographical study.

After completing Sumner, Donald wasn't sure what he wanted to do next. On vacation in North Carolina, he and Aida visited the novelist Thomas Wolfe's home in Asheville. He was not impressed. "It was a huge rambling frame structure with many, many rooms" to accommodate the roomers and boarders that Wolfe's mother took in to support the family. The rooms were small and bare, with a cot and a single light hanging from the ceiling. All Donald could think was, "Golly, how did a writer like Thomas Wolfe, so lush and rich in his prose, his thinking, his imagery, how did he ever grow up in this kind of arid, sterile environment?"

The question intrigued him, and when he returned to Harvard he decided to look into it. At the university's Houghton Library he discovered, to his surprise and delight, an enormous collection of Wolfe papers. "I started working on it right away," he says, "and for the next four years I worked on it full-time when I wasn't teaching." Although he did research in other places, "the basic work was done there at the Houghton Library."

Look Homeward: A Life of Thomas Wolfe, was published in 1987 and won Donald a second Pulitzer Prize.

Meanwhile, he had published a variety of other volumes. He edited the Salmon Chase diaries, *Inside Lincoln's Cabinet* (1954); published a book of essays called *Lincoln Reconsidered* (1956); and rewrote a large portion of Randall's *Civil War and Reconstruction* (1961); among many other projects and books.

After *Look Homeward* came out, Donald was again unsure of what he wanted to do next. Over the years, many people had urged him to write a life of Abraham Lincoln, but he had demurred; "there were a lot of good books already and I didn't think there was anything new for me to do." But when the Wolfe book won him a second Pulitzer, "I got the notion that there are people who think I'm fairly good at this sort of thing. Maybe I should try it." In 1995, he published *Lincoln,* which had a good reception, and he believes "it's going to stand up pretty well." It remained a bestseller on *The New York Times* list for sixteen weeks. He followed that with *We Are Lincoln Men,* in which he looked at Lincoln's associations with men close to him. "I thought it would show something about his character that I was not able to do in the big biography."

When Donald writes, he needs just three things—a desk, a computer, and relative quiet. He prides himself on being "pretty proficient in computer things."

When he decides on a subject, Donald reads rather broadly on it and around it for "quite a period of time without taking notes, without specifically focusing in, just to acclimatize myself." He reads whatever comes to hand, primary and secondary, until after several months, "I begin to think maybe I know enough to ask some interesting questions about the subject, and I begin formulating these, jotting them down as I do so." This gives his research a sense of direction, underscoring things that he needs to look into and dismissing the things he is not interested in.

Then begins his "dragnet research, just getting everything I can." He enlists research assistants by asking that when they do their own research, if they see anything related to his own topic—"however good, however important, however ugly"—that they make copies for him.

After a certain amount of time, "I get to the point where I seem to have enough notes on certain subjects, they seem to coalesce," and he begins to see what he can make of it. He reads through the notes for a particular subject, puts them back in the file, then sits down at the computer and decides what he wants to say about the material. He keeps the documents out of sight during this process. "I try to put down what this all means, and what it means to me, why do I want to talk about it." He believes "you get a certain fluency in language that you do not have if you have your notes in front of you." That becomes his first draft, after which he goes back to the notes to check dates, names, and so on.

Donald's take on writing without his notes at hand is this: "You took those notes yourself, you filed them yourself, you pulled them out and you just read them, so if you don't remember what's in them it's probably not worth knowing."

The second draft follows immediately, "while it's still fresh in my mind." That then gets put aside for anywhere from three weeks to two months while he works on something else. When he goes back to it, "I read it over, and often I say, 'Golly, how stupid I was to say this sort of thing,' and every now and then I'd say, 'Gee, I was pretty good on that paragraph.'"

He never starts a book at the beginning, but rather in the middle. After he "finishes it off," he knows what he needs to introduce in the earlier chapters. "Sometimes," he says, "it's like spaceships in outer space, because you've got one circulating around, and you're trying to hit it with the other one coming up—sometimes it works and sometimes it doesn't."

All of his notes go into his computer in a FileMaker Pro program. The program arranges the notes and can pull out every note in the collection that has anything to do with the subject he asks about. He has a hard copy of everything on the computer printed out, and when he's ready for notes on a particular topic, he uses the program to guide him to the hard copies in his file drawers. Before he begins writing, he has one-half to two-thirds of his research finished.

Donald always writes at home; there are too many interruptions and distractions at his school office. He has a wing of the house they had built that holds his library of ten to twelve thousand books. "It is my preserve, so to speak," he says. "Nobody comes in, except my puppy, without an invitation."

Donald tries to keep to a regular schedule when he writes, and likes to write in the morning—9 A.M. to about 1 P.M. works well for him. "I'm a demon typist," Donald says, "I type very rapidly." But he revises "very slowly," usually at least six different times. Some revisions are major, some minor, but "I'm always fiddling with things to the last minute." He works uninterrupted through the morning, and in the afternoon he reads and researches.

Donald treats conflicting material as if he were in a court of law—which witness is reliable, who was there at the time—and decides which source he thinks is authentic. What goes into the manuscript, he says, depends on the importance of the subject. A minor quibble might be footnoted with the information that not everyone agrees on that interpretation. A more major issue might have a paragraph discussing the fact that there are differing opinions on the matter.

Donald reads widely. He tries to keep up with current U.S. fiction and with most of the books that come out in other fields in U.S. history. "It's not that I have any research interest [in those other fields], but I definitely want to know what's going on." He reads "quite a lot" in psychology and psychiatry, two special interests that he believes "informed a good deal of my work."

Looking back on his life, Donald is "struck by the generosity of the historians' clan. I have had many professional colleagues who have been enormous help to me. By and large people have been very receptive, responsive, and helpful as I wrote on varied topics, and I've made a lot of friends that way. That is terribly important to me."

But most of all, Donald "enormously enjoyed teaching," and he learned from his students, undergraduate and graduate. One of the joys of publishing, he says, is receiving a letter from a former student, someone from perhaps a half-century ago, who is reminded by the book of Donald's class lectures so many years earlier.

Besides his two Pulitzer Prizes, Donald has won many other awards in his long and distinguished career, including several for lifetime achievement. Among them was one awarded by the newly built Abraham Lincoln Library in Springfield, Illinois; he was the first recipient, and the annual prize is now called the David Herbert Donald Award. He won a presidential award, was given many honorary degrees, and accompanied First Lady Laura Bush to Paris, France, to represent the United States when the nation rejoined the United Nations Educational, Scientific, and Cultural Organization (UNESCO).

Despite the many books he has published and the prizes he has won, Donald believes that his greatest contribution to the field of history has been his mentoring, "honing the minds of some very good graduate students who will be for the next generation the leaders and pioneers in their field. If you look over the country's colleges today, in many areas of nineteenth-century history, I'm very proud to say, the leaders are students who worked with me."

Donald's mentoring influence goes beyond the students he taught personally. Many of the students he taught have passed along to *their* students his philosophy of teaching, his emphasis on good writing, and his enormous respect for those they teach. And those third-generation students, a few of whom appear in this book, are passing those values and practices along to their students, who will, in turn, pass them along to *their* students.

Donald says, with modest pride, "I think that might be the best legacy that I could leave."

David Donald passed away in 2009, but his legacy lives on.

INDEX

CPSIA information can be obtained at www.ICGtesting.com
Printed in the USA
LVOW120018200212

269378LV00002B/11/P